BOBBY DARIN

BOBBY DARIN

Roman Candle

DAVID EVANIER

Cover photo of Bobby Darin (1958) is from PhotoFest.

Published by State University of New York Press, Albany

Originally published as *Roman Candle* with a new introduction by David Evanier.

© 2025 State University of New York

All rights reserved

Printed in the United States of America

No part of this book may be used or reproduced in any manner whatsoever without written permission. No part of this book may be stored in a retrieval system or transmitted in any form or by any means including electronic, electrostatic, magnetic tape, mechanical, photocopying, recording, or otherwise without the prior permission in writing of the publisher.

Links to third-party websites are provided as a convenience and for informational purposes only. They do not constitute an endorsement or an approval of any of the products, services, or opinions of the organization, companies, or individuals. SUNY Press bears no responsibility for the accuracy, legality, or content of a URL, the external website, or for that of subsequent websites.

EU GPSR Authorised Representative:
Logos Europe, 9 rue Nicolas Poussin, 17000, La Rochelle, France
contact@logoseurope.eu

Excelsior Editions is an imprint of State University of New York Press

For information, contact State University of New York Press, Albany, NY
www.sunypress.edu

Library of Congress Cataloging-in-Publication Data

Names: Evanier, David, author. | Evanier, David.
Title: Bobby Darin : Roman candle / David Evanier.
Description: Albany : State University of New York Press, 2025. | Includes bibliographical references and index.
Identifiers: LCCN 2024056433 | ISBN 9798855803099 (pbk. : alk. paper) | ISBN 9798855803082 (ebook)
Subjects: LCSH: Darin, Bobby. | Singers—United States—Biography. | LCGFT: Biographies.
Classification: LCC ML420.D155 E93 2025 | DDC 782.42164092 [B]—dc23/eng/20241122
LC record available at https://lccn.loc.gov/2024056433

*To Andrew Blauner, Harriet Wasser,
Dini Evanier, and Steve Blauner*

Time held me green and dying

Though I sang in my chains like the sea.

—"Fern Hill," Dylan Thomas

When you see me runnin',

you know my life is at stake.

—Howlin' Wolf

Contents

REVISED INTRODUCTION xi

CHAPTER ONE: THE HIDDEN CHILD 1
CHAPTER TWO: A "SCRAWNY THING" 6
CHAPTER THREE: THE NERVE OF A BURGLAR 13
CHAPTER FOUR: SPLISH SPLASH 30
CHAPTER FIVE: THE COMET RIDE 54
CHAPTER SIX: THE BIG TIME 68
CHAPTER SEVEN: THE *SHTARKER* 100
CHAPTER EIGHT: THE GENIUS 130
CHAPTER NINE: The Chameleon 141
CHAPTER TEN: A Higher Calling 151
CHAPTER ELEVEN: Slip-Sliding Away 169
CHAPTER TWELVE: The Lost Chord 181
CHAPTER THIRTEEN: Whirling Dervish 192
CHAPTER FOURTEEN: Roman Candle 213
CHAPTER FIFTEEN: The Curtain Falls 230

THE BEST OF BOBBY: A SELECTED GUIDE 253
ACKNOWLEDGMENTS 255

REVISED INTRODUCTION
David Evanier

IN THE FALL OF 2024, TWENTY YEARS after I first published this biography of Bobby Darin, the press reported that Jonathan Groff would star on Broadway in a musical about Darin, *Just in Time*. It was not a surprise. Bobby's music is still everywhere, timeless, and uncannily fresh. Hard as it is to believe, he left us in 1973 at the age of thirty-seven. He had been a chart-topping, multimillion-selling, Grammy Award–winning singer-songwriter, a Golden Globe–winning actor, and a dedicated political activist. He continues to be played more now than when he was alive—and he was a superstar then.

I remember Darin archivist Jimmy Scalia telling me,

> What happens is each generation you lose a decade. Lot of singers have fallen by the wayside. The reason Bobby never goes away is this: we're lucky in our lifetime to have just a few people that we can hold in our hands who create magic. They catch our attention and move us in ways no one else does. Sinatra, Tony, Dean, Sam Cooke were great at their genre of music. They'll stand the test of time. But there are people who just continually grow, like Bob Dylan. And Darin.

When you have somebody who has that much energy and creativity, we cherish them because what happens is it's real, it's passionate and it's a gift. Here's a guy who went from rock and roll to pop to folk music to Broadway, reinvented himself with swinging standards, turns around and becomes a rock star again in 1969 in levis.

The reassessments of Bobby Darin began as far back as the mid-1990s, when actor Johnny Depp told *Premiere* magazine, "Bobby Darin on the surface was this great personality who smiled and was cocky. He was a popular singer and actor who had such an incredible voice, like crushed velvet. Beneath that cool exterior was a bubbling brew of rage and imbalance. He was in a weird place inside, but all the while, on the outside, he played the role, because back then you had to play the role."

Jazz critic Will Friedwald wrote that "we need only the continually popular and incessantly exciting 'Mack the Knife' to remind us that Darin was easily, after Sinatra, the greatest of all swingin' lovers." James Wolcott wrote in *Vanity Fair*, "Among the bryl creem brigade that included Fabian, Frankie Avalon and Paul Anka, one talent shone brighter, better and truer. The jubilant rightness of his voice bursts through the past, providing a clear, direct link between him and the listeners, undiminished by time or fashion." Neil Young told *Rolling Stone*, "I used to be pissed off at Bobby Darin because he changed styles so much. Now I look at him and I think he was a fucking genius."

Back in the age of cool, there was Sinatra, there was Darin, and there were all the others. But Darin was not Sinatra, whose roots were primarily in jazz and swing and whose musical achievement is the most open and achingly vulnerable autobiography in the history of American popular music. Bobby's roots were rhythm and blues, rock, country, and folk, as well as jazz and swing. His inspirations were vaudeville, Black churches, music halls, Sam Cooke, Leadbelly, Chubby Checker, Fats Domino, Ray Charles, Little Richard—and Sinatra. His was a raw, restless talent, derived from a life steeped in music and performance history. Coming from the streets, he came to the blues naturally. It had the immediacy and urgency of real life. He had so little time, it spoke to him. He didn't have time for teenage bullshit or polite subterfuge; he would make it big or he would die trying.

The truth of the matter is that Bobby was living on borrowed time. Diagnosed with a critical heart condition when he was young, doctors predicted that he would never reach manhood. He did and lived his life at high-octane speed.

Dirt poor as a child, Bobby lived first in Harlem at 125th Street and Second Avenue, then in the South Bronx, and later at 50 Baruch Place around the corner from Ethel and Julius Rosenberg (whom he never met) at 10 Monroe Street in Knickerbocker Village, a housing project on the Lower East Side of Manhattan. Baruch Place was close to Yiddish vaudeville houses and to Sammy's Bowery Follies (where zaftig red-hot mamas holding little handkerchiefs belted out gay '90s songs atop the bar), Katz's Deli ("Send a Salami to Your Boy in the Army"), the old *Jewish Daily Forward* building on East Broadway, and Wild Bill Davison, Max Kaminsky, and other Dixieland greats played all night at Central Plaza on Second Avenue, near the fabled Boys Club of New York. He came from a neighborhood from which, forty years before him, Jack Benny, Jimmy Durante, Eddie Cantor, and George Jessel had scuffled their way to the top from nearby Catherine and Cherry Streets. In his 1969 autobiographical song "City Life," Bobby wrote that there was no heat in his apartment until the weather was so cold that it snowed. There was no backyard. If you wanted a tan, you went up on the roof, but the cement was hard up there. There wasn't time to "have time." And he expected a short life. A death sentence hung over him from childhood.

Bobby's crib was a cardboard box in a drawer. As a boy, he cleaned latrines and shined shoes. In his prime, he could swing and summon up a passion equal to Sinatra's although because he couldn't stand still he did not often achieve Sinatra's greatness as an interpretive singer. There wasn't the tranquility, the contemplative time, or a long life behind or before him for that. Miles Davis said, "It takes a long time to sound like yourself." Sinatra had Ava Gardner to torment him; Bobby had a red-haired snake dancer. But unlike Sinatra, he could also move with magical agility, he could do great impressions, he could rock, he was a swift and brilliant comedian, he could play seven instruments, he could write fine songs—167 of them. He wanted to be a songwriter, actor, singer, and musician, and he became all of these. He appeared in thirteen films and was nominated for an Academy Award in 1961 for *Captain Newman, M.D.* He wrote the musical score of the film he starred in with Sandra Dee, *Come November*.

At sixteen, Bobby performed folk songs like "Rock Island Line" at a Catskills resort. He always leaped ahead of his time, paradoxically by encompassing and loving everything that had come before, moving restlessly from folk to rock to the great American songbook to country and blues and back to folk and protest music. Like Ray Charles, he realized that no matter how far apart things are musically, they are very close at the same time. All music had a oneness to it; genres didn't matter. It was all one thing, and he dug it all.

He did it all, too, and spectacularly well. He was the quintessential glitzy nightclub performer in Las Vegas, one of the biggest draws in the history of that town as well as the hottest attraction at the Copacabana in New York City, the most important night club in the United States in the 1950s and 1960s. At his peak, he outdrew Sinatra and Sammy Davis Jr. He was the last great trouper, the personification of the golden age of show business. At twenty-five he married America's Sweetheart Sandra Dee and was dueting with Judy Garland, George Burns, and Jack Benny. He gave it all up and moved on. He was caught in America's most radical period of musical transition. Born at the end of one era, he bridged the gap between the 1950s and the 1960s.

Bobby spent his life searching for his natural self. But as he told a friend, "The key to me is that I don't belong anyplace. I don't belong in the streets of the Bronx, in high society, or suburbia. I don't belong among beatniks, and I sure don't think I belong in hotel suites."

— REVISED INTRODUCTION —

"I don't know if he was ballsy enough to touch on everything, or scared, hoping that if he kept moving quick, they couldn't find him," said Jimmy Scalia about Bobby's incredible range of styles and genres.

"He was a kid from the big-band era who could sing like a Black artist," Dick Clark said, "and also sing with a 20- or 30-piece band. I mean, those are divergent worlds that *hated* one another. And then he could make a funky little rock-and-roll record."

You can start at 50 Baruch Place, because it's still there, several blocks of housing projects, today largely Latino and Black. The ethnic cast has changed, but you can still see what it was and continues to be: the last vestige of dignity for the very poor who are tightly hanging on. The poor who haven't given up, who still work from nine to five, who still have family units, who push baby carriages; women in pink, in high heels, who look forward to christenings and fifty-year wedding anniversaries—who try to keep it together. They are the forgotten ones who hold on to the last rung of the ladder.

Bobby came from these honorable poor.

He shot up to the highest heights of show business.

To understand who he was and where he got to, you need to understand where he came from. Then the magnitude of the leap becomes amazingly clear.

Bobby came from Italians and neighboring Jews, from poverty, from terrible physical illness, and enforced isolation. What did he do when he was bedridden as a child? He read: fiction, history, poetry. He was a loner from the start, always outside his peer group. He devoured life but rarely enjoyed it. In thirty-seven years he conquered the world but could not quell the static within him.

He was Mister Cool to the world, but the world also watched that side of him give way and change before their eyes as life's realities—Vietnam, the civil rights struggle—shot bullets into that image. Bobby turned from the narcissistic show business mirror to look out into the burning streets of 1960s America, and he could not avert his gaze. He realized that the Copacabana and Las Vegas and *The Johnny Carson Tonight Show* could not encompass all that he knew and felt. He could not stop listening, seeing, changing.

He had protectors whose commitment to him was lifelong: among them the late Harriett Wasser, Bobby's publicist, and his manager, Steve Blauner. And above all there is his son, Dodd Darin, who has doggedly, with loving devotion, protected and expanded his father's legacy. In 2023 Direction Records reissued Darin's last album *Commitment*, his 1969 metamorphosis into protest rock that nearly wrecked his career with the Las Vegas crowd, who thought he'd become a hippie. Dodd wrote in the liner notes:

> In 1968 my Dad sold all his valuable possessions and moved into a trailer at Pfeiffer Beach in Big Sur, California. . . . In forming his own label, Direction Records, he had the freedom to create what he wanted to as opposed to what he felt he had to earlier in his career. . . . I didn't know it at the time but some of the best times I had with my Dad was from the 1968–1970 period. I lived with him in the trailer at Pfeiffer Beach and it was a blast. We'd chop wood, BBQ, go for long walks, listen to albums, throw a baseball around and work daily chores on the land where the trailer sat. . . . One day our project was to throw out awards and showbiz items he had been given over the years. I asked him why we were doing this and he said, 'These things don't mean anything to me. People will give you an award for just showing up somewhere.' I thought he was crazy but I understand it now.

"The reality is that there hasn't been anyone like Bobby since," Harriett Wasser said to me. "You hear people talk about other singers as 'A combination of Sinatra and Darin.' But once they get to Darin, there's nobody else."

May 14, 1936–December 20, 1973

Chapter One

THE HIDDEN CHILD

BOBBY'S GRANDMOTHER, VIVIAN FERN WALDEN, who called herself Polly, was a thrush. Saverio "Sam" Cassotto, his grandfather, was a small-time thug. Sam's family was part of the wave of Italian Immigration between 1900 and 1910, when more than two million men, women, and children came to the United States from Italy. Sam's father, a tailor, had opened a shop in Harlem to raise the money to bring his wife, daughter, and son to New York.

Italians, with their dark skins, at that time were regarded as one step above Negroes. Italian-American families averaged annual earnings of $688, insufficient to support a husband, wife, and two children. Italians were consigned to the most dangerous work. Despite their exceptional capacity for community, family, brotherhood, and joy, they had only their own to count on.

Sam Cassotto did not want such a fate. At first, upon arrival in America, he took odd jobs such as cabinetmaking, but found them financially unrewarding and physically draining. Then he found a friend in mobster Frank Costello. By the time Bobby was born, a piano would be waiting for him at the Cassotto household, a gift from Uncle Frank.

Big Sam Curly, as he was known, would not climb the mob ladder very high with Costello; he was primarily a gofer, although the two did briefly partner a liquor store. Sam had serious drug problems that made him unreliable and unstable, even by mob standards. He had undergone a botched appendectomy in 1907 that resulted in a painful internal infection. After taking morphine for the pain for three months, he became addicted. Opiate use was not against the law in those days, and he freely purchased the narcotic at the corner drugstore.

Sam's addiction undermined his usefulness to Costello, who was fond of him nonetheless. Concerned about Sam's deviant behavior, at one point Costello and his boys actually took Sam out on a boat for an extensive "drying out," but it did not take. (Surprisingly, Costello kept a personnel "file" of this attempt at trying to rescue Sam—more about this later.)

However lowly Sam's status, it was quite a coup to be that close to the Boss of Bosses. Costello was already becoming prince of the underworld. Like Tony Soprano, he even had a psychiatrist on Park Avenue—in times when psychiatry had even less cachet among gangsters than it does today. Costello in effect owned Tammany Hall; he was a murder mastermind and a brilliant crime strategist.

Polly Walden was born in 1894 in Pascoat, Rhode Island, to Julia Hanson, a native of Racine, Wisconsin, and Frank Walden, a mill owner. Polly was a blue-blood; her parents were of English descent. The couple separated soon after, and Polly lived with her mother in Chicago. A beautiful, petite woman, Polly had a restless, impulsive, independent spirit; her parents' heritage did not rub off on her. There was anarchy in her makeup. She bicycled by herself from Chicago to California as a teenager. She was a cheerful rule-breaker who would live a hurly-burly life of her own choice and decision, a life close to the edge, but also with spiritual and poetic dimension.

Polly suddenly left college and married a man who was almost a stranger to her, Ralph Kennedy. She left him after a few months. She loved vaudeville and was soon a featured dancer with the famous comedy team, Weber and Fields. While touring the circuit, Polly met Pasquale Cuomo and married him just as suddenly as she had married Kennedy. She left him, too, soon afterwards. Polly never bothered to divorce either of her first two husbands.

She now achieved some success on the stage as Paula Walden, songstress, "The Girl with Three Voices." Then, in 1912, Polly (the name she decided she liked after experimenting with Vivian and Paula) met Sam in Chicago. They fell in love, and Polly left the stage for good.

Sam and Polly were married on March 1, 1912, at St. Michael's Episcopal Church in Manhattan. Frank Costello and his wife were witnesses. The newly married couple moved to an apartment at 227 East 117th Street in the heart of what was then Italian Harlem. (A remnant of that Italian presence survives to this day, including Rao's Restaurant at 114th Street and Pleasant Avenue.)

Among the things the two had in common were their addictions. Polly contracted hers in much the same way that Sam did: as the result of a mishandled medical problem. She suffered great pain from poorly done dental work and tried out Sam's morphine. She too became dependent on it and would remain secretly addicted for the rest of her life.

Polly's first child, Vanina (Nina) Juliette Cassotto, was born on November 30, 1917.

Sam was not doing well financially. He was a compulsive gambler, and to compensate for his losses, he invented a "Lung Testing and Exercising Machine," which he tried unsuccessfully to peddle. He did better with a pop-up doll game that was sold at carnivals and shooting galleries. He also sold orange Popsicles at South Beach on Staten Island. When Prohibition came, he worked with Costello in rum running for the Mafia between Canada and the northeastern United States.

By 1934, Costello had risen to the top of his profession. His operations had expanded from rum running to slot machines. He invented a slot that dispensed candy mints along with slugs that could be redeemed for money. His company had installed more than 5,000 machines in speakeasies and candy stores.

But Costello did not take Sam along for the ride. Sam was not salvageable. On his own and reeling from the Depression, Sam fell hard. In 1934 he was arrested for pickpocketing. On October 14, 1934, he was convicted and sentenced to prison at Sing Sing in Ossining, New York.

Sam smuggled morphine into prison in the heel of his shoe, but his supply ran out and he went into withdrawal. He died of pneumonia, a complication of the withdrawal.

Bobby's grandfather will remain an elusive figure in Bobby's story, for he died a long time ago and no one remembers him now. Yet Big Sam Curly's spirit resurfaced one day recently, popping up like one of the dolls he invented. In a 2004 interview with one of Bobby's musicians, Bobby Rozario, Rozario talked about Bobby's performing skills on stage. "Bobby," he said, "had the nerve of a burglar."

AFTER SAM'S DEATH, Polly expected help from Costello, but none was forthcoming. She went on Home Relief. She was alone with Nina, who was 17 and, in the aftermath of grief for her lost father, looking for her first love. Nina became pregnant in 1935 by a college student she had been dating. She broke off the relationship and never told the boy of her condition, which was possible to conceal because of her congenital obesity. Abortions could be found even then; both Polly and Nina had already gone through them. But Nina wanted this child. To hide the disgrace, Polly decided that they would move to another neighborhood a few blocks away, at 125th Street and Second Avenue, where they could say that the baby was the son of Polly and the late Sam.

On the day of labor, May 12, 1936, Polly and Nina got off the bus that would take them to Bellevue Hospital and ran into the father of

Nina's child. "The last time Nina saw him was the day she delivered Bobby, the day she went into the hospital," Gary Walden, Nina's younger son and Bobby's brother, recalls. "They hadn't seen each other in five months. She never told him. She comes off the bus and there he is. There's her weight problem to begin with, and she tells him she put on more weight.

"Here's this college kid who obviously my mother must have cared for. They slept together, she got pregnant, he's lived his whole life, whether he married and had kids or not, whether he got killed in World War II, you don't know—continued living his life never knowing, 'My son was Bobby Darin.'"

The delivery took 40 hours, without anesthesia. On the morning of May 14, 1936, Nina gave birth to a baby boy weighing 7 pounds, 8 ounces. She named him Walden Robert Cassotto.

Chapter Two

A "SCRAWNY THING"

POLLY WAS ALMOST 50 when Bobby was born in 1936. For the next 32 years, Bobby would look upon her as his mother and Nina as his sister.

Polly and Nina settled down with Bobby in the Harlem apartment. It was a third-floor walk-up consisting of three rooms: a kitchen, living room, and bedroom joined by a long hall. Bobby's crib was a drawer.

In May of 1937, Nina met Charlie Maffia—that was really his name—at a dance. Charlie was a handsome, sturdy, likeable Italian man and a terrific dancer. He was a jack-of-all-trades who worked at the R&B Hardware Store as a clerk and truck driver for $18 a week. A hard worker, he loved food and music and a lot of women.

Charlie relished Polly's cooking, and soon he was practically living in the apartment. He was a nurturer, and he brought stability into the household. Within two and a half years, he moved in completely. "Charlie would work full time plus take on two, three extra jobs," says Gary Walden, Bobby's younger brother. "Anything he could do to make a buck. He could fix anything: refrigerator, car, you name it. He wasn't the most intelligent person in the world, but he was a good man. He was such a good-natured slob, and he loved Bobby and would do anything for him. He regarded Bobby as his son. A boy—that was so important in Italian families—someone to teach how to fish."

Bobby gained a kind and loving father. Charlie never stinted on anything for Bobby; he gave generously and from the heart. It would be Charlie who paid Bobby's large medical bills for all the years of his sickly childhood.

In a 1958 interview with Dick Clark, Bobby said, "You could walk into our house and you'd never see any great furniture or anything, but the love would hit you right square in the teeth."

A daughter, Vivienne "Vee" Carla, was born to the couple in 1943. A second daughter, Vana, arrived in 1944. It would never be easy for the two girls, with Bobby as the star of the household.

Polly was a devoted mother. She read poetry to Bobby, sang to him, and talked of her love of literature, music, and theater. She wanted to instill in him early a sense of the possibilities of life beyond the confines of poverty. Polly's German-Irish ancestry, and her literary and artistic bent, would set her apart in the hardscrabble neighborhoods the family lived in. Her secret addiction to morphine and her physical illnesses deepened her isolation from the surrounding world. She was at home all the time (Nina and Charlie both worked long hours) and constantly available to Bobby. Soon she was tutoring the boy in English, math, and history as well as taking him to vaudeville shows.

Bobby was a frail child, and at three he fell from a chair and broke his leg. Dodd Darin writes in his memoir that "neighbors expected the scrawny thing to die in the cardboard box that [lined] his crib-drawer." Bobby would later tell *Life* magazine writer Shana Alexander that he was so sickly as a baby that "the neighbors used to stop my mother on the street and say, 'Whaddya wanna wheel that thing around for? It's gonna die.'" Bobby had digestive trouble, major eye problems, and acute sensitivity to pain. Harriet Wasser recalls that "Polly would bathe his eyes constantly. Bobby's illness was a very major part of his everyday existence."

Dr. Morris Spindell, the family physician, gave a grim prognosis to Polly, which Bobby overheard: it would be a surprise if he lived to the age of 16; 21 would be even more unlikely. Spindell stated that if by some miracle Bobby made it into his mid-30s, medical progress might have advanced to the point where he could survive to full life expectancy. Unless that happened, he said, the ultimate life span Bobby could even dream of was 35.

The family rallied around him. Nina called him "The King," and he was treated that way. Bobby was the center of devoted attention from three loving parents; Polly, Nina, and Charlie. Much of his childhood was a solitary one, spent in bed, lying still to avoid the pain that any movement often caused. Five attacks of rheumatic fever battered him from ages 8 to 12. He took sulfa drugs daily. He couldn't roughhouse with the other boys and missed months of school. He spent most of the time reading and coloring as well as listening to the big-band music and Jolson records that Charlie played for him. Dodd Darin says, "From that point he started running. There was no time to waste. 'We're gonna do it now and yes, I'm brash, and yes I'm in your face, but not because I'm rude, but because I gotta get somewhere.' My dad needed to become a legend by 25 because he expected to be dead by 30."

Bobby's aloneness gave him the perspective of a much older man and an unusual degree of objectivity and thoughtfulness. He later told Dick Clark that most of the kids in his neighborhood "didn't ask questions . . . Most of them never knew how to do anything but grow up running scared. It's not that they were stupid; most of them had alert minds. But running with the pack becomes a habit."

Amid the isolation, pain, and poverty, Bobby's bedrock companion, his source of strength, was Polly. She was more than a caring mother to him; she was his mentor and guide. Polly was the one who encouraged Bobby to go to school and who nurtured his striving. She told him, "You don't belong in a tenement. You're not like other boys. You're special. You can't play ball; there are things you can't do because of your illness. But you're bright, you can learn, you can read, you can fill your mind with great, intelligent thoughts." She also gave him a sense of perspective about himself: "You're just one grain of sand in this huge world no matter how important you become. Every one's life is just as important to them as yours is to you. But you can make something remarkable out of your life."

Two years after Polly's death and shortly after he achieved success, Bobby was interviewed by Barry Gray, the nighttime talk-show host on radio station WMCA in New York City. Bobby said of Polly:

My mom was a very powerful influence because, when I was born, I was born different than anybody else, as far as she was concerned. I was a very sickly individual, and because it was hours and hours without sleep to take care of me, she just accepted the fact that God wouldn't do that to her or to me without making up for it later. So she just brought me up to try to think for myself, try to understand.

That was the key to her entire existence—the word understanding. *In other words, that I should understand myself, and then I can understand everybody. I enjoyed just a smattering of success before she passed away. And even in that time she never got so excited that she would go around saying, "Did you see what my son has done?" She didn't have to. She accepted it from the time I was born. Like it was supposed to happen.*

Bobby shared Polly's lack of surprise about his success. "I am two years behind," he said in 1958. "I should have been 20 when the first thing happened instead of 22."

Harriet Wasser, who knew Polly, recalls, "Everything Bobby had heard about his deceased 'father,' Sam Cassotto, was negative. Polly was really the one in the family, with no money, having nothing, who set Bobby in a different direction. This woman told Bobby from day one that he was going to be somebody. That's what sent him soaring."

As the rheumatic attacks receded, Bobby became much more active and social. He started to do Jolson imitations, play the clarinet, and do comedy, in spite of going to a tough school. In 1944 he entered Clark Junior High School in the Bronx. Actor George Nestor was in Bobby's class and recalls walking toward the school on the first day of class: "That was one very tough place, almost all working-class Irish and Italian tough kids. As I approached it with the other new students, I looked up at the windows on the second floor and saw dozens of boys looking down and shaking their fists at us."

Nestor remembers Bobby as an affable and friendly kid who wanted to break into show business. "Bobby was a slight, small guy, thin and pale. Very friendly, sweet guy. I knew he had a rheumatic heart; he had told us. He never had any clothes; he wore the same black suit every day. He always had friends. He talked about the performers he liked. He loved Clayton, Jackson, and Durante. He particularly loved Eddie Jackson; he said he was the old vaudeville, the strutting stuff. He was crazy about Jolson too.

"We had a little group of guys who hung out at the candy store, all aspiring performers: Bobby, who played the clarinet and wanted to be a comedian; Ivar Schwartzman, another aspiring comic; and John Bravo, who was dabbling in magic.

"Bobby did shticks in class, in the hall, with the other kids. Like he'd say, 'Ladies and gentlemen, we have here tonight a very famous celebrity. I would like to introduce him, the great boxer, Two-Ton Galento. Two-Ton, stand up and take a bow. Oh, I beg your pardon, ma'am, I'm sorry.'

"We were about to do a School Day show. I was interested in ventriloquism at that time, so I asked Bobby to be my dummy. He sat on my lap. I talked, and I tapped him on the back of his head and he moved his mouth. There was a strange French teacher, cool and attractive, always wore white gloves, claimed she hated men. Miss Winters. I said to Bobby, 'Have you heard about Miss Winters?' The dummy—that's Bobby—said, 'Yes, I heard about her.' I said, 'Half the men in town have asked to marry her.' And the dummy said, 'And the other half already have.' Big yuk. The next day Miss Winters called us in and said, 'I've heard that in your act yesterday, there were certain references to s-e-x.' She spelled it out like that."

John Bravo taught Bobby how to work a yo-yo. "Duncan Yo-Yo would go around setting up yo-yo contests. It was a big fad at the time. I was the Bronx yo-yo champion. Bobby couldn't do the yo-yo to save his life. He was so embarrassed. One day he said, 'Could you help me out?' So I helped him win the contest. He got this gold patch: YOU'RE A GOLD YO-YO GUY."

Bravo roamed the Bronx streets and parks with Bobby. "We'd just go from block to block; we'd razz each other. But Bobby was always physically weak. He didn't participate in athletics. I'm sure that wasn't easy for Bobby, because he wanted to be a dancer as well as a comic. So Bobby was isolated from the gang. He talked to me about the fact that he was going to die young and that he would have to accomplish what he wanted to do very quickly."

Bobby's love for vaudeville began in those years. Already fading and in its last days—movies were infinitely cheaper because they did not entail paying eight or nine acts and a band of musicians—movie theaters would feature vaudeville just once a week. Bobby glimpsed the last of it. "We'd go to movies and vaudeville," Bravo recalls, "the kind of places where they'd give away dishes to the people. The Bronx Opera House had serials on Saturday. In those days the kids would sit in a separate section and there was a matron who looked like a nun, in a black outfit with white lace. The RKO Royal and Loew's National featured vaudeville on Wednesdays. There were dancers, magicians, adagio dancers, guys who played the spoons. Strawberry Russell, a black vaudevillian who did everything from playing a cigar-box violin to tap dancing. You had a live orchestra; they played 'Strike Up the Band' and the red curtain opened, and the spotlight . . . It was magic."

George Nestor lost track of Bobby after graduation, but saw him one more time. "I was walking on 56th Street in Manhattan and ran into him. He was engaged to Sandra Dee and was going to play the Copa. He said, 'You gotta come and see my act.' So I went. Afterwards he was in his suite at Hotel 14 adjoining the Copa. He asked somebody about Sandra Dee: 'What do you think about my baby? Isn't she a doll?' He did the usual stuff when you've made it, snapping his fingers at the ass-lickers, the hangers-on. He got very jazzy; it was a different personality, all that Sinatra stuff. Not that he had become bad. He was still a very nice guy.

"That's the last I saw of Bobby. I remember thinking at the time, watching him run back and forth: if you have rheumatic fever, this is not what you should be doing."

Chapter Three
THE NERVE OF A BURGLAR

AT 12, BOBBY WAS ADMITTED to one of the most prestigious high schools in New York, a school for "brains"—the Bronx High School of Science. Bobby and his best friend, John Bravo, had been advised to go there by guidance counselors at Clark Junior High. Bobby fared badly, although in the long run he would find a group of friends with whom he would bond for many years.

Bobby felt painfully apart and different at Bronx Science. An overwhelming majority of the students were Jewish and from upwardly mobile homes, financially far better off than his family, and intellectually and culturally several levels above them. "These were future professional people, lawyers, doctors, scientists," Bobby said later. "Suddenly I'm with people not pressured financially, people uninvolved with food, rent, and clothing. I went overnight from the non-thinkers to the thinkers. It was shattering and abrupt."

Even among the inner group of his closest friends, almost no one was ever allowed to see the inside of his home. An experience he would never forget happened in lab class: a cockroach crawled out of his jacket to the amusement of his fellow students.

Bobby's long-time publicist, Harriet Wasser, or Hesh as she is affectionately called, has a different take on his reasons for going to Bronx Science: "Bobby went there because the school system was falling apart, going out of control, and there was so much machismo. Bobby was not a six-foot bruiser. He was the kind of guy that could easily be bullied. I was told by his friends that Bobby went there to get away from that tough milieu."

Bobby was shaken by the surreal experience of going to a school where the highest value was put on intelligence and returning in the afternoon to a neighborhood where education didn't mean anything at all; in fact, it was regarded as an effete pursuit. From these early years came a lifelong sense of shame about his family. "I didn't belong, at school or anywhere else," Bobby told Gene Lees, former editor of *Downbeat* magazine. "I enjoyed doing homework. That made me a freak to the kids on the block. And going to college was even more unheard of."

Bobby's alienation from and contempt for all of his family except Polly began at Bronx Science. In his memoir of Bobby, *Me and Bobby D*, Steve Karmen recalls the way Bobby would make fun of Nina's husband, Charlie Maffia, the only father figure he would ever know: "Now he [Bobby] was doing Charlie: 'I could drive the car for youse, take care of youse luggage, get youse stuff, hang around when youse need something, ya know? Ya know what I mean?"

Karmen's book, in fact, reeks with contempt for Bobby's family—a contempt Karmen may have imbibed from Bobby himself—referring to Nina as the "Burly Barracuda, the female Ralph Kramden," and Charlie Maffia as a "sometimes mechanic, sometimes garbage truck driver, and oft-times unemployed civilian." (Charlie was actually never unemployed.) Karmen says Maffia was "a big, crude, outgoing teddy bear, unshaven and wearing an old canvas jacket over a T-shirt. I could sense my mother's revulsion." Only Polly escapes Karmen's derision:

"[She] was a frail woman, with thinning gray hair, unfortunately sick with asthma. The illness made her seem quite old. Bobby was constantly worried about her health. Sometimes, I felt a little envious of how completely this kindly old lady believed in her son."

"Bobby didn't want to be where he was," Harriet Wasser says. "That provincial environment [of his family] was not going to be his fate. He hated it. He would do anything to get out of there. Nina wanted to be around him all the time, and he didn't feel comfortable with her. She was loud—it's hard to say all these things—she wasn't exactly the kind of person you would want around you. She'd butt in, say the wrong things."

Nina was obese, Charlie was a garbage man, the apartment was filled with cockroaches, with dust all over the furniture and a tub in the kitchen. The building shook with the fights and shouts of raucous neighbors struggling with the ravages of poverty. Bobby's own family was loud and "primitive," scratchers and screamers, sometimes eating with their fingers—this was Bobby's distortion of people who loved him 24 hours a day and would give their lives for him. But that was how he came to perceive them after visiting the homes of Bronx Science kids: rooms lined with bookshelves; radios tuned to Oscar Brand on Sundays and every day to station WNYC, the intellectuals' sanctuary, and listening to Drew Pearson and Edward R. Murrow; parents going to concerts at Town Hall and Lewisohn Stadium, reading Balzac and Dostoyevsky and Dickens and Thomas Mann and the *New York Times* from front page to back, fighting for racial justice—soft-spoken, dignified, and well-dressed mothers and fathers who gazed at Bobby with perceptiveness, kind interest, and high expectations. To Bobby it was a new world.

Bobby looked at his family and saw them as a bunch of losers. If they were his role models, he thought, he would never make it. Love was not enough; you needed intelligence, willpower, the desire to succeed, a thirst for learning, an ability to perceive what was in front of you and understand how to maneuver and strategize. The more he came to understand his own gifts and talents, the more Bobby detested the family that loved him and kept him alive. He looked at them lying around and was terrified that he would turn out like them.

There was self-hatred in Bobby: he had to obliterate those aspects of his family that he feared in himself. "When I first knew Bobby, he was so poor, he wouldn't let anybody come to where he lived," says Dick Lord, a childhood friend. "But he did let me come to Baruch Place for my 18th birthday party. Bobby wrote me a birthday card on a yellow napkin. This is what he wrote: 'Happy Birthday to the greatest from the ugliest.' Isn't that something?"

Harriet Wasser reiterates Bobby's alienation from his family. "He felt they were really low-class, constricting." Bobby didn't associate Polly, whom he thought was his mother, with the rest of the family. "She was different from the others," recalls Wasser, who knew Polly. "For one thing, she wasn't Italian; she was German-Irish. She was soft-spoken, unlike the rest of the family. To Bobby it was like, 'Why should I be a part of them when I can be a part of her?'"

"Everything he had heard about his deceased 'father,' Sam Cassotto, was negative," Wasser says. "Polly was really the one in the family, with no money, having nothing, who set Bobby in a different direction."

Although Bobby loved Polly deeply—and it was obvious to everyone that both Polly and Nina adored him—there was a deprivation hovering about Bobby that suggested the limits of Polly's ability to be a real mother to him. A recurrent motif in interviews with Bobby's acquaintances from his early years was the extent to which Bobby established close relationships with their Jewish and Italian mothers.

Polly, because of her morphine addiction and physical problems, was bedridden most of the time from her mid-40s on, subsisting on almost no food but zwieback and milk. She must have been a withdrawn, removed figure to Bobby, as much as she loved him and tried to be attentive.

Gary Walden, Bobby's brother and Nina and Charlie's son, has a mixture of love and resentment toward Bobby that is leavened by compassion. But he cannot understand Bobby's rejection of the family, which extended to Gary himself. Gary was born in 1956 and experienced the family from a very different vantage point. "Bobby was Nina's first born, a son and a beautiful little boy," Gary reflects. "And she had an unbelievable bond with her mother, Polly. Bobby was born into an atmosphere of total and complete love, and he had that growing up. How could you deny these people that gave you everything: their youth, their vitality, their encouragement, everything they possibly had? And yet he did.

"Bobby was given the best of everything as a child. If the girls needed to have their tonsils taken out, they went to the free clinic. Bobby had to go to a special hospital and have special doctors. Nina was working full time, Charlie was working two, three jobs, doing other errands, anything he could do to make a buck. He was never unemployed. It was all for Bobby."

In later life Bobby would constantly point to his youth as a time of painful poverty. Near the end of his life he took a trip to New York with his son Dodd to show him how low his origins were and how far he had come.

Gary Walden angrily disputes Bobby's version of a poverty-stricken childhood. "Charlie and Nina rented a bungalow every summer in South Beach on Staten Island," he says. "Not two weeks, the entire summer. There are several pictures of Nina and Charlie on a dock sitting with a reel. Who did this in those days? Nina insisted on it, because she said the kids needed to get out of the city, be in the ocean air. That's why it makes the trip Bobby took with Dodd to the *slums* he grew up in, in 1971 so weird. That bungalow was a great accomplishment. Bobby didn't take Dodd out to South Beach. Okay, it was just a bungalow; it had no heat. But because of Charlie's ability, he could always fix it up. Just two blocks to the beach. Everybody would come and visit. And Charlie absolutely loved Bobby."

To DISGUISE HIS FEELINGS of inadequacy at Bronx Science, Bobby became both class clown and, in his peg pants, sharply pointed shoes, and loud shirts, the smart kids' notion of a hood. "I remember Bobby and the other guys in his band dressing up as women on Topsy Turvsy Night at school," says classmate Alan Press. Bobby started a one-person extortion ring of his own. The take was usually a few quarters. He did little homework. He discovered music and acting, but these were very low on the list of Bronx Science's priorities. He did begin to realize that he wasn't less intelligent than the other students, but that they had been raised in a broader environment far removed from the world of his experience.

"To these kids," John Bravo says, "Bobby was a hood. So he acted like one. We were out of the ghetto. I don't think he was ever malicious or cruel. But they smelled it, that he was from a different stratum. And the two of us wore the pointed shoes, very garish suits, loud checkered shirts. We were the only ones that dressed that way, and we didn't even realize it. Those were just the clothes we knew."

"I met Bobby when he bumped into me in the hall at Bronx Science," Jerrold Atlas, another classmate, remembers. "I'd been there two weeks and was still wet behind the ears. Books went flying. As we were picking them up and sorting them out I said, 'Hey listen. I'm just glad to meet somebody who knows their way around this place. I don't know where I'm going.' Bobby said, 'Where do you want to go? I'll walk with you.'

"Bobby hung out in his world and I would sometimes be there as a shadow. That group of musicians—Behrke, Ocasio, Raim—and the weird guys who were smoking across the street at the coffee shop called Nuts and Butts. One day I was learning to play the guitar and didn't know what the hell I was doing. Bobby said, 'I'll show you.' So he came to my house. My mother made dinner. That was the start of their very special relationship. Whenever I would meet Bobby for the rest of his life, he'd always have a present wrapped up for my mother. He always said that she treated him like a person. She was like a surrogate mother, and I think he had many."

There were teachers who recognized Bobby's potential. "We had an

English teacher," recalls Atlas, "a tough lady named Molly Epstein. We called her 'Jolly Molly.' She talked to Bobby a lot. She taught him to use the language in staccato notes: short, fast words. I would see the two of them in class; they would always stand very close. She was very fond of Bobby. Bobby told me she sharpened his respect for language. And later, in 'Splish Splash,' when Bobby jumps out of the tub, it was 'Good golly, Miss Molly.' Well, that was Molly Epstein."

Bronx Science opened up Bobby's world and perspective and led him to an understanding of deeper values and goals. The family was now living in the projects at Baruch Place on the Lower East Side. For Bobby's family, the apartment, which was newly built, was a step up. Bobby hated it. The local kids would urinate in the elevator. Bobby, with his 137 IQ, had to get out of the ghetto and away from his claustrophobic family, even though they battled night and day to keep him alive. He was reaching out for an environment in which he could express himself and be known and understood. There was a world out there that would value his talent and intellect. Bobby told Nina, "It's like I'm in a tunnel, and all the way down at the far end is a small spot of light. I'm heading toward that light. I'll sacrifice anything I must to reach it. I can't let anything get in the way, because when I reach it, that light will be the world."

"Coming out of the ambience that he did," says Harriet Wasser, "he was always fighting the element that said, 'You can't go beyond us; you're one of us.' Remember, Bobby traveled all the way from the Lower East Side to Bronx Science. He also traveled all the way up there just to be with the kids he palled around with—Raim, Ocasio, Behrke, Atlas, and the rest. He never hung out in his own neighborhood."

Bobby had begun to pal around with Dick Behrke and soon with Walter Raim, Steve Karmen, and Eddie Ocasio. In junior year, the boys formed a band, with Bobby on drums, Steve as vocalist, and Dick on trumpet. It was a deep bond that would only be ruptured by Bobby's dizzying rise to fame and success. Within this small group, Bobby would become the charismatic center, the person others would want to be close to, sensing his special gifts. They were moths to the flame. The boys rehearsed together every night for three months and got their first gig at a high school dance. The teacher on duty, Mr. Feingold, gave them 20 cents and a stick of gum each as payment.

They were soon hired by Gertrude Newmark, day-camp director of the Sunnyland Farms Hotel, a small Catskills resort in Parksville, New York, for the summer of 1951. For $35 a week, they would bus tables at every meal, manage the candy stand, and create stage shows at night. Bobby borrowed a set of drums, which he could not afford to buy, from Dick Lord, whom he had met at the beginning of the summer.

"On my summer vacation," Lord recalls, "I would work in the Catskills. One night I was sitting on a kids' swing, and this girl came over to me and she grabbed my fly. I was 15.

"'What are you doing?' I said. She said, 'Take it out.' I said, 'No, no.' I was like frightened. She said, 'Well, that's okay. Because this drummer at Sunnyland Farms, he lets me do it. I'll go there.' As she walked off, I said, 'What's his name?' 'Cassotto,' she said. So I tell the guys in the band, and the next day we got off we drove to Sunnyland Farms to see this place and meet this jerkoff king. Bobby told me that every morning he had to get up and go to Monticello to take two courses he'd failed at Bronx Science, then he'd come to work at Sunnyland. We all became friends."

While he did his share of adolescent fooling around, Bobby also found his first girlfriend at Sunnyland Farms, Laurel Newmark, the daughter of Gertrude Newmark. "It was at Sunnyland that Bobby got the bug to act and sing and dance," Newmark recalls. "Before that he was a drummer and did a little comedy. People began to say that he was so talented. So he got bitten."

She describes Sunnyland Farms as a very small family hotel. "It was very *haimeshe*; the only non-Jews were Bobby and Eddie Ocasio. We put on our own shows. The boys did shticks. I did shticks. They would play and people would dance. Bobby worked in the concession during the day." Bobby needed the money badly; he had exactly one pair of jeans, and he would jump in the swimming pool with his jeans on to wash them.

"Bobby and I came to love each other a lot, but it was really young love. What do you do? You dance, you smooch. He wanted to marry me, but my mother said no way. He was always a gentleman."

Bobby's proposal to Laurel, the first of several he would make to girls, was delivered to her mother. "It was the normalcy he liked, my house, my mother's cooking. He wanted to be there. He would play the piano and sing. He learned some Yiddish from my mother."

Stanley Greenberg, another Bronx Science alumnus, writes in a recent memoir published in the Bronx Science newspaper of seeing Bobby in the Catskills that summer. He describes Bobby, who was called "Waldo," as exuding a "brash, feisty . . . tough-guy, hard-nosed quality":

> One summer evening Joe [Pastore] sang in the casino and Waldo the drummer did a comedy routine. Joe was sensational and Waldo was funny as heck. The Sunnylands glowed for a week after their performance. Somehow, Joe and Waldo then got a booking at Klein's Hillside Hotel . . . a huge hotel complex. Waldo borrowed my tan slacks because he had no suitable pants of his own. My pants enveloped his shoes as I was taller than Waldo . . . We all went over to Klein's to see our boys.

It was a disaster. Joe was just okay, but Bobby flopped completely.

But that was not the end of the story. Bobby would return to Klein's another night, determined to make it this time. Bobby's favorite performer was song-and-dance man and comedian Donald O'Connor. On this night Bobby performed a routine that came out of his love for O'Connor. All his innate gifts for singing, mimicry, comedy, dancing—for being the consummate showman—came electrifyingly alive. The response at Klein's Hillside was tumultuous. The applause came in waves at a grinning Bobby.

That was the night that Bobby got snagged. He knew what he wanted to be.

ONE REASON THAT BOBBY may have been such a little gentleman with Laurel was his terror of endangering his heart by having sex. Nina had drummed into him that it might very well kill him. There had been a "loose" woman on Baruch Place who invited Bobby into her apartment when he offered to help her with her groceries. Bobby left his friends and popped inside. Soon his friends heard a scream. There was shouting behind the door, and then it opened. Bobby stood there, his pants over his shoes. The woman attempted to pull him back. Bobby screamed, "I don't want to die!" His friends laughed hysterically at his being so chicken. It was the chance of a lifetime. Bobby could not explain to them why he was so afraid.

Charlie Maffia had heard of this incident and comforted Bobby about it. One morning while still working at Sunnyland Farms, instead of hitching to summer school in the morning, Bobby headed back to Baruch Place for the day. He knew that Polly and Nina were away at the cottage in South Beach. When Bobby entered, Charlie Maffia was on the bed, busily screwing the lady beneath him, his girlfriend Sally. Sally saw Bobby enter the room, stopped moving, and pushed Charlie's head. Charlie turned, saw Bobby, and said, "Hey Bobby, meet Sally."

Bobby started to leave, but Charlie called out to him, "Bobby, wait!" Bobby stood at the door.

Charlie leaned over and whispered something to Sally. Then he got up, smiled at Bobby, and slapped him on the back. "See ya later, alligator," he said, and closed the door.

Bobby was terrified, but horny as hell. He undressed slowly. He lay down next to Sally, his heart pounding. He thought it would blow up, that this was the end, but he couldn't stop himself. He exploded inside her.

Bobby rolled over and tried to regain his breath. He was wiped out. Sally got up and left; Bobby lay still for five minutes. Charlie waited outside. Bobby finally appeared.

"Well?" Charlie said.

Bobby grinned broadly. "What a way to go!" he said.

That fall, Bobby felt a tremendous sense of relief about his sex life and a new clarity about what he wanted to do. He would become the best entertainer in the world by the time he was 25. That would give him five glorious years to enjoy it all before he checked out.

Bobby went back to Bronx Science for his last year and graduated in June 1952. He spent another summer at Sunnyland, quietly reevaluating his goals and values. The sophisticated and tolerant milieu of Bronx Science had made a powerful impact on him. He encountered attitudes and behavior that suggested to him a broader range of options in life, a sense of possibility and dignity in human behavior. Bobby's feelings about civil rights and racism, about Jews and blacks, were unalterably reshaped during those four years at Bronx Science. In 1965, when he was 29, Bobby reflected on this experience in a radio interview on a program called *Ladies of the Press*. He said that until he went to Bronx Science, it was a natural thing to stand around the corner and "make derogatory references to other ethnic groups." He said it was brought to his attention by classmates at Bronx Science that he was "perpetuating a bias that was unfair." He hadn't even been aware he had been doing it. He "gave up a whole summer to thinking about it" and decided he would never use such words again.

"Later on in life," Jerrold Atlas recalls, "I said to him, 'You don't use that racist stuff anymore.' He said, 'I grew up.'"

"Bobby's education actually impacted on his relationship with his family," Harriet Wasser says. "By going to school, getting a scholarship—actually this really hurt him with them. In his own way he probably acted as though he was better than them. It would have been nice if Bobby could have said, 'Well, okay, my family is poor and has no education, they can't do much in their living situation, but I love them and they are great people.' Bobby never did that."

Rona Barrett, former movie columnist and a close friend of Bobby's, recalls the family (except Polly) as "basically real 'dem-dere-dose' people. There wasn't the intellectual stimulation that Bobby always needed. He had a tremendous curiosity about him. He wanted to know everything and anything. He wanted to be with people from whom he could learn."

At the same time, there were many resentments toward Bobby within the family. "Bobby's sisters saw that he was being catered to on every level by Polly, Nina, and Charlie," says Wasser. "Bobby had been carried around, he was in so much pain when he was a kid. On the surface, Bobby mainly seemed to be a perfectly normal kid, even in his own family. So the fact he was treated special was resented by the girls. There was this sibling rivalry." Wasser saw the relationship between Nina and Bobby as an intense one. "Oh my God, she was passionate about him. You just knew this was a special kind of thing; this was not a sister."

"But even later," Wasser goes on, "he was still the prince of the household. And Bobby was arrogant, he was always the star, even when he was nobody. That's why he became somebody, that charisma. When you're told all your life that you have something special, you ask yourself, 'What is this that makes me so special?'"

Drummer Ronnie Zito recalls that when Bobby began to achieve success, his family was very proud of him. "But they weren't amazed," Zito says. "Because all of them gave me the feeling that they expected it, that he was supposed to be a star. It was like, oh, of course."

Graduating from Bronx Science at 16 in a ceremony held at Loew's Paradise Theater, Bobby received a fellowship in theatre arts from Hunter College. Once there he played the second lead in Ibsen's *Hedda Gabler*. Bobby billed himself as Walden Roberts and won praise from the campus paper. Bobby recalled later that he went to Hunter so that he could "get up on the stage and ply what I hoped would be my trade. I was given that opportunity more than amply the first semester, and it was taken away from me in the second [to give other students their chance]. My purpose was clear and defined, so I retired from college life and went into the street to fight."

FREED FROM THE DAILY RESPONSIBILITY of school, Bobby rented a one-room apartment with Dick Behrke at 217 West 71st Street in Manhattan. It was Bobby's first stab at independence, a giddy moment for both boys. "It was a brownstone," Dick Lord remembers. "One flight up. The first day I walked in, I saw Dick and said, 'Where's Bobby?' He said, 'He's on the window ledge, tap-dancing.'"

Bobby and Dick Behrke did small band jobs together, Behrke on the trumpet, Bobby playing the drums and singing. They played at New York University and for rent-raising parties. They were sure now that show business would be their career. They didn't want anything to fall back on. It was total commitment and it was time to soak up experience in the real world.

"I would hang out with them sometimes all night long," Lord says. "Bobby showed me my first drag queen at a jazz club, Club 78 on Broadway at 78th Street, where Bobby sang and Behrke played for free. Both Bobby and Dick were in love with the same waitress who worked at Nedick's, an orange-juice and hot-dog stand. There's a circle when you get off the West Side Highway on 79th Street, and we stayed up there all night long, because they were arguing which one would walk her home.

"They never had any money. Around five in the morning there would be truck deliveries of bagels to the luncheonettes in the neighborhood. The deliverymen would leave these canvas bags of bagels outside the stores, and we would sneak over and steal bagels. Bobby and Dick hung a clothesline in the apartment. They would hang the bagels from the clothesline."

"None of us drank," Lord recalls. "So we decided it would be good to try. We bought a bottle of rye, but no one liked the taste. So Behrke had a great idea. If we ate peanut butter, he reasoned, we'd get thirsty, and then we'd have to drink the rye. So we did. All that happened was that we got dizzy and had heartburn. Bobby said he had drunk once before in his life, fell down a flight of stairs, and never drank again until that night."

Bobby was taking odd jobs: cleaning latrines, working in a munitions factory. He was often depressed and discouraged. Bobby canvassed agents' offices in search of an acting job. Dick Lord remembers that Bobby was fearless and unstoppable, and that his sense of timing and spontaneity, gift for mimicry, and boundless self-confidence that would soon serve him so well on stage were already very much in play. Still, in 1955, Bobby and Dick ran out of money. The electricity in their apartment was turned off, followed by the phone. The purloined bagels became their main source of food. Unable to afford the West 71st Street apartment any more, the boys had moved into Behrke's sister Lois's apartment in a racially mixed neighborhood in the Bronx. The Brooklyn Dodgers had won the World Series and there was pandemonium on the streets: bottles thrown out of windows, inebriated people staggering around, cars triple-parked. People were leaning out of windows on pillows, screaming down into the street.

Dick, Bobby, and Behrke passed a bar with a sign that read JAM SESSION TONIGHT. Behrke said, "Hey, we'll come back later and play," and Bobby said, "That's a great idea." Dick Lord said timidly, "I don't know. Look what's going on. And we're the only white kids around." Bobby and Behrke both jumped on Lord for this remark. "Aren't you ashamed of yourself?"

In the evening they returned to the bar. It was jumping: streamers and party hats, the jukebox blasting. The boys were the only white faces. "When we walked in," Lord says, "it was like a still shot, a frozen frame in a movie." Bobby asked the poker-faced bartender if they could sit in on the session. Without speaking, the bartender just pointed to the back room.

Bobby said to Lord, "Hold the drumsticks. I'll be right back," and left with Behrke. Dick Lord, not knowing what to do and not a drinker, ordered a beer. It was still very quiet in the room. "Finally," he says, "a big tremendous guy taps me on the shoulder and said, 'Who did you bet on?' I said truthfully, 'Well, I didn't bet.' And this guy said to me, 'Well, if you did bet, who would you bet on?' And I said, 'The Brooklyn Dodgers.' And he said, 'Too bad.' And he took out a Yankees pennant, unzipped his fly, and stuck the pennant in his fly. And he said to me, 'Kiss the flag.'

"Now my back is against the bar, and there's a circle of men around me, grown men, watching. And I know I'm not gonna kiss the flag. And the circle is getting closer. I was so frightened that I was cool.

"And all of a sudden, Bobby comes out of the back room and he sees what's happening. And he jumps on the bar, takes the drumsticks, and starts playing them on the bottles lined up against the wall. And the crowd is distracted. They're looking up at Bobby. They can't believe it: this crazy white kid is on the bar, fearless, playing on the bottles. And then Bobby takes a napkin, unzips his fly, and puts the napkin in his fly. And he does an impersonation of the guy who put the pennant in his fly. It was just unbelievable. And pretty soon they're all laughing. And I'm laughing. And the guy with the pennant—first he was amazed, and then he started to chuckle. I mean he couldn't help it. And then Bobby looks down to me and he says, '*Run! Run! Run!*' And he jumps off the bar and we all ran away."

Bobby was finally hired to play an American Indian in a touring production of *Kit Carson* produced by the Salome Gaynor Theater for Children. He earned $45 a week on the seven-week tour. Bobby later said, "I came out of that experience feeling, 'This is where I belong,' in show business. I had the world by the chops. Then I got back to New York and discovered there were only forty thousand other actors in this vast city."

During this tour Bobby met a 31-year-old Spanish snake dancer named Bernice. Bobby wound up playing the bongos for her and experiencing his first torrid love affair. Not much is known about this episode in Bobby's life except its traumatic impact upon him. He learned from it that he could only depend on himself, not on others. The lady was passionate and unstable and prone to suicide attempts in front of Bobby. He saved her life several times and once used a wire clothes hanger to help her have an abortion.

Bobby became emotionally ensnared. Bernice insisted that if he abandoned her, she would kill herself. The abusive relationship was over in six months, when she told him he was a hopeless loser and left him. The dancer took her life in January 1959, overdosing on sleeping pills, long after she and Bobby had parted. The police found her in a hotel room, surrounded by burning candles. She was wearing a nun's habit, and her hands held a crucifix. According to Shana Alexander in

Life, the end of the affair 'left Bobby feeling like an emotional basket case. The experience left him despondent for months. Then his despair dissolved in a newfound ambition: he would battle his way alone to the top of show business in the shortest possible time." Bobby told Alexander of the dancer: "Before I met her, I was just a kid in the Bronx. Afterward, I was the most disillusioned human being in the world. But I was no kid. I knew what I was singing about. I don't confuse a lyric with just words."

"That's the reason Bobby could sing with such depth for a young guy," explained Steve Blauner. "If you listen to Sinatra in the early days, he was this sweet little voice, this pure thing. He was that sweet thing—and then Ava kicked the shit out of him. So it takes a while. After that, Sinatra had lived those songs he was singing. You could feel it. Well, Bobby had that happen to him at an early age."

When the tour ended, Bobby and Dick Behrke were completely broke. Both needed clothes to play a band gig, and so did Dick Lord. Bobby suggested they steal them.

The next day they went to Klein's on Union Square, the lowest rung of the department stores, where clothes were dumped in wooden bins for the masses to pick through. Dick Lord and Bobby hunted through the clothes bins at Klein's and took what they could get: gold slacks and tan jackets. They headed for the exit. A security guard approached Bobby, who suddenly spied a white and red umbrella.

Bobby ran out of the store with the clothes and the umbrella, the security guard running after him. Out on the sidewalk, Bobby, transformed into Donald O'Connor in *Singin' in the Rain*, opened the umbrella and twirled it as he ran, leaping into the air and grinning. He ran into the street, stopping traffic and attracting a crowd. Losing the guard, he turned the corner, curtsied to the crowd, and opened the door of a taxi. He stepped over the occupants of the cab to open the door and get out of the other side. Now the cab driver got out to chase him. Bobby jumped onto the hood of a car, opened the umbrella, and dueled with the furious cabbie. Then he jumped off the car, danced his way through the traffic, twirling the umbrella over his shoulder, and climbed onto the back of a truck. The truck drove off with Bobby, as he dropped the umbrella onto the street.

Later that night Bobby appeared at the apartment with the clothes and threw them on the bed. To celebrate, he tap-danced again on the window ledge.

Union Square was Bobby's best performance to date. He was about to take that electricity, that boldness, that dazzling wild spirit, comedic spontaneity, and fearlessness—what Bobby Rozario called "the nerve of a burglar"—on stage. He was getting ready.

Chapter Four
SPLISH SPLASH

IN 1955 BOBBY DEVELOPED a songwriting partnership with Don Kirshner, another student with whom he had become friends at Bronx Science. At first Bobby and Don wrote commercial jingles for radio spots, but soon they were writing pop songs together and making the rounds, trying to sell them to music publishers. They copyrighted their first song, "Bubble Gum Pop," on January 17, 1956. At the same time, Bobby was working at becoming a serious singer and musician. He sang and played on the demos of the songs he wrote with Kirshner. Demos were aimed at name singers who might record them, like Billy Eckstine or Frankie Laine. Bobby, with his chameleon-like skills, provided demos that sounded like carbon copies of the original singers.

Bobby and Don went to see George Scheck, who managed Connie Francis and was the host of *Star Time*, a television variety show geared to teenagers. Scheck was impressed with their song "My First Real Love," and asked them to write a theme song for *Star Time*. He also began to place some of their songs with established singers: LaVern

Baker recorded "Love Me Right," Bobby Short did "Delia," Gene Vincent "Wear My Ring," and the Coasters "Wait a Minute." Most significantly, Connie Francis, the leading female singer of the day, recorded their song "My First Real Love"—it was her fourth single—with Bobby playing drums on the record.

Scheck soon discovered that Bobby could sing and agreed to manage him in 1955, when Bobby was 19. Producer Bruce Charet, who worked for Scheck later on, recalls that Scheck "had a very close paternal relationship with Bobby. George had many letters Bobby had written him on opening nights, and he always signed the letters, 'I hope you're proud of me. Bobby.' I always thought that was telling: that Bobby was so starved for a father. George taught Bobby all those dance steps that Bobby did in his act, the original stuff, the eccentric tap."

Bobby soon changed his name from Cassotto to Darin. He spotted a "Mandarin" Chinese restaurant sign in Beverly Hills with the "man" part of the sign darkened and liked the feel of it. Scheck signed Bobby to a record contract with Decca. Bobby's first record with Decca was the Lonnie Donegan hit, "Rock Island Line." As a result of the record, Bobby got his first TV appearance on the Dorsey Brothers *Stage Show*.

In his memoir, *Me and Bobby D*, Steve Karmen writes of that year he spent working with Bobby as his guitarist. He presents a vivid picture of the time the two were starting out and how they split apart. For Karmen, as for many of the people with whom Bobby came into contact, meeting Bobby was a life-changing, unforgettable experience. Karmen provides sharp details of Bobby's forceful, exciting personality at the start, when dreams were taking shape and seemed remotely realizable. Karmen participated in the "Rock Island Line" recording session with Bobby as well as on *Stage Show*. Bobby to Steve about the audition: "Do you hear me right? Network TV, Sa-tur-day night! . . . Wear a tie!"

Bobby had written the lyrics of the song on his shirt cuffs to be sure he remembered them. During the performance, however, he was sweating so profusely that the lyrics ran and he was forced to improvise some forgotten lines. Connie Francis would later write, "Only George Scheck and I knew how terrified he was—that just [before the TV show] he tried to run out of town." As Karmen tells the story, as a result of the TV exposure, Bobby is booked for a two-week engagement at a nightclub in Detroit and he wants Steve there with him for security. Karmen's phone rings. "This is it, Curly," Bobby announces dramatically. "It's Club T, Detroit!" The words leave Karmen "light-headed and flushed: 'D . . . Detroit!'"

What follows is a slow decapitation that Bobby executes on Steve with firm precision. Scheck conveys to Bobby that he thinks Bobby is using Karmen as a crutch. Bobby begins to cut down Steve's participation in the act.

To deepen the frustration, Steve is replaced as roommate by a girl, Monica, whom Bobby decides to take along for the rest of the tour. But it does not end here. Bobby and Steve are booked for a "sock hop" at a local high school. At these hysterical events, teens screamed in ecstasy as pop stars lip-synched to their current records. At the high school, the girls are more turned on by the handsome, taller Steve Karmen than by Bobby. They scream, "Let Steve sing!" When he does, the girls swoon.

When they get back to their hotel room, a furious, jealous Bobby tells Steve: "I should have known with all that jailbait looking at your curls that you'd inspire something. It was bound to happen sooner or later. Ah, better now. George was right . . . the man was right, and very smart. Now, the first thing is that tonight I'll sing all the songs alone, the whole act, no harmonies. What works, works. What doesn't, I'll deal with later. Just walk out with me and stay on till the end. And don't come out for the bow."

Karmen's feeling is one of abandonment: "No matter how hard I tried to distance myself from the truth, it kept creeping back in under every excuse I could invent to dodge it—Bobby Darin was getting ready to move on without Steve Karmen."

When the girls persuade Steve to dance and rush him for autographs at the next hop, the denouement is swift. Bobby deals Steve the lethal blow: "You're hogging my act . . . It's my act, not a double of Darin and Karmen. It's a *solo* act . . . You're my *accompanist*, Steve, not my partner. You can't *ever* forget that . . . Your purpose here is to help get my act off the ground, not to be seen as a part of it."

Bobby goes on to score the coup de grâce:

"Know what? You're too damn dependent on me . . . '*I couldn't have opened without you*,'" he sneered. "Is that what you want to hear? Well, it seems to me that I've said that quite a few times already. And it's true. But so what? Things are changing . . . Just accept that it's my act and that everything I do is meant to protect my future."

Bobby gives a choice: accept the new rules or leave. "Go fuck yourself," says Steve, heading for the door. He recalls that he was "hardly able to see where I was going."

"Look, anybody who knew Bobby knew he wasn't going to be a part of a team," Harriet Wasser says. "Bobby needed Steve at the beginning. He had no money. This happens with people every day of the week: you meet somebody and that person can do something for you. You have to seize the time; you go with it. Steve was six feet tall, blond hair, green eyes. Bobby was very insecure about his looks. Steve had the looks; Bobby had the talent and the drive. Bobby was not trying to be nasty or manipulative or cruel. It was inevitable that he had to split from some friends. And Bobby said it best. He was talking about me and him. He once said to me, 'You can't be manipulated unless you allow it to happen. You're getting as much a kick out of this thing as I am.'"

Wasser pauses, then continues. "Bobby felt that his talent had to win out in the long run, but he was never going to become a name because of being a nice guy, a good guy. He was only going to do it through his talent, and I think that when you feel that way, you test people. You're looking for the people who are going to stick by you through thick or thin. You don't look to the people who are going to stick by you only if you do the right thing."

John Bravo has a harsher take on Bobby. "For Bobby, everything was career."

BOBBY ALWAYS HAD BELIEVERS all through his career. But in the beginning, before he obtained recognition from the public, there was Harriet Wasser who passionately believed in him. She saw it, she knew it before she even heard him sing or saw him perform, and she held on as the rocket took off. Today Harriet is a walking encyclopedia on Bobby. A 50-year music-industry veteran, this tiny, endearing, waif-like woman of 74 wears her hair in a bun and is a combination of maternal gentleness and indomitable survivor's will. She is an astonishing character out of the world of *Broadway Danny Rose*—the Automats and Lindy's of the 1950s, the 52nd Street jazz scene of Jimmy Ryan's and Eddie Condon's—and of the old, raffish, Runyonesque Broadway where the dollar-sign did not determine all human relationships, and dreamers still wandered down Broadway singing "Every Street's a Boulevard in Old New York." She has a steady gaze, trusting, empathetic eyes, and the bull-dozing tenacity of the early civil-rights activists or old-time Marxists of the '30s. If Bobby had ever sung "My Yiddishe Momma," made famous by Belle Baker and Sophie Tucker, he would have been singing of Harriet. Darin archivist Jimmy Scalia says of her tenacity, "She's like a little terrier. Everybody I see who comes into contact with her, their life changes. It's amazing how such a tiny woman could have that impact."

"She will follow you into the bathroom to finish her sentence," one observer has said of her. Still, Harriet's doggedness is leavened with a healthy pragmatism and realism and an uncanny effectiveness—Bobby certainly would not have tolerated her otherwise. For many years, Harriet has been burdened with severe arthritis, which makes her lurching walk painful and difficult. This has not impeded her 48-year crusade—before and since Bobby died—to make Bobby Darin the biggest name in show business after Frank Sinatra. She holds herself erect and regal and appears to be looking down at you when she is perched beneath you, taking up a little corner of the chair she sits on.

Wasser worked for Steve Lawrence and Eydie Gorme, Sammy Davis Jr., Johnnie Hartman, Tito Puente, and Harry Belafonte, but has been in love with Bobby Darin since she first spotted him in a booth at Hansen's drug store on Broadway in 1956 and became his publicist. She and Steve Blauner played the pivotal roles in discovering Bobby and nurturing and plotting his rise to the top. Her devotion to Bobby is the stuff of legend, and she is not shy about stoking the flames.

A comedy writer named Robin Lorring told Hesh about Bobby. "She told me there was a young man I should meet and how great he was. She thought I would love what he did." Wasser recalls going down to Hansen's, the Broadway version of Schwab's Drugs in Hollywood where Lana Turner was discovered, and where all the aspiring singers, comics, and songwriters hung out. Robin introduced her to Bobby.

"Bobby had already made a couple of records with Decca and Atco when I met him, and nothing had happened. He was at an in-between stage of not exactly knowing what would happen. He was afraid Atco was going to drop him. He was living with his family on Baruch Place. [Bobby had moved back home from Lois Behrke's apartment.] He couldn't survive without them. I was involved with him more than anyone else. No one else had the time with him that I did. And from then on I was talking him up, and I was so convinced about him. I didn't even know what he could do as an artist. It was just that I recognized something special about this person.

"The impact Bobby had on my life was enormous," continues Wasser. "We see that 40 years later, he's still very much alive as an artist, and he's alive among the people who knew him. He was a person who always had to think in terms of how long he was going to live.

"He was consumed with his mortality," Wasser says. "Bobby for the most part kept his illness under wraps from the time he was eight years old. All you saw was the cocky image. He was not going to let anything get him down. And not only that: he was going to show that if he was not going to live long, he was going to give everything he had. Because he wanted people to remember him."

Rita Dillon, Steve Blauner's former secretary, says, "If ever there was an individual who discovered a passion that fulfilled her, it was Harriet finding Bobby. Very often people like her get dropped into the background. Her devotion is pure. She never sought any bit of limelight. She didn't need to have that sort of so-called reward."

"Harriet was just one of those human beings that I think God put on earth so she could signal to others that 'this person's got talent,'" says writer Rona Barrett. "And her ear for music was always incredible. Steve Blauner and Harriet just decided for the last 30 years that Bobby wasn't going to be forgotten."

"Harriet found Bobby at Hansen's," John Bravo recalls. "She absolutely fell in love with him, both talent-wise and sexually, but I don't think they ever had an affair. She devoted her entire life to Bobby. I mean all she did was Bobby Darin. She woke up in the morning and went downtown, just went selling and pushing Bobby all day long. Sold Bobby to producers, to agents, to record deals. Unbelievable.

"She just decided, 'This is what I'm going to do for the rest of my life.' Maybe Bobby wouldn't exist if it weren't for her. And Bobby adored her. He realized this was a gem. Hesh was jealous if you ate a piece of pie with Bobby in a restaurant. She had to consume his whole life. He had to consume her and she had to consume him. Even your wife, even your mother would not do for somebody what she would do for Bobby."

"People would run the other way when they saw Harriet," Dick Lord told Dodd Darin. "Not because they didn't like her, but because she was so completely obsessed with Bobby. She would talk to plastic, wood, a chair. Anybody, anything that would be standing still, she would tell about how wonderful Bobby was."

Hesh remembers that Bobby was not working much. "A lot of performers didn't want to work with him. They didn't want Bobby opening for them and having to follow him. They knew that he had something special.

"One day he was sitting at a table alone crying. The waitress stopped me from going over to his table and told me he didn't want anyone to sit with him. He was thinking about his future, and he was really in a terrible state. He would go in and come out of these states of mind.

"The true story of Bobby can't be told without understanding about his illness," Wasser continues. "He was sick; he couldn't breathe at times. The average person would never have known how sick he was. His friends didn't even believe it. It was a macho thing: you don't tell your friends. You might tell a woman; most definitely you didn't tell a man friend. You're not a complainer. He used to play in the band, play in the Catskills. He wasn't supposed to be doing all that stuff. But he felt that if he had to live, he was going to live.

"People used to say, How come his family come into the city and pick him up and drive him home? To them, it was like, Whazzamata, he can't take the subway like the rest of us? But I knew that Bobby couldn't walk up the stairs. He didn't tell me this; I guessed it. When I told him I knew, he admitted it. And he didn't have money to take cabs. And he wouldn't let anyone anywhere near the poor neighborhood and apartment where he lived, on Baruch Place. So he wouldn't even let people drive him home. But who knew this? I knew it."

Wasser went to work for Bobby without getting paid. "It meant more to me than money," she says. "I mean I wasn't starving. The mere fact I was involved and could have so much influence on somebody I believed in was more than enough. He couldn't pay me. He had no money." She found out a lot about Bobby from Polly. "Polly's the one who really told me about his illness more than anyone else. I mean he didn't sit me down at any one time and tell me he was really sick. She was the one who told me. She would say things like, 'When you're with him in winter when it's cold, you should be sure he wears his scarf.' I still see that scarf in front of me, because she said if he got sick, if he were to get pneumonia, he could die."

Those who had glimpses of Bobby in this period remember his poverty and his longing to be part of a family. Joyce Becker was a reporter for her Bronx high school paper when her friend suggested that she interview Bobby. It turned out that Joyce and Bobby lived five blocks apart.

"I said, 'Would you come to my house for lunch? He said he'd love it. He was very impressed that my father had a car and would pick him up. Bobby did not want my father to go to his house—I think he was embarrassed about that—but rather suggested meeting on the steps of the post office on Grand Concourse. My father brought him to my house. It was a bitterly cold winter day. Bobby was wearing a very thin cotton shirt, slacks, and a paper-thin gray coat, a summer coat. He was using a neck scarf to wrap around his hands. He was freezing. My mother made him hot cocoa and lunch. My father asked him, 'Why aren't you wearing gloves?' My father went into the bedroom, came out with gloves, shirts, and underwear for Bobby. Bobby didn't have false pride. He said thank you and he left that day with a shopping bag of clothes."

It was the start of a close friendship. Becker's family warmed to Bobby immediately. "They adored him," she says. "Because he was a *haimeshe* boy. A home person. He came into my house, he plopped down, he hugged my mother. It was just family, and I think in his craziness, his crazy life, there was no family. He said, "I have no home. I've been on my own forever.' I said, 'But you have a mother.' He said, 'Yes, but it's not like your house. My mother is not like your mother. It's different.' So he was an old man. I think he grew up when he was nine. I think the secrets his family were hiding from him were so intense that there was not a normal life in his house. He seemed to long for what my family was. I don't think he had a home to go to with warmth and chicken soup cooking. He also had this inward feeling of death. That he was not going to live long. He said that over and over again. He was a lost soul."

Becker convinced the principal of her all-girl high school to have a sock hop for Bobby. The principal granted permission to hold the hop on the stage in the gym. "In comes Bobby, Vana, Nina, Harriet Wasser, a whole entourage. Like a big star. The principal, Mrs. Heffernan, who looked like a nun, said, 'Who are all these other people?' Bobby says, 'This is my sister, these are my nieces, this is my secretary.' There was also a black girl and a Chinese girl. Mrs. Heffernan says, 'And who are these people?' Bobby says, 'Oh, they're also my nieces.'

"Well, you know in those days rock and roll was considered horrible, like drugs; it was evil. Bobby got up and sang two songs. it was pandemonium; the girls were rushing the stage. Mrs. Heffernan threw him out of the building, and I was suspended. I was in shock. Bobby and his family could have left, but he put his arm around me and said, 'You're with us. Come with us. We'll get a pizza.' I said, 'How will I get home? It's late; my mother will kill me.' 'Don't worry,' he said, 'I'll take care of you.' He was a protector, always. Hugged me, kissed me, held me. He was a man that had to have love."

After Becker graduated from high school, she would go into Manhattan on Fridays to Don Kirshner's office at 1650 Broadway. "I'd go up there and answer Bobby's fan mail," she remembers. "Bobby would always be there, and he'd put his head on my lap and sing to me and I'm like in love. I was 16 years old. It was the biggest thing in the whole world to me. I'd been going to an all-girls' high school. Hello!"

Joyce would be the second girl that Bobby would propose to—through her father. "Bobby started going with Connie Francis, but I didn't know this. I took a job as Connie's secretary. Then they broke up. Bobby was in my house one day and he turned to my father and said, 'I love your daughter and I want to marry her.' My father looked at him and laughed. 'You gonna do what to who? I don't think so. You see that door? Get outta here. Or you wanna be friends? Be friends. My daughter's not getting married. When she does, she's gonna marry a Jewish guy. Goodbye.' And he threw Bobby out of the house. But we remained friends."

Becker pauses. "I realized later that I came into Bobby's life after he broke up with Connie, and maybe it was like a vendetta: I can't have you, so I'll have her."

Connie Francis was an Italian girl from a background, ethnicity, and milieu close to Bobby's own. She writes in her 1984 memoir, *Who's Sorry Now?* that when she first met Bobby in 1956, she found him an "egomaniac" and "fresh." She soon begins to have a more sympathetic understanding of him.

He tells Connie, "By the time I'm 25, I've gotta be a legend . . . The doctors say it will be all over before I hit 30. I gotta leave something behind the people will remember, and all I got are the songs in me."

The two of them discuss a new kind of show business that had emerged since the advent of Elvis. It was a world dominated not by the bland weekly hit parade with Guy Lombardo or Snooky Lanson and Patti Page singing "How Much Is that Doggie in the Window?" or by the Las Vegas tuxedo crowd. This was a scene dominated by kids in jeans who wanted something more real and sexual; hit singles were the paths to success, and 45s were bought by kids. They liked rock, they loved Elvis, and they were determining the new market. Bobby tells Connie, "Race music, hillbilly music, the blues. It's the music of the future! Just look at Elvis and Ray Charles and Fats D! The real thing is still waitin' in the wings. You'll see, someday the blues will be pop music. And you can't sound too educated—like you took voice lessons—'cause the kids don't dig that."

Their relationship is deepened by the common bond of struggling to make it in show business:

> We constantly analyzed, compared, mimicked, learned from each other, and encouraged each other; and were both hopeless workaholics . . . Before the mirrored walls of the big rehearsal studio next to Mr. Scheck's office, we'd practice hand and body motions for hours. Bobby would do comedy, impersonations, and little dance routines like Donald O'Connor . . . He'd dance like Bill Robinson and say, "Don't tell me I'm not part Negro down deep somewhere. Man, I really feel for these people and their music."

Connie would be the first of the many women Bobby would protect, from Polly to Sandra Dee to Andrea Yeager. Connie came from the most insular and provincial of backgrounds.

Their relationship is doomed from the start by the hostility of Connie's father, George Franconero, who regards all men who look at his daughter as the scum of the earth, but forms a particularly obsessive hatred for Bobby from the moment he sets eyes on him. George appears willing to kill him if necessary to get him out of his hair.

One evening Bobby takes Connie home from their date and they find her packed luggage outside the front door. Bobby reacts to this by suggesting they get married. Connie replies that her father will kill both of them. She also fears that the marriage would stand in the way of his career, and that he will resent her for it.

They sit in the car talking. Bobby pleads with her to marry him. Connie is too afraid of the consequences to make a move. She says she has to go home. Bobby tells her, "In that case, Connie, we can't be with each other anymore." He adds, "Someday, Connie—someday very soon—I'm never going to have to say 'sir' again. Not to anybody."

Soon her father visits the office of George Scheck and demands that Scheck drop Bobby as a client, and gives him an ultimatum: "Get ridda that bum. Make up your mind, Scheck. Dump Bobby or I'm taking my daughter away from you. You can't manage them both."

Scheck follows Franconero's orders. When Scheck tells Bobby of his dilemma, Bobby says, "What are you going to do? I have no father. You're like my father." Connie Francis later recalls Bobby's devastation. "He just walked out on the street a broken man." The final blow comes later, when Connie is booked to appear on *The Jackie Gleason Show*. Bobby comes to the rehearsal, and the two are reunited as if they had never been apart: "Bobby and I cuddled together . . . clutching each other's hands tightly." Later, at rehearsal, Connie's father barged through the stage door, brandishing a firearm like some kind of hit man from out of town, hotly announcing his intention to obliterate Bobby once and for all.

George Scheck, Dick Lord, and another fellow restrain her father while George Scheck excitedly shouts, "Run, Bobby, run!" Connie sees Bobby leap up and dart through the rows of empty seats and up the aisle toward the men's room, where he escapes through a window.

Joyce Becker remembers that night. "I was working with Connie and she insisted I come with her that night. I asked why. She said,

'Bobby is going to be there and I've gotta see him. I don't want my father there. My father will know if you're with me it's safe and he'll stay home.' So we went to the theater. Bobby came in, and she saw him. She almost died. There was such a love. That was Romeo and Juliet. On both sides.

"An hour later, George Franconero comes flying through the door, carrying on. He was crazy. If he could have shot Bobby, killed him, he would have done it. He would have rotted in jail. Bobby and George were both crazy. Bobby hated people too—people that disappointed him, who would lie to him. People that pushed him too much. He liked to be in control. When he hated, he hated. Well, he hated George. That would have been High Noon if it had happened."

The relationship is ended forever.

In an epilogue, Francis writes of seeing Bobby again four years later, in January 1960, at a dual appearance on *The Ed Sullivan Show*. Both of them have seen their careers skyrocket, and they are both surrounded by their large entourages: "We simply stared at one another, as if caught off guard by a chance, unexpected meeting. Then, very slowly, Bobby walked to where I was standing, his eyes never leaving mine. Slowly he wrapped both arms around me, burying his head in my neck, and rocked back and forth."

The duo sing "You're the Top." When the song is over, Connie's father is waiting.

Connie and Bobby would never see each other again.

Connie's view of the love between her and Bobby is not shared by everyone. While some, like Joyce Becker, Hesh Wasser, and Neil Sedaka, confirm Connie's claims, there are others who, while never denying Bobby's deep affection for Connie, have a more cynical take on the relationship. "Women in Bobby's life," John Bravo says, "I would guess, were only to be used, as sex objects, connections, and financial arrangements. And I could almost guarantee that he left Sandra Dee when her clout in Hollywood was over."

"That's the only love Connie ever had, with Bobby," Steve Blauner contends. "If her father hadn't interfered, and they'd been together, she may have been sorry for it in the long run. But at least she would have been sure. Now she always talks about what it could have been. I don't know how Bobby felt about her. I wasn't there. But if somebody unequivocally said, 'I know he was using her,' it wouldn't surprise me. And it wouldn't make me think any less of him."

"I think Bobby was crazy about Connie," Rona Barrett says. "He really adored her and thought she had a great voice. But he liked her as a person and somebody he understood. They were two Italian kids who came from the same side of the street and had an awful lot in common. I think it was obviously not meant to be for them to get married. But I do think that at some point they had talked in their teen days about getting together on a permanent basis."

FOLLOWING BOBBY'S DETROIT GIG with Steve Karmen, he went on the road in 1956 with Don Kirshner backing him on guitar. Bobby's singles for Decca, which were released in 1956 and 1957, included "Rock Island Line," "Silly Willy," "Timber," and—by far his best—"Dealer in Dreams," a strong ballad with big-band horns written by Darin and Kirshner. While in Nashville, Bobby recorded four additional songs with a rock-and-roll beat: "Talk to Me Something" and "Wear My Ring" (also written by Darin and Kirshner), "Just in Case You Change Your Mind," and the old Broadway standard by Billy Rose, "I Found a Million-Dollar Baby (In a Five-and-Ten-Cent Store)." Bobby paid for these recordings himself and planned to use them as demos. Kirshner brought the masters to Atlantic Records, and Bobby was signed to Atlantic's Atco subsidiary by Herb Abramson and Ahmet Ertegun, founders of Atlantic, as a result of their "Million-Dollar Baby" record.

Rock-and-roll legend Alan Freed included Bobby on his TV show, *The Big Beat*, along with Frankie Lymon, Chuck Berry, and Andy Williams. Freed also booked Bobby on his rock-and-roll revue at Harlem's flagship theater, the Apollo, where he sang songs by Ray Charles and Fats Domino, "Short Fat Fannie," and his Atco releases.

Bobby went on a bus tour with Fabian, Dion, Paul Anka, and

Frankie Avalon to plug his "Million-Dollar Baby" record. Avalon remembers meeting him for the first time on the tour in Youngstown, Ohio. "Bobby's aspiration then was to become a finger-snapping, Sinatra kind of a guy, and I also didn't want to be a rock-and-roll singer myself. So we both identified with that. In those days we slept in the bus on the top where we stored our luggage. Each town we hit, we'd look for a radio tower, and we'd walk in with our records and say, 'Could you play them?'

"I shared a dressing room with him and I remember Bobby looking in the mirror, combing his hair, and all of a sudden I heard a bang. I looked around. Bobby had thrown the comb down, stared at the mirror, and said, 'Look at me. I'm losing my hair already.' That was a very traumatic thing for Bobby. We were all pretty boys. He was not in that category. We would have these screaming kids on the tour. They didn't scream for Bobby. He didn't have the adulation we got. He wasn't on all the covers of *Movieland* and *Screenland*. We looked like teenagers. Bobby didn't even look like a teenager. He was older than the others. He knew how to manipulate his image with the public, but inside he was a struggling guy that wanted to be somebody else, really. When he looked in the mirror, it was 'Jesus—I would like to be that handsome guy,' but he wasn't. But then he'd walk into a room and just light it up with his charisma."

Avalon noted that there was a more fundamental way in which Bobby differed from the other teen singers he was associated with. "He always knew that he did the rock songs to get himself known. His goal was to get to do the things that he really wanted to do, the standards. For Bobby, the other stuff was a means to an end. And he would talk about having rheumatic fever. He would say, 'What's the difference? I'm not going to be around here a long time anyway.' But oh my God, he was so great. He knew what he was doing, he had an attitude, he was glib, he was funny, he could come back at any situation. He was a rarity."

Bobby's search for a father figure resulted in a lasting relationship that began at the very start of his career when he was really scuffling. Andy DiDia would become his valet and stay close by him through most of the years. "Bobby was just like a son to me," recalls DiDia, who is nearing 90. "He first appeared at the Gay Haven in Detroit in 1956. He had no money. He was staying at the Wolverine Hotel for $21 a week. I told the owner of the restaurant to feed him and make believe it was on the house. And I paid the owner. I gave Bobby some of my clothes and bought new clothes for him.

"When he finished a show, he would say to me, 'Feel how my heart is beating.' Nina would call me and ask how he was. Once I said, 'Not good, his heart is beating so fast.' When Bobby heard I told her this, he was mad. He said, 'Look, I could be dying. Don't ever tell anybody I'm not well.'

"Once we had a dispute. He said, 'Andy, who's your favorite star?' I said Clark Gable. So he fired me. He hugged me, but made me go home. He said he was going to use someone else. Because I didn't say he was my favorite, that he was the best. And I really thought he was the best. We got together again a little later.

"Bobby liked his girls. He used to tell me, 'See that one over there? I want her.' I said, 'Bobby, I can't just get her for you.' Bobby said, 'I don't care how you do it.' So I would go over there and talk to her, and there was no problem. I'd get them, they'd get together, and then when he didn't want them anymore, I had to find some excuse. That was the only part of the job that was rough for me."

DiDia continues. "Bobby hated his hairpiece, just hated it. He kept asking me, 'How does it look?' After Bobby died, I had cufflinks with his snapping fingers and his initials made and I gave them to Dodd and to Tony Orlando."

Neil Sedaka first heard of Bobby from Don Kirshner in 1958. "I was the first singer-songwriter to join Donny's stable at Alden Music. One day Donny told me he collaborated with a young kid who was very talented. Then he brought in the record of 'Splish Splash' and he didn't tell me who was singing, and I said, 'Oh, that must be the new Fats Domino record. It sounds terrific.' He said, 'No, it's not Fats Domino; it's my friend Bobby Darin.' And then I met Bobby at 1650 Broadway. Oh my goodness, Bobby was the most confident, the most talented.

He became my idol. Bobby recorded one of my songs that year, 'Keep A Walkin'."

By December 1957, Bobby was edging toward a toehold in the business. He appeared for the first time on the most important TV show aimed at teenagers and their musical tastes, Dick Clark's *American Bandstand*. Bobby's appearance was a landmark, significant both for its impact and as the beginning of a lifetime friendship of enormous career importance to him with Dick Clark.

When Harriet Wasser saw Bobby weeping that day at Hansen's, he was not experiencing an irrational depression. He had come so close, but without a hit song, he was still broke and in the wilderness. His manager had dropped him. Decca had dropped him. Atco, one of Atlantic's labels, had lost patience with him and was about to cancel his contract. And he knew it.

AHMET ERTEGUN, ATLANTIC'S DIRECTOR, a true visionary, is another legend in the music business. He came to America from Turkey (his father, Munir, was the Turkish ambassador) in 1936. Ahmet and his brother Nesuhi fell in love with jazz, and the two brothers would haunt New York's historic Commodore Music Store. "Ahmet's obsession with black culture was as powerful as my own, his ear bent by what he called their 'secret language,'" recalls producer Jerry Wexler.

Ahmet and Herb Abramson founded Atlantic Records in 1947 in a two-room apartment above Patsy's Restaurant on West 56th Street in Manhattan. The flamboyant Atlantic became the nation's premier rhythm-and-blues label in the late 1940s, as well as one of the great soul and jazz labels in the 1960s. Atlantic soon added other legends to its staff, among them Jerry Wexler in 1953 and engineer Tom Dowd. The collaboration between Ertegun and Wexler was fateful. The hits came instantly; they ripped through them together one after the other.

Atlantic developed its own sound, backing up all of its singers with boogie-based, sax-led band arrangements that were intrinsic parts of a song. It was able to link aspects of traditional blues and rhythm and blues to conventional forms of popular music.

Rock and roll's triumph in the late 1950s was inevitable. "Much of pop music," Jerry Wexler reflects, "was little more than steady 32-bar boring songs sung to Victor Herbert behind-the-potted-palms, put-you-to-sleep charts." First rock was called "cat music," the pre-rock-and-roll label for rhythm and blues that was popular with whites. Soon it became rhythm and blues and then it turned into rock and roll. White people were listening to, buying, and playing black music. It was a much closer approximation of reality than pop, and it had universality. It could utilize vernacular phrasing and language, the sensual, the gritty, edgier aspects of life.

Wexler writes in his memoirs, *Rhythm and the Blues*, that "just when I stepped into the scene, the tables finally began to turn. Music heretofore ignored—a new kind of rhythmic blues emerging from the black urban centers, and hillbilly music coming out of the white South—was making commercial sense . . . Suddenly there was another force at work—old but new, primal yet complex, a music informed by the black genius for expressing pent-up frustration, joy, rage, or ecstasy in a poetic context marked by hip humor and irresistible rhythm." In the 1960s, '70s, and beyond, Ertegun and Wexler had incredible success in soul, jazz, and rock.

It is impossible to overestimate the impact of Atlantic on American soul, rhythm and blues, jazz, and rock music. Their dizzying catalog is simply much of the sum total of the glory, the royalty of American music in the 20th century, from Ray Charles, Milt Jackson, Joe Turner, John Coltrane, Ornette Coleman, Jimmy Witherspoon, and Thelonius Monk to Charles Mingus, Solomon Burke, Wilson Pickett, Aretha Franklin, King Curtis, Otis Redding, the Allman Brothers Band in the '60s, to Brook Benton, Eric Clapton, Dr. John, Willie Nelson, and the Rolling Stones in the '70s.

Wexler, who had been a reporter for *Billboard* and who coined the phrase "rhythm and blues," became an Atlantic partner in 1954. That year, he and Ertegun produced the definitive Ray Charles session for Atlantic with Charles's own band, including "I've Got a Woman," "Greenbacks," "Black Jack," and "Come Back Baby."

This was the amazingly procreative company that 21-year-old Bobby Darin soon joined. The possibilities of its happening were remote. Atlantic was featuring black and rhythm-and-blues artists. Only characters like Ahmet Ertegun and Jerry Wexler, with their ability to spot talent, would have responded with alacrity to a scene they witnessed by chance. "Bobby had done four standards with a large band for Herb Abramson, my original partner, when Herb was heading our Atco label," Ertegun recalls. "To my mind they had no chance of being successful. But while they were being processed, Bobby would come to the office to see Herb, and Herb would keep him waiting. The waiting room was next to my office, and it had an upright piano in it. And I would hear through the door Bobby doodling and singing while he was waiting to see Herb. What I heard had no relationship to his records. Bobby was playing blues, some Ray Charles numbers, some original compositions. And he was playing early versions of what would become 'Splish Splash' and 'Queen of the Hop.' He had all these ideas. And I thought, 'My God, he's terrific! This is not the same guy on those stupid records.' So I would go in and talk to him and he would play me songs. And we struck up a friendship.

"After Bobby's records were released and flopped, Herb announced to me and Jerry Wexler he was releasing Bobby from his contract. And I said, 'Just a minute. Before you do that, I want to make one session with him.' In that one session we recorded two hits. And it was done in less than two hours. There was 'Splish Splash' and 'Queen of the Hop'; the next session we recorded 'Dream Lover.'" This recognition by Ahmet Ertegun and Jerry Wexler was the beginning for Bobby.

"He was really poor," Ertegun continues. "I would lend him money to pay for subway fare. At that time he was really struggling to get started in show business. But he had done enough to have stage presence—from the very beginning, the minute he stepped on the stage, it was like he owned it."

Bobby's love of black music and tremendous identification with it were major factors in Ertegun's immediate interest in Bobby. "Bobby sounded to me as close to black music as Elvis Presley was. We at Atlantic had tried to get Presley but it didn't work out. So to me this was the answer. I had somebody just as good or better. Except that Bobby didn't stay with that music; he went on to pop. Bobby got pulled away, because he wanted to go here, there, and the other place. It could have been partly my fault, not to keep him closer to the funk, which is where he really came from. Because he had a real feel for that. Of course he also had a real feel for the pure pop, swing pop. There's a great deal of jazz in that music; it's swing music. Very valuable music. He loved it all. He always cut records that he felt with all his heart and soul. But he was one of the few talents who knew how to use the rhythm-and-blues roots of most popular music."

"Our first white artist was Bobby," recalls Wexler, "and certainly one of the essential players in Atlantic's history. Bobby was a Mensa [the high-IQ society] person, and he wore the pin. Now Ahmet, Nesuhi, and I were all college graduates. Bobby would listen to us talk; he was kind of wistful, like the kid with his nose up against the window pane while they're cutting up the Christmas turkey. He kept after us to take the Mensa test, surely hoping we would fail. Our disclaimer was we didn't like to wear our IQ as an insignia on our lapels. We didn't tell him, but Ahmet and I regarded the button as the nerds' badge of honor. But I'll put the P.S. to that: we also didn't want to take the risk of fucking up and failing. Bobby was very very adaptable. He learned fast. And he was a bitch of a pianist. He brought in that song, 'Splish Splash,' which I thought was a piece of unspeakable shit. But Ahmet saw it right away. It all started with Ahmet. Ahmet believed in Bobby from the beginning. Ahmet was everything in Bobby's career. It was Ahmet's stewardship. I worked on some of those sessions—Ahmet and I coproduced them—but Ahmet was the man. I can't give him enough credit for what he did with Bobby. He was the front man, he was the leader, and he was the point man. And he was Bobby's horse."

Ronnie Zito agrees: "Ahmet was the producer, but he would just let Bobby do whatever he wanted. He just liked him so much. Ahmet was a jazzer too, completely. Ahmet really knew Bobby. He understood him completely."

Jerry Wexler spoke of the scene Bobby was entering in 1957 to '58. "Bobby came at a very exciting moment. Donny Kirschner, his manager, really grabbed hold of the Brill Building scene. Don was a street genius who, with no music experience, got into the business and built an empire of songwriters and singers. He was zealous and jealous and amazingly effective. He became the czar of Brill Building rock and roll, which was a very important early stage in primal rock. People like Carole King, Gerry Goffin, and Jeff Barry, who wrote those ditty-bop songs, came on the scene highly evolved. They brought great musicality to it. If you listen to some of those tracks, they were terrific. You like to look back and think, well, early rock and roll was some primitive caterwauling. The Beatles were unspeakable at first, but look how they developed and what they turned into, not without some good help from George Martin. Lieber and Stoller and Phil Spector were starting to come, Bob Crewe, people who not only entered the picture but endured for decades."

"Million-Dollar Baby" didn't make it for Bobby, but it brought him to the attention of New York's leading rock-and-roll disc jockey, Murray the K [Murray Kaufman]. Murray the K had included Bobby on his rock shows at Harlem's famed Apollo Theater. Most significantly, Murray the K—or more precisely his mother—led to "Splish Splash."

Bobby was at Murray the K's house when Murray's mother called. When she heard that Bobby was there, she suggested that he write a song about taking a bath. While Murray went into the bathroom to shower and shave, Bobby went into his bedroom and in 35 minutes composed the song called "Splish Splash." It would change his life.

"Bobby Darin was in my office at 1650 Broadway the afternoon before he was going to record 'Splish Splash,'" songwriter Doc Pomus recalls. "While we were gabbing away, Bobby started to break out in ugly red blotches. I made him sit down and try to relax. He kept saying he was getting a heart attack. I thought it was all nerves, because he was going to cut new sides for Atlantic that night with Ahmet Ertegun. The previous ones, 'Million-Dollar Baby' among others, were hip and showed off Bobby's cool chops but never inspired the record buyers. This was supposed to be Bobby's last chance for the big dance on the label and he was scared. Mort Shuman, my partner, and I told him some bad jokes and got him to loosen up. Then the three of us got into a giggly mood and we exchanged some dirty lines and tore apart some characters that even looked low to lowlifes. When Bobby left us, he had the cocky half-grin on his face and everything was copacetic. 'Splash' was a monster, and Bobby was an instant star after many, many years of tough grinding. The usual overnight success story."

Ertegun supervised the recording session for "Splish Splash" on April 10, 1958. Bobby also cut "Judy Don't Be Moody" and "Queen of the Hop" at that session.

"Splish Splash" was a smash. While superficially it seems to verge on a novelty hit, it transcends that genre with its intensity, humor, originality, torrid sense of fun and good times, and its genuine rock-and-roll musicality—the wailing sax, big beat, pounding honky-tonk piano, and Bobby's driving, snarling, rough-edged, inspired delivery. It is simply one of a kind. Its endurance over the years as a rock classic testifies to its artistry. "Splish Splash" never dates or loses its volcanic force; it tears off the roof. It contains an homage to Buddy Holly (Peggy Sue), Fats Domino, and Little Richard. Humor is not always a mainstay of rock, and this song explodes from a humorous premise that it exploits to the hilt, imbuing the song with irony. Yet the irony is undercut by the sense of fun and playfulness—it *is* a song about taking a bath. You smile the first time you hear it, and you're still smiling the hundredth time. It's all about spontaneity, sensuality, and joy.

The feeling is orgiastic. The sense of humor is implanted in it from the beginning, thanks to the contribution of another Atlantic genius, Tom Dowd. "When the recording date was over," Dowd said later, "I mixed down a version of the song from the 8-track tape and, just for fun, went over to the water cooler, filled a paper cup with some water, and jostled my fingers in the cup, making a splashing sound. I recorded this onto a piece of tape and spliced it onto the front of the mix-down I made the acetate from, before I sent it over to the main office for evaluation.

"They may have played it twice before they called and said, 'It's a smash; master it right away. Pull out all the stops, make masters for all the plants, and get them out tonight!' When I mentioned the 'noise' on the front of the song, the comment was 'Don't change anything, just master it.'"

"Splish Splash" was one of the few records by a white artist that sold well in the black community for the simple reason that most listeners assumed Bobby was black. But Bobby was not pretending or imitating here. He was singing it the way he felt it. Bobby certainly had the capacity to be a chameleon, and that could work to his detriment, but at his best—as he is here—he is just singing his heart out. According to Hesh Wasser, "Sure, he was influenced by Ray Charles, by a lot of people—Belafonte, Sam Cooke, Jolson, Durante, George Burns, Judy Garland, Louie Prima. He was inspired by so many different people—not just one—that he could be himself."

There was calculation on Bobby's part. Dodd Darin quotes George Scheck on the origins of "Splish Splash": "Once Bobby and I were in Atlantic City. It was in the summertime, and black people were singing on the rooftops like it was New Orleans. I said, 'Bobby, you're a great mimic. You can do anyone. You'll be different. You want to sing, and "blackie" is going to be in for a long time.' And black people were just starting to make it mainstream. I said, 'You ought to sing like these people.'

"He hits me on the back and says, 'You know, I've been thinking about that.' Later, when he did 'Splish Splash,' he came into my office with the demo in his hand. He was shaking when he put the record on my turntable. And he played it, and I says, 'Bobby, Atlantic City!'

"And he says, 'Yes, Atlantic City.'"

"Bobby was a rebel," says producer Len Triola, who was a programmer in the 1980s at WNEW-AM, the most influential pop music station in America. "Here he comes along and forged his own way.

Painted out a picture of what he wanted to do and he did it. Bobby's was the first rock and roll that maybe even your parents could understand. You could hear the words. It was melodic. You stand still when CBS-FM plays him. They're going to play him a hundred years from now. That's the visionary he was; he had that musical vibe."

"Splish Splash," a funky little rock-and-roll record if there ever was one, landed at No. 3 on the Top Ten in August 1958, No. 1 on the rhythm-and-blues chart, and No. 17 in Britain. Bobby was on his way.

Jerry Wexler recalls that Atlantic's records had "suddenly stopped selling [in 1958], and we started to panic . . . Two records got us back in the game. These tunes were so winning, so widely popular, so immediately irresistible, no one could keep them off the air . . . The first was 'Yakety Yak' by the Coasters; the second, Bobby Darin's 'Splish Splash.' Each sold well over a million. At wholesale, that meant $400,000 or $500,000 in revenue."

They all celebrated at Hansen's that night. Hesh photographed Bobby in front of the jukebox and said, "This may be the last time we see you in here." Don Kirshner, Dick and Ellen Lord, Neil Sedaka, Dick Behrke, and Steve Karmen stood there, memorizing the moment.

That night, Hesh would introduce Bobby to his idol, Sammy Davis Jr., for the first time. That introduction led to Bobby's finding his third savior and best friend, Steve Blauner.

Chapter Five
THE COMET RIDE

BEFORE "SPLISH SPLASH" BEGAN TO MAKE NOISE, Bobby, uncertain about his future and fearful that Atco was about to drop him, recorded another song he'd written with collaborator Woody Harris, "Early in the Morning." Murray the K sold the master to Brunswick Records. As soon as "Splish Splash" began to rise in the charts, Bobby's contract with Atco was renewed after all. "Early in the Morning" was released by Brunswick, but with Darin's name changed to "The Ding Dongs." Ertegun and Wexler, of course, immediately recognized Bobby's voice, refused to let Brunswick release the record, and bought the master back from them. Hesh Wasser remembers that she was with Bobby when Jerry Wexler came up to Bruno Photography on West 57th and confronted him about it, but not with a sense of acrimony; they weren't really angry with him. For one thing, Bobby was now a valuable property; for another, they understood how uncertain he had been about his status at Atco and that he had cut the other record behind their backs for insurance. To avoid competing with the fast-rising "Splish Splash," Atco released "Early in the Morning" with another pseudonym for Bobby, The Rinky Dinks.

Later, in July 1958, Dick Clark announced on his Saturday-night TV show, on which Bobby was appearing, that Bobby really was the Rinky Dinks. Then Atco proceeded to release "Early in the Morning" a second time, with the label reading BOBBY DARIN WITH THE RINKY DINKS. Atco also released Bobby's first album, *Bobby Darin*.

At this point, Bobby went on several rock-and-roll tours, appearing in October 1958 with Dion and the Belmonts, Frankie Avalon, the Coasters, Buddy Holly and the Crickets, Jimmy Clanton, Joanne Campbell (whom Bobby dated), and Clyde McPhatter.

"Queen of the Hop" was Bobby's third hit of the year. Realizing that Bobby now needed professional management, Ahmet Ertegun took him to Csida-Grean Associates, a three-way music conglomerate. Csida and Grean owned a talent-management agency, a music-publishing firm, a record and television production company, and two music-publishing outlets—Trinity Music with BMI and Towne Music with ASCAP. Bobby signed with them, but the arrangement would not last long.

Bobby cut more first-rate rock-and-roll records in 1958: "I Want You with Me," "Pity Miss Kitty," Doc Pomus and Mort Shuman's "I Ain't Sharin' Sharon," and best of all, Neil Sedaka and Howard Greeenfield's "Keep A Walkin'." While Bobby continued to record rock, and to praise it as well, "I put Ray Charles on a pedestal," he said. "Ray Charles is the greatest thing since Beethoven." Bobby did not want to be pigeonholed as a rock singer.

Music producer Bob Marcucci first met Bobby in Youngstown, Ohio, when Bobby was touring with Frankie Avalon and other young rock stars in 1958. "We had just done a record hop," Marcucci recalls, "and come back to our room. It was so small you had to jump over the bed to get to the next bed. Bobby said to me, 'I just don't think I want to stay in this business. This is not what I like. I love music, not this rock stuff.' These rock-and-roll shows, they were hard to take, if you were someone like Bobby. All these little kids yelling and screaming. Bobby wasn't like that. He liked and respected all those people, but that wasn't him. He wasn't like a Frankie Avalon or a Fabian. He was more introspective.

"On stage, Bobby was a trouper," Marcucci continued. "But that's not what he wanted to do. Think of Sinatra coming out and doing a rock-and-roll show. Frank was lucky. What he did was only for himself, with himself. I'm sure even the girls going crazy was a little strange to him because he didn't look at himself as the idol type. But Sinatra was; he started it all. But Bobby became totally involved when he did the standards. He loved that. He had heavy emotions. I loved that bitey, sexy quality of his, the edge. Sinatra had that too, but in a different way, much smoother than Bobby was. But Bobby had that bite that you like on stage. Man, he owned that stage."

"Bobby and I go back to the late '50s, when he first started," Paul Anka remembers. "We did a lot of shows together, toured together on the rock-and-roll packages, *Coke Time, Hullabaloo*. Frankie Avalon, Fabian, myself, and Annette would hang out more. Bobby had his own agenda. He wasn't a participant socially with us as a group. He'd come in and do the show. And once he did *That's All*, it was a departure from what we were doing and gave him a different kind of cachet. He was way ahead of his time. And he carried himself that way; he didn't want to be part of any ongoing social things with us as a group."

"Bobby was a person with great ambition and endless vision," Ahmet Ertegun pointed out. "He could see no limit to his potential. But he wanted to be a bit of everything. He wanted to be a rock and roller, he wanted to be a pop singer in the mode of Sinatra and Dean Martin, he wanted to be a folk singer."

Bobby's desire to succeed in the adult world of nightclubs began to be realized in December 1958, when he had a highly successful engagement at a major venue, Ben Maksik's Town and Country in Brooklyn. The year was also a financial breakthrough for him. In 1947 Bobby had earned a total of $1,600, but in 1958 his income had jumped to $40,000 after expenses.

Bobby's meeting with Sammy Davis Jr., which came about after his recording "Splish Splash," was the beginning of a lifelong friendship. "I invited Bobby to Sammy's recording session," Hesh Wasser recalls. "I had worked with Sammy on his Broadway show *Mister Wonderful*. During the break in the record session, I introduced Bobby to Sammy. Sam didn't even know what Bobby did, didn't know anything about him. 'Who is that guy?' he asked me. I could tell he was really digging Bobby. When we were leaving, he mentioned that he was going to be at the Apollo. I said something about coming to see him and would it be all right if I brought Bobby. Sammy said, 'If you come without him, you don't get in.' As soon as Sammy saw Bobby perform, he became a passionate supporter. He would mention Bobby every night at every club he performed in; if Bobby was appearing at a club in the same city, Sammy would urge the audience to go see him." Sammy said of Bobby, "I'm black, and he's got the rhythm."

According to composer and arranger Buddy Bregman, the relationship between Bobby and Sammy was "absolutely smashing. Those guys were really close; they loved each other. There was no animosity. Sammy welcomed him. He was not a rival. Bobby Darin a rival to him? What Sammy did was a one-man entertainment. Bobby was a great singer and entertainer. Not the ultimate entertainer that Sammy was, because he didn't dance like Sammy. And I think that Sammy liked the fact that—I don't mean Bobby was like Frank—but that Bobby was sort of the first Sinatra clone that came along that became famous. Not really a clone, but with some of what Frank had inherently, and with even more energy."

Wasser met Steve Blauner when she was working with Sammy. Now she would make another of her many fateful *shiddachs* (Yiddish for matchmaking) for Bobby. It was an extraordinary talent she had for bringing people together in combinations that would change their lives—in her words, "send them soaring."

STEVE BLAUNER BEGAN HIS CAREER as a little boy doing Al Jolson imitations after seeing *The Jolson Story* 13 times and sneaking a radio under the covers in bed to listen to broadcasts of the famous Wednesday amateur nights from the Apollo Theater in Harlem. Steeped in show-business lore and the magic of vaudeville and old Broadway, Blauner has had a remarkable career since managing Bobby. He served as vice president of Screen Gems in charge of new projects and went on to form a movie production company, BBS Productions, with Burt Schneider and Bob Rafaelson. Blauner and his partners produced some of the best films of our time, among them: *Five Easy Pieces*, *Easy Rider*, *The Last Picture Show*, and *The King of Marvin Gardens*. He earned an Academy Award for documentary in 1976 for the film *Hearts and Minds*.

Blauner is a passionate lover and a passionate hater. When he likes you, he really likes you, and the same applies when he hates you. Blauner and Jerry Wexler did not hit it off. Today Wexler comments, "We went to Bobby's Copacabana opening and proudly presented a check for $80,000 to Bobby. It was for just one quarter of the year, not half a year. Steve said, 'Is this all?' I'm sure he was awed by the amount, but what he was trying to do was demonstrate his cool." No one else seems to conjure up such a negative image of Steve Blauner, although people agree that Blauner could be killer-tough as well as brilliant—great assets in a manager, and that if Blauner was on your side, if he loved you as he loved Sammy and then Bobby, you had a manager who would take a bullet for you and protect you until your dying day. Besides, Bobby always said he wanted a manager who would "leave a trail of blood." That was Blauner.

You also had a manager of uncanny intelligence, professional skill, and absolute integrity—and, of course, someone with a capacity for vengeance and unreasoning rage. Steve Blauner actually became connected to Bobby in the first place out of vengeance.

"I adored Steve, but Steve was always frantic," recalls Rona Barrett. "He was quitting every three minutes. I felt that Steve was very jealous of anybody who came into Bobby's life, jealous and controlling, and therefore he would go into tirades. Bobby could have the histrionics, but he didn't necessarily want it around him. So it always amazes me that Steve was able to stay as long as he did. One thing that Bobby did respect was intelligence, and underneath it all Steve was a very intelligent guy. But he was very bombastic. So anybody who came into Bobby's life, there was always something wrong with them and he always had to protect Bobby. And Bobby needed a tank. On some level Steve was exactly what Bobby needed."

"Bobby was already signed to Atco when I met him," Blauner remembers. "I was an agent at General Artists Corporation (GAC), a talent agency in Manhattan. I was really a gofer; my shared office had no windows and my salary was $75 a week. One step away from the mailroom. I was just a *pisher* who would stand in people's doorways to try and learn. People would say, 'What are you standing there for?' I'd say, 'I'm trying to learn.' I'd been in the business a minute and a half. We handled bands and acts at GAC, singers and comedians. My job at GAC was to assist various talent bookers.

"Pat Boone was one of GAC's clients, and Sammy was coming into town to do *The Pat Boone–Chevy Showroom* TV show. Sammy was with the William Morris office. So I took the time to call the people at the Morris office that I knew and say, 'Look, Sammy's coming to New York. I'm going to be with him night and day. That's our relationship, we're friends; it has nothing to do with business.' I was assuring them I wasn't trying to steal Sammy away for GAC.

"And I thought that was a very nice thing to do. And Sammy came to town. And we ran together. Went clubbing and everything else. And all of a sudden some wise guy at the Morris office is saying, 'That kid Blauner is trying to steal Sammy.' And I got pissed off. So—they were drawing up the contracts to sign some kid called Bobby Darin. A rock-and-roll singer. Fuck him. I hated rock and roll. I wasn't into it. Harriet Wasser was always telling me about this kid Bobby Darin. If it wasn't for Harriet, there's no question that I never would have known or met Bobby Darin. She brought Bobby up when I was at a recording session with Sammy Davis Jr. She's responsible for it."

Blauner's lack of interest in Bobby was overcome by his strong interest in screwing the Morris office. So he did. He borrowed another agent's office that actually had a window. He called Harriet and said, "Get Bobby up here."

"Bobby came to the office and I sold him a bill of goods," Blauner recalls. "And I signed fucking Bobby Darin to a personal management contract for GAC.

"I hadn't heard him. I didn't care to hear him. What am I doing? This is a man's life I'm fucking with. I was just trying to fuck over William Morris because of this attitude.

"Now I feel guilty. What do I do? They get Bobby a booking in Bridgeport, Connecticut. I got a friend to drive me there. Bobby was so low on the totem pole, he opened the show. Bobby walked out on the stage singing crap that I couldn't stand. But my mouth fell open. I couldn't believe what I was watching from the minute he hit that stage. I mean, you've probably had that experience where you see someone and you just say, 'Oh my God.'

"I came back to the office the next day and went up and down the aisles screaming, 'If this kid can sing one note legit he's going to be one of the biggest stars of all time.' So everybody laughed at me. I wasn't booking talent at this point, but I was Bobby's biggest booster."

Hesh Wasser says she had met Sammy right before she met Bobby, and she met Steve Blauner while working for Bobby. "There's a lot of overlap," she explains. "When I took Bobby to meet Sammy, Bobby had not hit yet. So when Bobby finally hit, Steve was at GAC. That meant that Steve was getting himself involved with Bobby at a time when he really wasn't supposed to be. Bobby was being managed by Csida and Grean. I was just watching the scenario unfold. After Bobby signed with them, Bobby asked them and they agreed to give me a small office in their suite."

At Csida and Grean, Wasser operated as a tiny double agent with a sweet smile, burrowed away in her little office. "I didn't feel they were the right management for Bobby," she says, "because the direction they were looking to send him in was teenage rock and roll. And Atlantic was also seeking to keep him going in the same direction. In the meantime, I was corresponding with Steve Blauner. So I was operating out of Csida and Grean's office and I was acting against them. Steve envisioned Bobby going in the direction I thought was right for him: the standards. I knew where Steve wanted to go, and I knew that was where Bobby wanted to go. I would tell Bobby, 'You can only go so far as a rock-and-roll artist.' Fabian, Avalon, were for the most part just rock and rollers. They were limited. You can't just do it with teenagers. You don't really establish yourself as an artist with total acceptance until you have the adults. It's really the standards that come back in the long run. They are what last.

"Steve would say things to me like, 'I wish I could manage him, but I don't think I can handle it.' Steve was very young, only a little older than Bobby. He was scared to death of managing an artist of Bobby's magnitude. Steve had called me and said he was so frustrated, he couldn't stand what he was doing at GAC. He wanted so much to be there for Bobby, to guide him and his career. Bobby came up to the office that evening. We started to talk and I said, 'Bobby, Steve wants to manage you so bad. He's just dying to do it.' And Bobby said to me, 'That's why he's going to be my manager.'"

"I was transferred to L.A.," Steve Blauner says. "Bobby would come out to do a gig, just one-nighters or sock hops at gyms at four in the afternoon. He wasn't making much money. It hadn't happened for him. He'd sleep on the couch in the living room of my apartment.

"'Splish Splash' was all he had then. And even though I had nothing to do with singers at GAC, it got to a point where I was a bore because all I ever talked about was Bobby. I still didn't actually know that he could sing legit. I just knew there was something about him when he hit the stage, that he was born for it.

"He would stay with me in L.A. in Laurel Canyon when he came out. And I had some problem, mental, emotional or whatever. Bobby turned to me and said, 'Listen, you know when I get up in the morning and look in the mirror, what do I see? I see a short, big-nosed, bad-chin, pot-bellied Italian. When I walk out that door, I'm Rock fucking Hudson.' He made himself feel that way and in turn people believed it.

"And I dug him," Blauner says, "as I got to know him. One day we were driving down Sunset Boulevard and Bobby asked me to manage him. I almost crashed the car." Blauner put Bobby off at first, thinking that he wasn't qualified to do it. "The real reason," he says now, "is that I was scared."

DARIN'S FIRST SINGLE OF 1959 was "Plain Jane," a rock number that didn't travel very far commercially or artistically. He followed it by writing and recording a song that would turn into a pop standard, "Dream Lover." The song was, of course, about teenage angst, but sung with a lilting flow in an edgy but softer voice becoming characteristic of Darin, a sound that would predominate in his nightclub appearances. "Dream Lover" reached No. 2 on the charts by July 1959.

Meanwhile, Bobby was making the rounds of TV shows doing guest appearances. He was not exactly obsequious with those who had lesser talent. According to Ahmet Ertegun, "From the very beginning, he behaved like he was an old star. He had a short temper. And that was fine: to me he was a star, so he could behave like that. When he appeared on *The Perry Como Show* in April 1959, before anyone had a chance to introduce him, he walked right up to Como and said, 'Hi, Per,' and just walked right by him. Well, you know this kind of thing, there's an age difference, there's a way of going about that. This was pointed out to Bobby. I said, 'Look, try to behave around the star of the show. Fabian was here last week and he was very nice to Como.' Bobby said, 'Fuck Fabian. He can't sing! I sing better than he does.' So, you know, that's how he really felt."

In the spring of 1959, Steve Blauner scored a huge coup for Bobby. "I was told that George Burns was going to play a nightclub for the first time ever," explains Blauner. "He had played vaudeville, theaters, radio, television, and it was the first time he was going to work without Gracie because she was retiring. Burns was with MCA. He was going to hire a group of people, a dance act, a boy or girl singer as the opening spot in his act, and put together a show."

Blauner persisted in trying to reach Burns, whose first reaction was, "What's a Bobby Darin?"

"I got in to see Burns," says Blauner, "and I played him Bobby's new record of 'Some of These Days.' I figured he could relate to it because of Sophie Tucker; it was from his era. And I got Bobby the gig."

George Burns later recalled this meeting: "I wanted to meet Bobby Darin. When Blauner came in, I thought he was Bobby Darin. I was terribly disappointed. I said to myself, Jesus, he's a big, fat kid. I don't want to take him to Vegas. Finally Blauner told me who he was, that he was his agent, and I took Bobby to Vegas."

According to Blauner, "The engagement included two weeks in Lake Tahoe to break in the act and four weeks in Vegas at the Sahara. It was $1,500 in Tahoe and $2,500 a week in Vegas. So, I can't believe what I've done. I go to New York and see the head of the nightclub department, Buddy Howe. I say, 'Buddy, I've taken care of Darin for the summer.' He says, 'What are you talking about?' I tell him the money. He says, 'Uh uh. Bobby's going to England on a rock and roll tour.' I said, 'What, are you out of your mind? He can always go to England on a rock tour! Do you understand what this is?'

"Howe replies that opening acts in Vegas get a lot more money than that. I say, 'Buddy, if I'm a Bobby Darin, I'd pay George Burns ten thousand to take me. It's worth it just for opening night. George Burns first time ever working without Gracie, and in a nightclub. That publicity alone. And it gives Bobby the transition out of rock and roll.' Buddy goes on to say, 'Will you stop interfering in the nightclub department?' And I say, 'Yes I will.' He says, 'Well, you've said that before.' And I say, 'Well, this time I mean it. I just quit.' And I got up and left. I couldn't compromise myself. So I had no place to go."

Bobby told Howe to cancel the British tour. Ed Burton, Bobby's manager at Csida and Grean, said that they were committed. "Then get uncommitted," said Bobby.

The engagement in May 1959 was a triumph for Bobby. "I remember opening night," Blauner says. "Spencer Tracy, all the big stars came from Hollywood. It was just jammed. Burns opened the show with a monologue and then he introduced Bobby, who sang six songs, including 'Splish Splash,' 'Mack the Knife,' and 'Some of These Days.'" Burns returned for a song-and-dance routine, climaxed by a closing duet with Bobby and Burns doing a soft-shoe and singing "I Ain't Got Nobody." *Downbeat* wrote, "Self-assured, almost cocky in manner, young Bobby Darin cradled a sophisticated house in the palm of his hand and made his bid as leading contender to the title, Young Sinatra."

The engagement was the beginning of a close personal relationship for Bobby, as George Burns became the father figure Bobby had been looking for desperately all his life. He would always call him "Mr. Burns." Bobby gained not only major entry into show business with this engagement, but a mentor and a cherished friend. He told Barry Gray, "He is to me the closest thing I've ever had to a father. George Burns taught me more in six weeks in Vegas than 20 others could have done in ten years."

"When he mentioned George Burns, his whole face changed," recalls Bobby's lifelong friend Jerrold Atlas. "You know, Bobby had this funny smile: one side of his mouth would curl up a little bit. Not both sides, just one. When he talked about George Burns, that little smile would come up. That was the closest I've ever seen to his showing love and respect for someone. This was deep and genuine. It was very uncommon for him. He generally was a mask. In response to this, I said, 'Well, I know Burns is very funny and a great entertainer, but what else is it about him?' Bobby said, 'I know I'm loved.' I never heard Bobby say that, ever."

Meanwhile, Steve Blauner, having left GAC, was looking for a job. "Sam Katzman, king of the B-movie makers, who made *Rock Around the Clock*, hired me," he remembers. "He'd get an idea Monday; by the following Tuesday it would be in the theaters. I had more money than I'd ever had before, a big office at Columbia. But B pictures were over. Katzman couldn't get anything off the ground. And he picked me up at lunchtime to take me to the racetrack. And I said to myself, well this is no way for me to get ahead in life. And so I picked up the phone.

Bobby was playing Blinstrub's in Boston. And I said, 'Bobby, if you still want me, I'll manage you. But it's gotta be right away.' Bobby had four years left with his managers, who were really music publishers. It was a five-year contract. He went to them and said, 'Look, I want Steve to manage me. How can I buy you out?'

"Remember, Bobby had no money. He hadn't made any real money yet, although Bobby had already written and published many songs under the aegis of Trinity Music. So he and his lawyer, Frank Barone, made a deal with them that anything that he wrote and recorded would be published by them until the $100,000 mark. Then the deal would be over, but they would own those copyrights forever. So that hundred thousand could be worth millions, who knows, depending on what the songs were.

"Here's a guy, I've been in the business a year and a half, he went out and sold his *soul* to get me to manage him. For Bobby to take me, 24-year-old kid wet behind the ears, but who he believed in, to pay $100,000 to get rid of his managers so he could hire me, that took guts and confidence, which Bobby was full of. He believed in me before I believed in me. We never had a contract. A handshake. And when we decided actually for me to manage him, I said to him, 'Look, Bobby. You sing and dance, you pick your songs and do what you have to do. I'll do what I have to do. I'll be all over you, pestering you, telling you to do this, do that. But in the final analysis, that's [the singing] yours. Well, I need mine. I need my own persona. I don't want to come and ask you for anything. Whatever I say, you're gonna do. The day you start making decisions, I quit. Total power. In other words, you'll play here, play there, do this room, do that room, whatever.' And he lived by it. He gave me his life. I insisted on power of attorney, I signed all his contracts, I carried the checkbook with me.

"And later I went from Bobby to Screen Gems to my own company and *Five Easy Pieces* and *Easy Rider* and *The Last Picture Show* and *Hearts and Minds*, Academy Award. Nothing was ever like the time with Bobby. Academy Awards, it didn't matter. It was a comet ride. It was a fucking comet ride."

Blauner immersed himself totally in Bobby's career. He took complete control. "Bobby and I had a ritual. He would say, 'I never have to ask Steve what he thought of my performance. He would come in and say nothing. I know, uh uh, no good. If he shakes my hand, well it was okay. If he hugs me, it was good. But when he hugs me and picks me up off the ground, I know I'm going through the roof.' That was the way we did it."

Together, Hesh Wasser and Steve Blauner would make it happen for Bobby. "It really was a team effort," Wasser says. "It was two people working with the same thrust in mind. We both wanted to make it happen, and we both did it in a way that we felt would work for us and for Bobby. And Steve was not easy. He was one of the most insecure people I knew. He did things that shocked me and laughed about them, and I would say to him, 'Steve, I would never dream of doing anything like that.'"

Bobby was rising quickly, but there were many rungs up the ladder. There was the critical question of his next album. Once again, it would be Hesh Wasser who would be the catalyst.

"I was never a rock-and-roll person; my first love was jazz," she says. "I was not going to flip over Bobby doing 'Splish Splash.' I knew what else he was capable of doing—that's what drew me to him. I wanted him to have the hit, which 'Splish Splash' was. But once he had the hit, he would have the opportunity to go and do his own thing. I was at a meeting with Bobby, Ahmet, Nesuhi, and the others at Atlantic Records. They were discussing what Bobby's first major album should be. They said, 'Let's do an album in a Fats Domino mode. A rhythm-and-blues, rock album.' To anyone else in the record business, it would have made sense. You followed up what you'd done before. And of course, I couldn't say a word. I'm just sitting there as an observer.

"When the meeting was over, Bobby and I were walking up 57th Street, across the street from Carnegie Hall. And I was very unhappy. I was crying; I was literally almost hysterical. I said to Bobby, 'I think it's ridiculous. It's a mistake.' Bobby said, 'So what do you think? What kind of album do you think I should do?' I said to Bobby, 'I think you should do an album of standards.' Now, this wasn't happening then in music; nothing could have been more unfashionable. It was unheard of. The natural thing, from a commercial point of view, was to exploit Bobby's popularity as a rock singer. But Bobby just looked at me and said, 'Hesh, don't worry. You'll get your album.'"

A few days later, Bobby went up to Atlantic and told them what he wanted to do: an album of standards. "They almost died," Wasser says. "They couldn't believe it." Ahmet stared at Bobby and said, "What are you talking about? You're a rock-and-roll singer. You'll ruin your career."

"I'm going to do this album," Bobby replied.

Chapter Six

THE
BIG
TIME

It was probably the most surprising switch that any popular singer on the rise ever made—a total departure from what was expected of him. Just as he was beginning to achieve great success in rock and roll, Bobby was ready to take his chances on eroding his image with his public to keep growing as an artist. At 22, he was already ready to move on. Watching his studio rehearsals, one could immediately catch the moment that Bobby was getting happy with the music, whether it was a new song he was writing or an arrangement he was trying out. The smile spread all over his face, his body bounced, and he could not keep still. Bobby was an artist who needed to be happy when he sang, to be inspired. Staying in one place stifled inspiration; changing genres, experimenting, jumping into the water, taking chances: this restless quest defined him as a singer.

"Bobby made a terrific transition from a kid rocker into a suave nightclub performer who could give Sammy Davis or Frank Sinatra a hard time," Jerry Wexler states. "He was just great on the floor, his composure, his moves. I thought his moving away from rock almost right away to the standards was very intelligent. The progression from rock and roll to either jazz or sophisticated nightclub ballads and crafted blues is to me a mark of maturation."

In reality, Bobby would become the last of an era of nightclub performers. He was entering a world in which nightclubs were the glittering center of show business with a circuit stretching across the country from the Copacabana and the Latin Quarter in New York to Bill Miller's Riviera in New Jersey, Skinny D'Amato's 500 Club in Atlantic City, Mister Kelly's and Chez Paree in Chicago, the Latin Casino in Philadelphia, the Town Casino in Buffalo, Blinstrub's and the Latin Quarter in Boston, the Three Rivers Inn in Syracuse, and Ben Maksik's Town and Country in Brooklyn. It was still the era of Walter Winchell, Damon Runyon, Leonard Lyons, Sidney Skolsky, Earl Wilson, Meyer Berger, Jack Lait, and Lee Mortimer. But the composers of many of the most popular standards were themselves beginning to pass away, and the New York they once celebrated was now heading into decline. Oscar Hammerstein II died in 1960, Cole Porter in 1964. The lights were going out on old Broadway.

The songs sung in the nightclubs were culled from the great American popular music catalog: Irving Berlin, George Gershwin, Rodgers and Hart, Cole Porter, Schwartz and Dietz, Sammy Cahn, and Jerome Kern. In truth, Bobby had always loved those songs, and in them he found his own voice. He would bring to them a richness, depth, and personal stamp that had eluded him in many of his rock records. Bobby always needed to move beyond and resist his chameleonlike ability to copy the sounds of other artists in his hurry to reach the top instantly. He sounds more like Presley than Presley on "Mighty Mighty Man"; and "Baby Face," despite its vigor, sounds like a reincarnation of Little Richard's arrangement. When he was emotionally moved, he forgot the treadmill and was swept up into the meaning and beauty of the music. "Bobby grew up listening to Charlie Maffia's record collection," Steve Blauner says, "Crosby, Jolson, Sinatra. So then he's doing 'Splish

Splash.' Well, that's because it's the only way he can get his foot in the door. But the minute he had the strength to call his own shot, what did he do? The *That's All* album."

When Bobby did *That's All*, many assumed he would try a Sinatra album. There was no question that Bobby revered Sinatra; what singer did not? But for Bobby, Sinatra was the gold standard, and some observers thought Bobby was obsessed with him. Yet the album is largely devoid of a Sinatra feel or even of songs Sinatra had chosen to sing. (He would record "Mack the Knife" long after Bobby died, and in his record he would pay homage to Bobby's version.) "When Bobby made the switch-over from rock to standards," Hesh Wasser says, "it really set him apart. It separated him from all the Sinatra clones. Because they could do only one thing, and Bobby could do every genre. Even Sinatra himself could never have done what Bobby did."

That's All was totally against the grain. "Totally against everything, because he had never done anything like it," Steve Blauner says. "Here's a guy who was doing 'Splish Splash,' 'Dream Lover,' 'Queen of the Hop.' What do you mean he's doing these standards? Think about it. He picked all of the songs. And he had a way of doing songs differently than they'd ever been done. 'Mack the Knife' had been a dirge. 'That's All' was a ballad."

Bobby was rebelling against not only his own image but against the musical times. Rock and roll had taken over the music business. A musical amalgam that comprised many strains of American music—rhythm and blues, country and western, gospel, jazz, folk, and swing—its strong sexual overtones (in the black community, "rock and roll" was a common term for both dancing and sexual intercourse) had made it greatly appealing to white teenagers. Frank Sinatra was one of those who expressed his distaste for it (and, indirectly, at his chief rival, Elvis Presley) in 1957:

> *It is sung, played, and written for the most part by cretinous goons and by means of its almost imbecilic reiterations and sly, lewd, in fact, plain dirty lyrics . . . It manages to be the martial music of every side-burned delinquent on the face of the earth.*

But Sinatra was in the rearguard. In 1954, "Sh-Boom," a rock-and-roll song recorded by both a black group, The Chords, and a white one, The Crew Cuts, became the fifth best-selling song of the year and the first rock-and-roll hit. In 1955, 12 of the year's top 50 hits were rock-and-roll songs. Among them was Bill Haley and the Comets' "Rock Around the Clock," which was featured in the film *Blackboard Jungle*. The record reached the top of the charts and sold 15 million copies by the late 1960s, becoming one of the best-selling single records of all time.

From 1956 to 1960, black artists such as Chuck Berry, Ray Charles, Sam Cooke, Little Richard, Little Willie John, Fats Domino, and the Platters rose to fame and fortune. White singers, most notably Presley, borrowed black styles and utilized them to catapult themselves into the ranks of the new icons. And the white rock-and-roll singers, like Presley, Jerry Lee Lewis, Buddy Holly, and Pat Boone, were popular with their cover versions of black hits, sometimes more popular than the original artists were. Presley's blend of rhythm and blues, rockabilly, and country music led to 14 consecutive gold records from 1956 to 1968.

Record sales soared. With the success of rock and roll, annual revenues climbed from $219 million in 1953 to $277 million in 1955, reaching a staggering $600 million in 1960. By 1955, the ballad singers were already beginning to lose their hold on the public. The record companies, Tony Bennett says, "started going for this obsolescence idea. They didn't want records that would last, they didn't want lasting artists, they wanted lots of [consecutive] artists. So they started discarding people like me and Duke Ellington and Leonard Bernstein."

Within a few years, the impact of rhythm and blues had totally transformed American popular music, and Tin Pan Alley was displaced as the music center of the universe.

This was the high tide that Bobby was swimming against.

Bobby played a key role in creating the new album. "Now that he had 'Splish Splash,'" Hesh Wasser says, "I was there with him when it was a matter of him searching, trying to figure out where he was going to go, not knowing what would happen. After he and Dick Behrke gave up the apartment on West 71st Street, Bobby was living with his family again on Baruch Place. He couldn't survive without them. He needed to have medical care; if he was sick, he had to be under constant care, he had to be watched. So he was depending on them. It was Charlie who mainly took care of him. Bobby couldn't take the subways because he couldn't walk up the stairs; Charlie would drive into Manhattan and pick him up."

But outside the house, it was Hesh Wasser who was Bobby's guardian angel. Once again, she played a crucial part in what transpired. Nelson Riddle had created the great arrangements that marked Sinatra's transformation as a singer in the Capitol years of "In the Wee Small Hours," "Songs for Swinging Lovers," "Nice and Easy"—albums that changed Sinatra's image in the public's eyes from a gentle romantic balladeer into both a macho swinger and a heartbreaking ballad stylist of enormous depth and passion. Wasser set about finding Bobby his Nelson Riddle. She decided on Richard Wess.

"I was the one who found Wess for Bobby," she recalls. "I knew that Wess was a big-band arranger and had done some albums. Richard had absolutely no interest in rock and roll, while Bobby was basically a rock-and-roll artist at that time. He would never have really talked to Richard Wess about music. Bobby knew who he was, but Wess was just a person who passed through his life; I don't remember them ever sitting down and having a conversation. So I was the one who really inquired of Wess. I went to him and asked him to show me something he had recorded. I liked an album that he had done with a singer named Sally Blair. Wess seemed to be right for Bobby, and so I got Dick together with Bobby. He never even listened to the albums Wess had given me. He trusted my judgment. Dick said to me, 'How do I know Bobby is going to pay me?' I said, 'Just don't worry, it's going to happen, take my word for it.'"

Wasser never doubted that Bobby would return to the standards. "Even when he was doing rock, he never really gave up on everything he had listened to as a kid. He liked rock, and he wanted to be part of the current scene. He wanted the kids to like him, but he also wanted the adults to like him. He was going to do a little rock and roll, but then go out there and sing Jolson's 'Rainbow Round My Shoulder' and show as a 22-year-old, 'I'm going to knock their socks off.' And he knew this was how he would do it."

"Bobby had a great regard for the old performers, for what came before him," says singer Steve Lawrence. "You soak that in, and bring your own intelligence, your own abilities, your own creativity, to what has influenced you. And then you become, it's like the tenth man. You listen to nine other things out there, put yourself into it, and become the tenth man."

Many of Bobby's other peers, in addition to Frankie Avalon, Steve Lawrence, Dion, and Paul Anka, also regarded him as apart, someone with unique gifts, focus, and unusual seriousness. "Bobby was much more hip—even though we all considered ourselves hip—than any of us," says singer James Darren. "When you perform, many actors and singers are afraid to show their real selves, afraid they won't be liked if they reveal what's underneath. Bobby did not have that problem. The best thing you can ever do is to show yourself—because you have what you are, and that's what's unique about each person. Bobby did all that onstage. And that's why Bobby was such a standout. And it all came from the fact that Bobby was confident with himself and not afraid to show it. If you listen to his records today or see him on film, he's sustained, he holds up. Do you know what his impact comes from? It comes from whatever his vibes were when he sang those songs or his vibes whenever you saw him. *You* come through him. That's *you*. So that's why Bobby lives, the magic the human being has.

"Bobby was older than what he was. Bobby was 25 going on 55. But he was inventive in the way a young kid is. His head was like he had been there before. Like he came back, reincarnated. The body's young, but his brain—he was hatched. I was cracking the fucking shell of the egg. And this guy was shaking the shit off his wings."

Bobby initially recorded "Mack" with three other songs on an EP— an extended play album of four sides, very much in currency in the '50s.

Al Kasha, two-time Academy Award–winning composer, recalls that Bobby's determination was so great that he paid for the EP himself. "This is really the big story about how 'Mack the Knife' came about," Kasha says. "When Bobby signed with GAC, there was an agent there named Roz Ross who booked the rock-and-roll shows for Dick Clark. Bobby felt he was getting older and was already losing his hair. He knew he wanted to make the transition to being a nightclub singer and wanted to get into the Copa, and he told Roz. Ross said to Bobby, 'Jules Podell doesn't understand songs like 'Splish Splash' and 'Queen of the Hop'; he doesn't get rock. You have to do something for me to show Julie, some sort of demo, to get into the Copa.' Bobby went to Ahmet and Jerry with 'Mack the Knife' and said that he would never get into the Copa, never get anyplace, unless they released the EP. And he said he'd give up his royalties on 'Splish Splash' and 'Dream Lover' for it. He took a gamble. He was always a gambler, Bobby, on himself, because he was a visionary. The EP went through the roof. Then Atlantic finally put it out as a single."

"He would go and record a session, and it would be charged to him," Steve Blauner recalls. "He didn't pay at that moment, but before he saw any money, it was deducted from his royalties. In those days, you could make an album of 12 songs in three days, and it would cost about $25,000. So if he was getting a dollar an album—and he wasn't, because in those days the albums sold for under five dollars—and I think he had 5 percent of 90 percent. Plus, the 90 percent came from old deals when they were making shellac, and there would be breakage from shellac, so automatically you didn't get paid 10 percent. Of course now they were moving into 45 rpm's, and there was no more breakage, but they were still getting away with it. So he had 5 percent of 90 percent, whatever that came to. You had to sell a lot of those to make up the $25,000 before you started to get any money. So with 'Splish Splash' and his other hits, Atco owed him money. They knew this album would pay for itself, and so they went along with it."

From December 19 through 24, 1958, Bobby recorded all the tracks for *That's All*, although the album would not be released until 1959, and no singles from it, including "Mack the Knife," the song that would immortalize him, were released until August 1959. Bobby did more than record the songs. "People say Sinatra was one of the only artists who ever produced and took a hand in his albums—he didn't just get up and sing," says Hesh Wasser. "He really contributed, produced, collaborated, he did everything. Well, Bobby certainly did just as much in that ballpark, if not more. Bobby Scott would say, 'You write a chart for Bobby Darin, you're working with him. Because he's sitting there, he's telling you the notes.' He'd direct it all. And we're not talking about some 40-year-old. We're talking about someone who from day one, when he entered the studio, he always had control. That's why all these other artists—Durante, Burns, Jack Benny—were surprised and in awe of him from the beginning."

Dick Clark recalls that "Bobby and I were very close; we could say anything to one another. He called me once on the phone. He said, 'Listen to this record.' He plays 'Mack' over the phone. I listen and then he says, 'This is my next release.' I say, 'Are you out of your mind? What are you trying to be, a saloon singer? You're a rock-and-roll star, you're huge, you're on the roll. That's the sort of stuff you'd hear from a lounge lizard singer."

In February of that year, Steve Blauner and Bobby were at the Moulin Rouge in Los Angeles watching Jerry Lewis perform. "Somebody said there had been a phone call for Bobby," Blauner recalls. "And I didn't think anything of it, because I didn't know anybody knew where we were. And who would be calling Bobby? So I didn't pay any attention to it. After the show, we went to a Chinese restaurant on Sunset Boulevard and I said to him, 'You know, somebody said someone was trying to reach you. Isn't that strange?' So he said, 'Let me check at home.' He called New York and found out his mother [Polly] had died. So I put him on the plane next morning to go home for the funeral. And he buried her."

Polly, who had a heart condition that was a contributing factor in her being bedridden from her mid-40s on, died of a stroke. She was in her mid-60s.

"Bobby had done the *That's All* album but it wasn't released yet, and we had the acetates. He gave one to me, and he took the other one and put it in Polly's coffin. She never heard the album."

"I was at the wake," Joyce Becker remembers. "Bobby was sobbing, oh my God. Uncontrollable. He was white as a sheet."

"Bobby was devastated at the funeral," says Hesh Wasser. "He was crying. It was very important to him to have Polly hear *That's All* before she died."

An indication of how deeply Bobby felt about Polly's death and the lack of connection to the rest of his family came a year later, when he was interviewed by radio talk show host Barry Gray. Asked about his family, 24-year-old Bobby replied: "I am an orphan, in the sense of being without a father or a mother."

"I met Bobby when he first came to Miami in 1959," Hal Taines, one of the men who would be a surrogate father to Bobby, remembers. "I was nine years older than Bobby, but he wanted to be a buddy right away. Talked a great deal about Polly, what a wonderful woman she was. They used to live on potatoes so that she could pay for Bobby taking music lessons.

"There was a bond between Steve and Bobby about both of them losing their mothers at the same time. If Bobby had a feeling that you and he had something in common, he was like a brother to you. And he loved Steve. He didn't like Steve, he loved Steve. When he introduced me to Charlie Maffia, Bobby said, 'My sister's married to a garbage man. What do you think of that?' Bobby made Charlie Maffia his road manager. Charlie said, 'What does a road manager do?' I said to Bobby, 'Charlie can't be your road manager. He doesn't even understand what it is.' Bobby said, 'Tell him.'"

DESPITE MOURNING POLLY'S DEATH, Bobby did not let it stop him. In the summer of 1959, he was invited to sing at the Hollywood Jazz Festival. The single of "Mack the Knife" had taken the country by storm. It surfaced on the *Billboard* charts in August, and within six weeks it was the No. 1 single in the country. It remained there for nine weeks and stayed on the charts for 52. "Mack" was accepted both by adults and kids and sold two million records.

"When he had signed with General Artists Corporation," Al Kasha recalls, "Bobby said, 'I don't have the greatest voice, but I dance real well and I move real well.' Because he'd been a drummer too, he understood the pauses, the highs and the lows, the loudness, the softness, the eighth-note pushes. So he sang like a drummer. He hit what's called all the accidentals. If you look at a written drum sheet, it would be like Bobby's singing. And he danced really well on stage. He had perfect time too; he could back phrase but catch up, and he was always on top of the song. Sinatra had great phrasing. This is a lot to say about Bobby Darin, but Darin, even more than Frank, was the greatest singer when it came to the time of the song. Sinatra wasn't a musician; Darin was a natural musician. He's the ultimate drummer-singer.

"Similar to Sinatra, Bobby mapped out the arrangements too," Kasha continues. "He would point to the sax section when they were coming in. He knew the whole orchestration as if he wrote it. I mean, he really lived the orchestration. He was very complimentary to musicians, as Sinatra was. Very appreciative. They loved to work with him because of that. I would call him a singer's singer and a musician's singer.

"Another quality that Bobby had was that he was an intellectual. He did understand the words. He was a moment-to-moment actor. He sounded like the words. He captured the mood of the word: I want to be *happy*; I want to be *sad*. He'd recreate the mood, sounding like the word at that moment. You say 'hush,' it sounds like 'hush.' Loud it's loud, soft it's soft. Bobby and I talked about it, because he wanted to be an actor. And it didn't have to be one mood only. From line to line in a song, he would do like, 'I've got you under my skin . . .' He would do that long; then, the second time—'I've got you . . .'—he'd do it fast. So there was always variation in the rhythms."

By the end of the year, Bobby was heading for the very top, the pinnacle, of show business.

Steve Blauner was charting every move, designed to keep up the momentum and accelerate Bobby's rise. And every move was right. "Bobby was already a star in Hollywood before anybody ever saw him," says Steve. "There was a nightclub out there called the Mocambo, the famous watering hole of the stars. Then some kids from Chicago came out and bought it and opened it as the Cloister. And Bobby's first major engagement in Hollywood was at the Cloister. We would take ads in the trade papers every day for two weeks: 'Fourteen days Till D-day.' The quote of a famous person about this anonymous singer. No mention of Bobby's name. In fact it got to the point where people were calling up, wondering if they could make a reservation for Doris Day. And so finally, one day before he opened, full-page ad: 'One Day Till D-Day.' And it had all the quotes on the page about how great Bobby was, without Bobby's name. And then the day he opened: 'Today is D-Day. Bobby Darin Swings . . .'

"And then there were lines around the block at the Cloister. Now I'm in Jerry Lewis's office at Paramount. Jerry's on the phone with somebody and he's talking about Bobby Darin, what a great det det det. He hung up the phone and I said, 'You never saw him.' Jerry says, 'What are you talking about?' I said to Jerry, 'You're saying how great he is. You've never seen him.' 'Well, I—' 'Jerry, this is me. You've never seen the man!'

"That's what was created out here by all that stuff. Being seen and going and doing. Bobby was a star in Hollywood before he had any right to be. That's why Bobby soon ended up with two seven-picture deals—option deals—at two different studios."

The August 12 engagement was an unparalleled sensation. George Burns introduced Bobby: "I'm very pleased to have been asked to make this introduction. I predicted a year ago that this boy would go through the roof, and he has. He's only 23, and he has a very exciting style. So, here he is, a real nice boy, Bobby Darin." In addition to George and Gracie, Jack Benny, Danny Thomas, Shirley Jones, Jerry Lewis, Shelley Winters, Donald O'Connor, Natalie Wood, and Robert Wagner were there for the opening.

"I was one of the guys in the beginning with Steve Blauner," Jack Gilardi, executive vice-president of ICM, remembers. "Not so much that I recognized Bobby's talent, but Steve recognized it. Every day, twice a day, three times a day, Steve Blauner would be on the phone: Bobby Darin, Bobby Darin, Bobby Darin. He was obsessed. And I believed Steve. Steve never BS'd me, never lied to me. He kept saying: You gotta do this, you gotta do that. I had only met Bobby once through Frankie Avalon. Frankie told me that Bobby and he went on a tour with Paul Anka and others and Bobby was much more sophisticated, much more accomplished, sort of the outsider. So my friends from Chicago were opening a joint called the Cloister. I tell them, you gotta buy Bobby Darin. We put him in there for $2,500 a week for 10 days. Everybody came. You couldn't get in, I don't care what night it was. But Bobby wasn't a beginner. He was a trouper. He belonged on the stage.

"And I came to love Bobby. We had a rapport, being both Italian. I think Bobby knew and smelled who was really true and honest with him, and he was hostile to the guys that wanted to use him because he was hot. His good judgment came from the street. Every time I think of Bobby, I want to smile. Bobby was always warm, embraced you. And Blauner was always the big teddy bear."

Buddy Bregman was the arranger of Bobby's act at the Cloister. "I got involved with Bobby through Sammy Davis Jr. He used to spend as much time with Sammy as I did, so I saw him all the time. Bobby took the audience by storm," Bregman says. "He was a bombastic hit. Some of the time I saw him from the back. He had rhythm from his head to his toes. Bobby has that 'huh!' He used to hunch his shoulders a lot. When he hunched, something happened vocally that was terrific. It gave it a little 'huh!'—a lift. It's like someone gives you the *push* inside—I think that's what he did."

Bobby went from the Cloister to the Sands in Las Vegas. This might have marked the moment he began to be known as a troublemaker. "There were a lot of drunk Texans in the audience," remembers Steve Blauner, "and they were making noise. And he just said, 'Fuck you, people.' And like the fourth song in, he said, 'Get me "Mack the Knife."' He did it and he walked off the stage. Jack Entratter didn't pick up his option."

That was not the only incident at the Sands. "We went down to the rehearsal," Jack Gilardi says. "In Bobby's act, he gave a tribute to Ray Charles. I sat that night with Jack Entratter in his booth. Bobby opened up and did the finger-snapping, and at the end he did his tribute to Ray. Entratter turned to me and said, 'I didn't know this guy brought along the Ray Charles Singers' [a bland white backup pop group, not related to the soul singer]. He thought it was those singers from *The Perry Como Show*. Entratter didn't realize that Bobby hadn't brought along any group at all. And Bobby went into that loud Ray Charles music. 'Not in my room you don't!' Entratter shouted. Afterward in his dressing room, Bobby said, 'Clear everybody out.' Entratter walked in and said, 'I don't want you to do that part of the show. It's not that kind of a room.' Entratter wanted to show he was boss. Bobby said, 'I'll never play this joint again.' And Bobby never did. And Bobby did business, big business."

On September 5, Bobby was paired with one of his all-time idols on television on *An Evening with Jimmy Durante*. Bobby sang "Mack" and "That's All" and did two duets with Durante, "Bill Bailey, Won't You Please Come Home" and "Personality." Soon after, Bobby did an extraordinary imitation of Durante for a charity benefit. The most amazing thing about this performance is that Durante comes out and starts singing, and then a second, agitated Durante comes out and observes him with perplexity. The first Durante is actually Bobby, and his imitation of Durante is so perfect—in appearance, voice, feeling—there's no way you know it's Bobby until the real Durante reveals himself. Steve Blauner recalls Durante exclaiming, while watching Bobby rehearse from the control room, "That's me! I can't believe it. That's me!"

On September 8, 1959, Buddy Bregman orchestrated a Hollywood Bowl concert in honor of the composer Jimmy McHugh with Bobby, Vic Damone, and Anna Marie Alberghetti. Bregman conducted the

Bobby and Steve Blauner

Elvis would sometimes visit Bobby in his hotel room while they both were performing in Las Vegas. In the center is an unidentified fan.

Joanne Campbell and Bobby during one of their private moments at the Paramount Theater in Brooklyn

Frankie Avalon backstage with Bobby at Ben Maksik's Town and Country Club in Brooklyn

Harriet "Hesh" Wasser shown with Bobby at Ben Maksik's Town and Country Club. This was Bobby's first major nightclub engagement following the success of "Splish Splash."

Bobby with Nina and Charlie Maffia at the Copacabana in 1960

Bobby faces his adoring fans while on tour as a rocker.

Sammy Davis Jr. was one of the featured guests when Bobby was the subject of *This Is Your Life*. Here we see Gary Walden, Nina's youngest son and Bobby's half-brother, being lifted onto a chair by Sammy and Bobby.

Bobby having some fun with Dick Clark during one of the tapings of *The Dick Clark Show* on ABC-TV, circa 1960

On November 30, 1959, Bobby received two Grammy Awards, one for Record of the Year for "Mack the Knife" and the other for Best New Artist. Here he is shown with (left to right) David Rose, André Previn, Jonah Jones, and Shelly Berman.

Bobby at an early Decca recording session in 1956

"When the shark bites with his teeth, dear . . ." Bobby poses with the catch of the day, along with songwriter Woody Harris (rear, second from right, in striped shirt), his collaborator on "Clementine." The rest are the owners of the Singapole Motel and the crew of the charter fishing boat.

Hollywood Bowl Pops orchestra. "Bobby was terrific to work with," recalls Bregman, "better than Streisand. Better than almost anyone. Bobby had a nonchalance onstage that I liked a lot. And you felt he meant every word he said. Even on the up-tempo songs, because even if he combined the rhythm with the meaning of the lyrics, Bobby got more meaning out of the song." Regarding the vocal differences between Sammy Davis and Bobby, Bregman says, "Sammy Davis put a patina to the music and the lyrics. Bobby didn't. Bobby didn't have any layers; he didn't have any sheen on his work. He was pure, heartfelt. Sammy's heartfeltness was, you knew, made up. Sammy was a better dancer than anyone. But Bobby moved great. He felt the music; he moved with every beat."

In November, Bobby would join four show business heavyweights—Burns, Benny, Eddie Cantor, and George Jessel—on another TV special, *George Burns in the Big Time*. Bobby was seated at the table with the stars, and as always, he fit in perfectly like an old trouper. On this night, nostalgia reigned. Jessel and Cantor reprised the song they had sung to sold-out crowds for months at the RKO Palace in 1932, "Pals." Bobby performed with Burns, reprising their nightclub act.

Steve was aware that Bobby had health problems, but it was only because of a rehearsal for *The Ed Sullivan Show* that he discovered the extent of Bobby's illness. Bobby had gone to the rehearsal after closing an exhausting seven-day, seven-shows-a-day engagement at the Steel Pier in Atlantic City. "I had originally told Bobby, 'You can't talk about your illness,'" Hesh Wasser recalls. "As soon as Steve said something about wanting to manage Bobby, that was one of the first thoughts that came into my mind. Bobby and I pretty much agreed at that time that we just wouldn't tell him. Then an incident came up where Steve had to be told. And it was Nina who really did it.

"When Bobby did *The Ed Sullivan Show*," Hesh continues, "his dressing room was on the top floor, two flights up. The elevator was out of order, and Bobby bounded up the stairs. He saw his three-year-old nephew [actually brother], Gary, waiting for him at the top and lifted him up for a bear hug. Bobby started gasping for air. He called for help, clutching his chest. They rushed oxygen to him. He lay on the couch in pain, breathing into the mask." Sullivan sympathetically told Bobby to cancel his appearance. But Bobby was used to the pains and recovered enough to go on anyway. No one would have dreamed he was sick as he sang "Clementine" and the Arthur Schwartz standard "By Myself." "And Nina said, 'This can't be. Gotta tell Steve Blauner. He's gotta know. Bobby can't be put on the top floor ever.' So Nina was the one who made the point. By the time Bobby went to California, Steve already knew everything, and he was the one who called the doctor and got the best people."

From that time on, Bobby would always carry an oxygen tent and mask with him, which he kept backstage. Even Wasser did not know this.

Bobby was acclaimed everywhere, but at night he went to bed with chest pains and the realization that no matter how sweet it all was, it could not last. He went from the television show to the Moulin Rouge in Los Angeles in September 1959, where he set an attendance record and a one-week earnings record. He went from there to the Sands Hotel in Vegas. Jerry Lewis told him, "Do you realize you're alone in your generation? Sammy, Dean, and I are all 10 years ahead of you. Unless you destroy yourself, no one else can touch you. If you louse it up, it's going to be your fault. Because you have the talent, kid. You're alone. You're alone."

Bobby had two enemies, and Jerry Lewis had touched upon the one other than death: himself.

He was now the hottest entertainer in the country.

Bobby began gathering around him the musicians who would stay with him for the critical years ahead. Drummer Ronnie Zito was playing Utica, New York, with Bobby in a club date. "The people around Bobby—Steve, Harriet—had such belief in him," Zito says. "They were so supportive of him in his career. Everyone was on his side. He just had such good time, such great rhythm. He was so rhythmic that it was perfect. He asked me to come to Washington with him, and then he said, 'I want you to be my drummer.' I was with him through the hottest period, the Copa days. He used to sit down at the piano and jam during rehearsals. Fool around. He might sit down at the drums. Or he would do 'Come Rain or Come Shine,' just me playing bass behind him. Nobody was doing that in those days. It was almost like a jazz thing.

"He was so natural. I'd be playing the drums and I'd be looking at him, watching him. I'd be catching things. We would hook up. He was very open and up for grabs, whatever worked, whatever felt good to him, if he could just dance to it. Sometimes he used to dance in the studio, without an audience, just to see how it felt. Music to him was his life.

"When he sang," says Zito, "he used to stand in front of me, in front of the drums facing me. And he would sing to me and dance at the same time. And I would be playing. That was our meeting, our conference. That's the way it was done! He stood in front of me and sang with a smile on his face and danced. It was kind of a magical thing."

THE FIRST THING ONE NOTES on the album jacket of *That's All* is a benediction from Sammy Davis Jr. in the form of a Western Union telegram:

> JANUARY 27, 1959. BOBBY DARIN, CARE STEVE BLAUNER, GENERAL ARTISTS CORP. BEVERLY HILLS CALIFORNIA—DEAR BOBBY HAVE JUST HEARD THE DUBS FOR YOUR NEW ALBUM. WHAT CAN I SAY? THEY'RE SO GOOD I HATE YOU. BUT SERIOUSLY BOBBY, I THINK THE ALBUM'S ANOTHER BIG STEP IN A CAREER THAT WILL LAST A LONG TIME. I ANXIOUSLY AWAIT THE PUBLIC'S REACTION TO THE ALBUM FOR IN THIS DAY AND AGE OF GIMIC [SIC] SOUNDS AND GIMIC RECORDS THE CHOICE OF MATERIAL AND THE ARRANGEMENTS OF DICK WESS ARE A PERFECT COMBINATION OF SHOWMANSHIP PERFORMANCE AND TASTE. IN OTHER WORDS I DIG IT SEE YOU SOON. SAMMY DAVIS JR.

What meant a lot to Hesh Wasser was a second message, this one from Bobby on the LP (not reprinted now on the CD). He wrote, "A little Darin, a little [Richard] Wess, a little Wasser, makes this album what it is. Love, Bobby."

That's All begins with one of the most powerful doubleheaders in recording history: "Mack the Knife," formerly a dirge, and "Beyond the Sea." In Germany, where "Mack" premiered in 1928, Brecht had entitled it "Moritat," which means "Murder Ballad." Lotte Lenya, wife of Kurt Weill, was in the original production, playing Jenny Diver, and repeated her role in the New York production that opened to great success in 1954. In his book *Jazz Singing*, Will Friedwald writes that "such songs are part of a shared English-German tradition, ballads for performance on music hall stages . . . that cry out the news, offering grisly details of the latest crime." (The most famous murder ballad in the traditional English repertory is "Sweeney Todd the Barber," the source for that most Brechtian of Sondheim musicals.) Friedwald writes that in the New York production, "Mack" was sung "with a reporter's detachment . . . a very straight inventory of the master criminal's evil deeds—a very Brechtian approach." Louis Armstrong gave Mack more immediacy, treating him like a "rascal," "singing of MacHeath laughingly, and perhaps ever so faintly admiringly."

Bobby pointed out in an interview with Barry Gray that he'd heard many versions of "Mack" that were "dry, almost like a minuet." But in Bobby's swinging version, Mack turns into an inspired, even joyous Brechtian piece of libertine comic lunacy, mayhem, and murder—nothing so celebratory or warm-hearted about murder and murderers would come along until *The Sopranos* 30 years later. The roots of the record can be seen in the first great recordings by the trumpet player Jonah Jones and Louie Armstrong's (1955) definitive jazz version, which conveyed much of the fun. (There have also been excellent versions by Ella Fitzgerald and Bing Crosby.) Armstrong rejected the song at first because the lyric was too bloodthirsty. However, when he heard a recording of it by Gerald Price, a member of the New York cast of the musical, his face lit up, and he said, "Well, I'll be! I used to know some cats just like that in New Orleans!"

"Bobby's track of 'Mack' is so good," Ahmet Ertegun recalls, "I knew we had a hit before Bobby started singing, before they ran the arrangement down. Before he opened his mouth, I said, 'This is magic!' I knew that this was it, that it was undeniable. It was so in the pocket." Ertegun explains its history. "I had been at the home of Lotte Lenya one day, and she asked me why I'd never made a record of Kurt Weill's songs. A couple of days later, Bobby Darin came up to me with the wonderful Louie Armstrong recording of 'Mack' and said, 'I know this sounds pretty weird, but I think I could make a great version of this—I should do it.' So we made a big-band arrangement, using Don Lamond, a great drummer from Washington, and Richard Wess completed the arrangement, although Bobby had a lot of influence over that too. Bobby sang his heart out, with so much feeling. It was just one of those forever records."

Singer Julius LaRosa recalls the first time he heard "Mack": "It came on the radio and I said to my wife, 'My God, I can't believe that's Bobby Darin.' Because by me he was 'Splish Splash.' I wanted the Splish Splash man, but now there's this other color, here's this other side. And the son of a bitch was good."

Bobby brings "Mack" up many notches. The Wess arrangement changes keys, rising chromatically with almost every new section. He starts small and keeps rising and rising, crescendo upon crescendo, swinging it, until it almost explodes on a sharp 11th chord. This is Bobby tearing the roof off, coming home, finding his voice and style absolutely. This is the mark of the artist: it's a work of art that no one else could do. It's his alone. No one else could swing it this way, this hard, this comically, with such total originality, vocal authority, and abandon, give it those "eeks," "hup-hups," "ho-hos," "ahs," and "uh-uhs," those body sounds that complement the sensuality, the physicality, the immediacy of it. *Nothing* has been done this way before. The track is so fresh it's as if it happened yesterday.

"Mack" established Bobby as a great pop singer. He was influenced here by Armstrong and Sinatra—the swagger and the machismo certainly started with Sinatra—and he would always be influenced by others. This was sometimes to his detriment, but in his best work the reality is that Bobby was more inspired than influenced. In an interview with Barry Gray, Bobby pointed out that Armstrong was inspired by King Oliver in his recording of "Mack," and that he was inspired by Armstrong. There cannot be the birth of an artist if the artist does not at first recognize beauty and want to create something beautiful himself or herself. Sinatra listened to Billie Holiday; Dean Martin listened to Bing Crosby. Shortly before his death, the great Ray Charles had a dialogue with his biographer, David Ritz, in *Rolling Stone* about "copying" other artists:

> **Charles:** *I can do a lot of little things well. But I copied.*
> **Ritz:** *And then innovated.*
> **Charles:** *The innovation was copying. Good copying. Great copying. But I wouldn't put me up there with Bird and Diz.*
> **Ritz:** *And when they say you invented soul music, you're going to argue?*
> **Charles:** *Maybe I put together two things that hadn't been put together before, but hell, give credit to the church singers and the bluesmen who I got it from. I got enough credit. Let people know that it didn't come from me. It came from before me.*

Bobby listened to Ray Charles and Sinatra and countless others. He seemed to love it all. The end result transcended influence and resulted in something utterly original. Bobby's work at its best was more than the sum of its parts—sometimes it was better than all those parts were in the first place. "The Sinatra-styled 'Mack the Knife' and 'Beyond the Sea,'" says Jerry Wexler, "proved that Bobby, a minted diamond, could swing in styles ranging from rock to big band-jazz."

"Mack the Knife" was only the start of *That's All*. "Beyond the Sea" was once a solemn French pop song ("La Mer") by Charles Trenet and sung so slowly it could wither on the vine. It had previously been recorded by Benny Goodman and Tex Beneke with the Glenn Miller orchestra, in lush arrangements heavy with strings. Here, in the American version by songwriter Jack Lawrence, "Beyond the Sea," like "Mack," is turned upside down and swings with overflowing buoyancy and exuberance. "Beyond the Sea" is a kind of follow-up twin to "Mack," but without the nasty sentiments. On the contrary, it's an ode about homecoming. The singer is sailing toward shore, where his lover "stands on golden sands." It's a friskier version of "I Left My Heart in San Francisco"—the action's going to be a lot hotter when this singer gets home. The single of "Beyond the Sea" was almost as popular as "Mack," rising to No. 6 on the charts. It's a lot happier than "Mack," to say the least. Yet Bobby swings it just as hard, with irreverence and impudence, raising the roof all over again. The record begins with muted trombones, and then Bobby comes in, strings, horns, and brass kicking in. Following the instrumental break of thundering drums and soft strings, Bobby blasts away on the final chorus.

Bobby's songwriting ability was evident in "That's the Way Love Is," which holds its own with the beautiful classics Bobby includes on the album, from "Through a Long and Sleepless Night" and "She Needs Me" to Gershwin's "It Ain't Necessarily So" and "I'll Remember April." And with the title song, Bobby once again defies expectations and turns the Nat King Cole ballad into something new with a frenetic, up-tempo reading. Bobby's homage to Sophie Tucker, "Some of These Days," is captivating, conjuring up the golden days of vaudeville at the Palace, the Ziegfield Follies, and the Winter Garden. He does it better than Sophie, but only because Sophie did it first and Bobby is reaping the benefits. He is building upon what has come before and tipping his hat to the originators—not as chestnuts, but as the first creators. As with many of the songs on the album, Bobby projects his youthful image and perspective on songs that have never been rendered this way before and gives them new life and vitality. "Some of These Days" would be identified with Bobby at his best.

"BOBBY WAS ALWAYS REAL, and his songs covered a wide range of concepts," Jerrold Atlas, Bobby's childhood friend, says. "Bobby's importance to American culture lay in the fact that he was an ordinary guy. Even though he was not, he appeared to be this ordinary guy who was not handsome but had incredible talent. This was a guy you knew.

You watched him and related. The way we watched *Happy Days*. So when he did Kurt Weill and modernized it, he just blew people away. People understood Kurt Weill and Lotte Lenya as a result of what he did. Before that, Kurt Weill was for the literati. After Bobby, Weill became interesting.

"Bobby just took simple American singing," Atlas continues, "which it really was, and moved it to a whole other level. He didn't have a voice like Sinatra or Pavarotti or Bocelli, but Bobby could sell something, even on the radio when you couldn't see him. It was his delivery that was very special; it was the delivery of the kid next door. Before that it was the Tony Bennetts, the Jimmy Rosellis, the Jerry Vales; wonderful music, music we all loved, and those singers had voices that were melodic beyond belief. Bobby wasn't that at all. But it was a guy in America singing, a talented, street-smart guy. He made that character his."

Michael Cuscuna, jazz writer and director of Mosaic Records, says, "I first got into Bobby when he was having rock-and-roll hits, because I was 11 and that's what I was into. When *That's All* appeared, the album came out before the singles. I was in a store on Broadway in the 40s, and of course when you're 11 you're measuring every dollar you spend. My cousin and I were looking at it and I said, 'I don't know. I never heard any of the tunes. And they're all long; they're all over three minutes. There's something fishy about this. Ah, it's Bobby Darin. I'll get it.' I was kind of put off by it at first, but I kept playing it because I invested four fucking dollars in it and I was gonna get my money's worth. It was one of the first things that got me into 'adult' music. I was just getting into jazz at the same time, and this dovetailed perfectly into adding to my musical education. And I ended up within a couple of months falling in love with the album."

On November 29, 1959, the music industry's second annual Grammy Awards ceremony was held. Bobby and "Mack the Knife" were up for four awards, including Best Vocal Performance, Male category. Sinatra won that one, but Bobby received the award for Best New Artist.

Four records were nominated for Record of the Year: "Mack the Knife," Presley's "A Fool Such As I," Andre Previn's "Like Young," Sinatra's "High Hopes," and The Browns' "The Three Bells."

The winner was "Mack the Knife."

Bobby had received two Grammys.

"After the Grammys," recalls Steve Blauner, "we were walking through the lobby of the Beverly Hilton. We were stopped by Vernon Scott, a reporter for the United Press. He says to Bobby, 'Do you want to be bigger than Frank Sinatra?' Bobby says to him very respectfully, 'Why would you ask me that? We're a different generation. All I want to do is to be the biggest and best Bobby Darin I can be.' Scott said, 'Well, you want to do everything that Sinatra has done.' Again, Bobby replied, 'It's not fair. What does one thing have to do with the other? I want to do whatever I can do.' The next day—which I loved, of course—in 2,000 papers across the country, the headline read: "Darin Wants to Be Bigger Than Sinatra." Scott claimed Bobby had said, 'I hope to surpass Frank in everything he's done.' I just loved it. My attitude was always, I don't care what they print about Bobby as long as they spell his name right."

Bobby told the *New York Post* he hadn't made the remark. "There's no question of beating Sinatra. Please don't use the comparison. I want to do everything that anybody's ever done, but better." The *Post* got back to Vernon Scott, who said, "I don't blame him for denying it. It wasn't the brightest thing in the world to say. But he didn't say it spitefully. He just said it exuberantly, flush from the victory of his awards."

"So I never talked to Vernon Scott again," says Steve Blauner. "Bobby never talked to him again. Anyhow, this started a whole thing. I said to Frank, 'Why don't you and Bobby sit down?' So I arranged a meeting. And they met and talked. And everything was fine. I don't know what Frank thought."

What Frank thought may be gleaned from what he said on one occasion: "I sing in saloons. Bobby Darin does my prom dates." And what Bobby really thought can be found in his response in *Downbeat*: "I'm only too happy to play his prom dates . . . until graduation."

Bobby's alleged remark to Vernon Scott followed him everywhere, and he kept denying it. "It's an insult to Frank to compare him with a 24-year-old punk like me," he said in another interview in the *New York Post*. "I don't want to be a second Frank Sinatra. I want to be a first Bobby Darin."

The discussion helped Bobby in a number of ways. It marked him as a controversial figure, a mantle previously held primarily by Sinatra himself. In addition, the controversy actually elevated Bobby's status in another major way—there could hardly be such discussion if there weren't some legitimate basis for comparing the two singers. Bobby would have been the subject of ridicule if the comparison was ludicrous. It wasn't, and Bobby emerged as more of a comer than ever.

Bobby would tell *Downbeat* later, "It is Sinatra as a person more than Sinatra as a singer that has influenced me. His outlook on the business and his attitude to performance are the important things. My approach to singing is not the same. Sinatra has a clipped speech. I'm a slurrer. But let's face it, he's the boss. Frank Sinatra is the greatest living lyric interpreter."

According to Jeff Bleil, who wrote *That's All: Bobby Darin on Record, Stage, and Screen*, "Some critics were starting to suggest what Darin himself would have gotten slammed for saying—that comparisons to Sinatra were absolutely valid."

Composer Bobby Scott ranked Bobby higher than Sinatra in some ways, noting that he was more of a performer than Sinatra. He told Jeff Bleil, "Bobby belongs, as a performer, in the age that produced a Sophie Tucker, an Al Jolson. He was in the great performing tradition, and I kind of think of him as the last hurrah of the preceding Golden Age of Performing. I don't put Sinatra in that category. Sinatra is a product of the record industry. Had Sinatra been born earlier and tried to perform during the vaudeville era, we'd have never heard of him . . . I think Sinatra needed a band. I don't think Bobby ever needed a band. I think Sinatra had to learn things that were inherent in a guy like Bobby."

In a similar vein, even Sammy Davis Jr., who worshipped Sinatra, said, "Certainly Bobby's style is more physical than Frank's ever was."

"Sinatra was an influence on everyone," Buddy Bregman says, "but I think Bobby tried for his own sound. In the rhythm pattern that Sinatra floated over, Bobby hit the rhythm more than Frank. I think Bobby was sinking into the rhythm, while Frank played against the rhythm."

Producer Bruce Charet echoes many of these sentiments and maintains that Sinatra's strength was more as a singer than as a performer. "One of the things that people don't remember about Frank Sinatra is that during the height of Frank's power in the '50s, he rarely played to a standing ovation. That's not the way Frank worked. He did 38 minutes, he sang beautifully, he was charming—this is pre–Rat Pack Sinatra—he didn't try to be terribly funny, it's not what he did onstage. He sang great, but he didn't give of himself in the Jolsonesque manner that guys like Darin, Sammy Davis Jr., and Judy Garland did. When you list the great variety performers of the prerock era, with Jolson sort of as the grandfather, that's not where Frank lived. Jolson and Darin were invincible on stage. Frank's greatness is his recorded body of work. Fred Astaire's greatness is his dancing. And Bobby's greatness was as an in-person performer."

The notion of a feud between Darin and Sinatra would never fade away, but there was little factual confirmation of it. Sinatra seemed to have genuine respect for Bobby as a singer and performer. Bobby would become very close in friendship to Nancy Sinatra Jr., Dean Martin, and Sammy Davis Jr., but he was never a part of the Rat Pack circle, and he was never invited to be part of it. He was far too experimental and restless to be pigeonholed, he did not drink, and he was not a Hollywood-Vegas type.

As to whether Bobby was "obsessed" with Sinatra, Michael Cuscuna offers this insight: "You can't put Sinatra on without being obsessed by him. He was one of the most musical singers in the world, with amazing control and originality. When your foundation is Sinatra and Ray Charles, you can't go too far wrong.

"What Darin and Sinatra had in common," continues Cuscuna, "was passion. Both singers are jazz singers in the sense that when they sing a song, they sing it with their own very strong interpretation. It almost sounds like it could be a tenor sax or a trumpet playing the melody, not a singer following the lyrics and the melody. I think it's what makes Darin and Sinatra great. And both loved that real swing-band feel, especially with Billy May. May was the perfect arranger for them."

"The only down part for me with Bobby," says songwriter Rudy Clark, "was his obsession with outdoing Frank Sinatra, on becoming bigger than Sinatra. He had a fixation on Sinatra. If you mentioned Sinatra's name, Bobby would get moody. I would hear people talking to him many times, telling him to forget this fixation, that he was a special talent in his own right. Everybody knew that trying to outdo Sinatra was futile. Sinatra was a legend. Bobby was only tormenting his own self. No white artist could swing like Bobby."

According to Ahmet Ertegun, "At one point in his life, Sinatra represented to Bobby all the things that he would like to have achieved. And Sinatra didn't look upon Bobby with a kind of love that Bobby would have expected, which he got from people like Johnny Mercer or older vaudevillians like George Burns. Because in a real sense Bobby was a trouper: he did everything, he was ready for everything, he put on a great show. But Sinatra was a strange person in many ways. He either loved you or hated you, and the people that he really loved were people who had to join his club and be subservient. Bobby was not going to play second fiddle to anybody.

"Sinatra felt there was a conspiracy among people who made rock-and-roll music to destroy what he called 'good' music and that they did it for the money. Bobby was certainly a part of the birth of rock and roll. So that gave him an aspect which made him persona non grata with the Rat Pack. It's too bad that he fell in a place where on one side there were the Mick Jaggers, who thought he was too much of a Rat

Packer, and the Rat Packers, who thought he was too much of a Mick Jagger type."

Ertegun recalls that he gave a big press party for Bobby at the Dorchester Hotel in London. "Bobby said he really wanted to meet Mick Jagger, who's a friend of mine," says Ertegun. "Mick didn't usually go to these kind of press parties for other artists, but I asked him to please come, Bobby would like to meet you. Now that was becoming the era of long hair and Carnaby Street dress, a kind of hip, not-too-dressed-up kind of look. And at this cocktail party, Bobby had somehow decided to put on a dinner jacket, black tie, with a red jacket that was kind of glittery. When Mick arrived with Andrew, who was his sidekick, they were both dressed up in a very in-London, Carnaby look. And when I introduced them to Bobby, they started laughing. And it was a very embarrassing moment. I kind of deflected it. But they were ready to just sit back and just look at him and laugh, because to them, what he was typifying was what they were putting down."

There was certainly ambivalence in Sinatra's feelings about Bobby. When Bruce Charet asked Sinatra about Bobby many years after Bobby's death, Sinatra replied, "He was a very talented kid. The problem he had was he didn't have quite enough voice to be an important singer." Dick Clark doesn't see it that way at all. "I think Bobby had plenty of voice," he says, "and he could do every conceivable kind of music that Sinatra couldn't do. There was probably no love lost between the two of them. Because the older guy looked upon the younger guy as possibly a challenger. And Bobby made no bones about the fact that he thought he was going to be king of the world shortly." According to actor Dick Bakalyan, "Frank had a lot of respect for Bobby. We were on a yacht in the Mediterranean in 1965. Frank said Bobby was one of the greatest talents in the business. He said, 'If you could get what Bobby did onstage bottled, captured in its fullness and richness where you could share it with the whole world, it would be an amazing thing.'"

"I always wondered what Frank thought about Bobby," recalls producer Steve Metz, "and when I did meet Frank and we talked for a little while about Bobby, it turned out Frank really respected the guy. He didn't have the hatred for Bobby the public was led to believe. Frank said he was a fine talent. I had always thought Bobby and Frank didn't like each other. Frank said, 'Nah, that's more of Bobby's thing. I'm way past that competition. I think he's a fine talent. Will he be bigger than me? I doubt it.'"

Perhaps a performer is best remembered by those who have seen him or her, a sentiment captured best in the late Peter Allen's haunting tribute to Judy Garland, "Quiet Please." In that song, Allen wrote, "The last of the singer is the last of the song." "Seeing Bobby on video is not the same as when you're in the room and feel the heat of the performer," singer Steve Lawrence says. "Film and TV too; it's not the same, it's another dimension. You don't get fully that intensity, that power, the fever of the experience. You really had to see Bobby in person to know the magnificence of him as a performer."

In that light, singer Bobby Rydell recalls that "Bobby was a triple threat. He was just scary onstage. I mean the things he did were just unbelievable." And Dick Bakalyan remembers: "When Darin was onstage, you couldn't hear a fork or a glass, he was so spellbinding. There was a presence that was just extraordinary. When you record that on film, it's a different dimension. It doesn't have the depth of sound and feel."

Still, a telling indication of how Sinatra really felt about Bobby as a singer was that when he formed his own recording company, Reprise, and chose his favorite singers, including Dean Martin, to record on the label, Bobby was one of the first Sinatra approached.

To another observer, who will be anonymous, it was also something else: Bobby was smarter than everybody else, and the '60s were happening. "Look, Bobby had an intellect," he explains. "Way above all those guys. Sensitivity and intellect. Way above Frank, way above Dean, way above Sammy, way above Jerry [Lewis]. It all has to do with the fact he had an intellect. Lounge singers don't have intellects. That's what makes Bobby different than Buddy Greco. He was really smart, and all those guys were not, none of them. I knew every one of them. I knew Frank, I knew Dean, I knew Sammy, I know Jerry. You know what they had in common? Some of them had some street smarts, but they were all dumb. You could not be alive in the mid-60s and not feel a burning need to be part of what was happening culturally in America."

THERE'S NO CLEARER INDICATION of how Bobby really felt about Sinatra than in Ed Walters' account posted on the Darin Web site BobbyDarin.net. Walters was a pit boss in Las Vegas:

I came in contact with Darin a few times. In the early '60s he came to Vegas to play the Flamingo. He came by one afternoon to the Sands to meet me about setting up a pool table in his suite at the Flamingo. He got the word that I played very good and could help set him up. So we got together a few times and after his shows we would go to the Greek's, a local poolroom, and play. As we got to know each other, it became apparent that he wanted to find out from me all he could about how Sinatra worked at the Sands and what he wore, etc. He would ask me who made his tuxes (Sy Devore), his shirts (Nat Wise), his shoes (I didn't know). He wanted to know who introduced him and how. Now, to most of this I would tell him to just go and see Sinatra. But Bobby would not go.

When Sinatra was in town, he [Bobby] came to the Sands to see me and wanted to see the Copa Room. It was in the afternoon and I took him to the stage. He got on it and walked around. He was in heaven. He stood center stage and got the feel of the room and what it was like to play there. He took down the name of the speakers that were on the floor, right in front of the mike. He wanted to know the name of the speaker used in the room. I didn't know any of this. He wanted to know what mikes Sinatra used. He wanted the name and model number. He even took down the name of the mike stand used in the Copa Room. Did Sinatra use this? I told him no. Sinatra had his own special stand and special mikes brought in and set up by his own people. Bobby wanted all of this. I told him I would do what I could. "I want to use what Sinatra is using." I don't care what he told the press. Sinatra was his model and in many ways his idol.

As a result of *That's All*, *This Is Darin*, and above anything, "Mack the Knife," within months Bobby had emerged from the ranks of kiddie-pop rock-and-roll singers and stepped into the top ranks of major show-business singers and performers. He had eclipsed everyone from his generation except Elvis Presley and was now perceived as a potential superstar. Benny, Davis, Burns, Garland, Sinatra, Durante were show business royalty. Bobby already seemed perched to join them. And apparently they perceived him that way.

In December 1959, Bobby's emergence as a major star was marked by Ralph Edwards's *This Is Your Life* TV show paying tribute to Bobby by documenting his life story on national television. Nina, Charlie, Gary, Vee, and Vana were secretly flown to the West Coast to take part in the show. Although the program's format involved surprising the guest celebrity—Bobby was in the studio rehearsing for another CBS show, *The Big Party*—by a fluke Bobby actually knew about the show. He pretended that he was surprised. "Years later," Dick Lord says, "I said to Bobby, 'You acted really surprised,' and he didn't answer me. I said, 'You really knew, didn't you?' He said, 'You're the only one who ever said that to me,' 'Did you know?' 'Yes, I knew.'

The program offered a rare glimpse for posterity into Bobby, his family, and his friends at this pivotal moment of his life. Steve Blauner, Nina and Charlie, Don Kirshner, Murray Kaufman, Dick Lord, Dick Behrkre, Sammy Davis Jr., and George Burns were all gathered together, and despite the sentimental format of the program, there were moments of real feeling throughout. Bobby, as usual, had a hard time appearing modest. In fact, there was a surreal element to it all: it was almost impossible to realize that many of the events depicted in the show were not those of a lifetime but only the past four or five years. Bobby's high-school experience, forming a band, playing in the

Catskills, his record and nightclub successes were not long past, but measured against his rapid rise to the top, they seemed as if they must have occurred a long time ago. Bobby exuded confidence—he seemed (and certainly behaved like) the "old star" that many people perceived him to be.

The first person to step forward was Steve Blauner, who in a youthful, emotional voice said, "The first time I saw Bobby I believed in him, and he's just starting to fulfill the promise." Ralph Edwards went on to ask Bobby what his real name was and drew laughter from the audience when Bobby said, "Walden Robert Cassotto," quickly adding, "It's not a sickness."

Sketching out a sanitized biography, Edwards said that Bobby's father, "an Italian carpenter," died before Bobby was born, and introduced Bobby's "sister and brother-in-law," discreetly changing their last name from "Maffia" to "Mafi." Nina was bursting with pride ("I'll have you know that he did six years of grammar school in four years and got a scholarship medal besides!") and overflowing with love for Bobby as she embraced him. Bobby tried not to squirm with her and with Charlie. Charlie faltered a little at first, speaking in simple, untutored, unpretentious English: "Well, it wasn't gettin', we didn't get by too easy in the beginning." Bobby cracked, "You got along very hard in the beginning, that's what it was." Charlie went on: "Well, we were all proud, we bought him his new first suit he ever had. But the dog took the seat of his pants out—it seems funny now—on the way home from church, but at the time it was a family disaster." Nina, addressing Bobby, recalled that "You used to ride downhill on your bicycle standing on the seat without touching the handlebars. To make it even more frightening, you used to twirl a cane in one hand and a hat in the other."

It's impossible not to love these people, and one realizes with a pang that, as much as they clearly loved Bobby, Bobby really did not love them.

Veteran film producer Norman Taurog was next, announcing that Bobby had been signed to a motion-picture contract with Paramount.

The warmest moments of the night came when Sammy Davis Jr.

and George Burns appeared. Bobby and Sammy embraced with great affection. Bobby noted with gratitude that Sammy "mentioned my name for like a year straight, both shows, every night, wherever he was." The love between Burns and Bobby was apparent even as Burns joked, "I love Bobby. I'd like to adopt Bobby. I'd make a fortune." Burns went on more seriously, "The reason I love Bobby is the first time I saw him work, he was so good that I knew you couldn't be that good unless you loved show business." George and Bobby went on to do a piece of the sand dance (they would both keep sand in their pockets for the occasion) that they did in their Vegas act.

But the moment when Bobby looked as if he were about to cry was when Edwards referred to the death of Polly, "his mother." Bobby bowed his head—not a rehearsed moment.

At the end, Bobby's "nephew"—really brother—Gary, who was three, came on the stage with Vee and Vana, and Bobby cradled him in his arms. Gary looked up and Bobby kissed him and asked, "Do you love me?" Gary replied, "I love you."

Inevitably, there would be those who felt left out. Recalls Ahmet Ertegun, "I was the one who really zeroed in, and we as a label worked very hard to make him big. He was a very important star for us, and we also had a cachet of being hip. We didn't lack anything that the majors had. As a matter of fact, we had a lot that they didn't have. When Bobby got to California, I was there, and in front of me they would all be discussing what studio would be making Bobby's next picture, and who would be doing this, and who would be the agent. And they're saying, of course, the only real drawback is that he was with a small, insignificant record label, Atlantic. I was standing there listening to this and thinking, Where are these shmucks going to be in a few years?

"When *This Is Your Life* was done, nobody asked me to be on it. Or anybody from Atlantic. Look, it didn't mean anything to me personally. I watched it on TV. And I saw a lot of these people who were not that important in his life. But he was surprised and very happy to see them, and nobody ever said to me, 'Oh, we should have invited you.'

It was never mentioned. Steve Blauner never liked Atlantic or any of us. But I loved Bobby Darin and I had a good time whenever I was with him."

It had been an amazing year. Bobby had risen to the top of his profession as one of the hottest singers in the history of American popular music. At the close of 1959, Bobby was on his way to becoming a legend in his own time.

Chapter Seven
THE SHTARKER

Now there was success, and with it the dangers that success brought. Every move, every statement Bobby made was scrutinized by the press and the public. "Bobby and I went to the Cloister in Hollywood to see a show," Steve Blauner recalls. "We walk in and he does a number with the headwaiter, then he sees Don Rickles, goes over to this and that, ring a ding ding, the whole thing, instead of 'hello, good to see you.' And I don't say anything. It became obnoxious. Finally I called him outside and I said, 'Bobby, everybody knows who you are. You don't have to fight for that anymore. When you walk into a room, you don't have to do anything. But you're so nervous that you gotta be on.' And so he got pissed. I said, 'Go fuck yourself,' got in the car, and left him there. We had a screaming fight the next morning. His press agent was upstairs waiting for us and thought we were coming to blows. In fact, I put my chin out and said, 'Go ahead, hit me.' But nothing happened." In the end, Bobby trusted Steve's judgment.

Now that Steve Blauner was his manager, Bobby shifted his base of operations to Los Angeles in 1960. With that change inevitably came a change in the relationship with Hesh Wasser.

"When Bobby moved to California, we had many run-ins and disagreements," says Wasser. "Bobby knew in his heart and soul there had to be some kind of a break in our relationship if I was going to stay in New York and he was going to be in L.A. Because I had too much time on my hands here. I couldn't just concentrate on him here, which is what he wanted me to do. I could have gone to L.A. I think part of it had to do with the fact that I didn't think it was going to work between me and Steve Blauner. Truthfully, it wouldn't have worked if we ever really became competitive, and he wasn't using me to serve him. And I don't think I could have put Bobby in the position of choosing between me and Steve, because he needed Steve very badly. I wasn't going to do for him what Steve was going to do for him. I would be lying to say that I could. Steve needed me, but he resented it. I'm sure he did. Later on I said to him, 'I'm surprised you didn't drop me at the start,' and he said, 'I was too scared. I was a novice. And all of a sudden this guy comes along, he's going to be a superstar, how do I know I can manage it? I would never drop a person like you.' In other words, under the circumstances."

There were fundamental changes, too, in Bobby's personality as he became a success. "If you knew Bobby before he made it," Hesh Wasser remembers, "you saw a lot of the nice, real good qualities. He was very sweet and considerate. If you got to know him later on, the chances of that being the case were not as likely. The arrogance only came, as far as I was concerned, after he made it. Look, Bobby was many people, very different in different situations. There were things that he did that were ugly; there were things that he did that were wonderful. You had to ask yourself, How did this person get to this point from real poverty, from the Baruch houses, from his serious illness? And once it happened, it had to be an incredible feeling. It wasn't only getting there; it was staying there. Sometimes he was a bitch; sometimes you wanted to kill Bobby. He did little things that were so aggravating once he made it. I brought in pictures for him to autograph, and he said, "Not now." I was just standing there. He wasn't busy; he was just on a power trip. On my way out, he smiled and said to me, 'This is what you always wanted.'

"There's no question in my mind that Steve was creating this monster of his own," continues Wasser. "Steve played the heavy on behalf of Bobby. But in many instances he also put Bobby in the position of playing the heavy. He would deny that, but he was doing it by his very attitude, which was one of showing a lot of hostility and anger. I think Steve convinced Bobby that being the nice guy was not going to work. Before Steve came into his life, the most important thing to Bobby was to be liked. That was part of making it, as far as he was concerned. Once he made it, he felt he wanted to make it because he was talented. When Steve came into his life, there was more pressure on Bobby.

"The bottom line with Steve is that with all his problems, he has always been honorable. People do acknowledge my role in Bobby's career. If it were someone other than Steve Blauner, they might try to discredit me, to take all the credit themselves. He could easily have said, 'Sure, she knew Bobby; so what? So did a lot of other people. A lot of people helped him." Steve didn't say that. He was truthful."

"When you get to the point of being the star," says Steve Blauner, "you are catered to from the minute you wake up to the minute you go to sleep, staff all around you, sucking up to you, fawning over you. You're driven to work, everyone says, yeah, you look great, people are crashing, waving to you. And at some point, how do you not succumb to this and not think your shit doesn't smell? So Bobby had that side of him that would drive anyone up a wall. And probably all of it derived from fear."

"Bobby never looked at the bright side of anything," actor Shirley Jones, in whom Bobby often confided, recalls. "There was never a glass half full; it was always half empty. I don't think he ever saw himself as being as successful as he was. He would say jokingly, 'Sure, I'm the top of the heap. Nobody's gonna touch me.' That kind of thing. But he didn't believe it."

On January 11, 1960, Shana Alexander published a profile of Bobby in *Life* that highlighted a statement by him he would never live down. Bobby told Alexander what he had told Connie Francis years before: that he "wanted to establish myself as a legend by the time I'm 25." He went on to say, "I want to make it faster than anyone has ever made it before," and "I want to be in the upper echelon of show business to such an extent it's ridiculous." Taken out of the context of his physical condition, Bobby's comments underscored the reputation of arrogance and bullheadedness that was accompanying him everywhere. A year earlier he had cautiously hinted at his condition in an interview with the *Los Angeles Times*: "I have the feeling I'm going to die young. So I've got to do what I'm going to do now." But he didn't follow through on this line of thought in his public statements.

Bobby and Steve were always courting controversy, so the remark was not exactly uncalculated. They realized that the brasher and cockier Bobby appeared, the more press he would get. Nor was the Alexander article all that damaging to his reputation. Read in its entirety, the piece is actually very favorable toward Bobby. She gives Bobby ample credit for his talent and ambition and sketches in vividly the struggles of his childhood and young adulthood. Writing of his performance, she says, "It becomes clear why he has been one of the fastest-rising singers in recent years and has earned the right to dream big . . . Darin is moving in the right direction at a dead run." She quotes Sammy Davis dubbing Bobby 'the *shtarker*,' which she politely translates from the Yiddish as "the strong one" ("ball-breaker" would be more accurate).

Alexander writes that Bobby yearned for the respect of successes like Sinatra and George Burns. She quotes him: "These people should say: 'Yeah, you belong in the center of the circle, kid.' "To this end," she says, "he has begun to work harder toward achieving a stage personality all his own. Darin's forte on stage, he believes, is to be 'a singer who moves well, a singer who moves like a dancer. That's my billing, and I intend to sell the hell out of it.'" She goes on to quote sympathetically Bobby's own analysis of himself:

"At the bottom of Darin," he explains, "is a bewildered, confused, soul-searching, grasping artist who is desirous of truth in art . . . Now you gently simmer and you lay over this bottom stratum a little bit of human being who craves social acceptance. Sprinkle with a few years of childhood environment. Add years of plain poverty and simmer some more. Add the ability to think as an individual, bake for 19 years, top it off with a very bad experience emotionally, place in oven for three and a half years, and you've got me. Now, stratum by stratum, it must all be torn down." Tearing down the stratum, in Darin's vocabulary, means growing up. When that day comes, he believes, "there'll be no more need for the pressure, the yelling, the ring-a-ding stuff. Everyone will say, 'Who's that quiet, powerful guy over there?'"

"When Shana Alexander wrote that piece," says Steve Blauner, "that article did more for Bobby than any other piece ever written. I couldn't have paid for that kind of publicity. And Bobby didn't say he was going to be a legend by 25. He said he'd like to be a legend by 25."

Other journalists had mixed reactions to Bobby's honesty and volatility. Al Aronowitz and Jack D. Fox wrote in the *New York Post* that "the white heat of his temper has become part of the glow of his charm." Bobby seemed to relish the controversy. He told the *Post*: "When you write about me, make it tough. Ruin me."

There was an honesty to Bobby that wouldn't quit, and along with it there was a steadfast loyalty to his friends. "Nancy Sinatra Jr. and Tommy Sands were throwing Bobby a party," recalls Blauner. "At 5 P.M. Bobby's friend Rona Barrett calls and says to Bobby, 'How come I wasn't invited?' Bobby just had this intense loyalty. So he hung up the phone and said to me he wasn't going to the party. I said why. He said Rona wasn't invited. I said, 'So? How dare you? It's not your party, Bobby. This is Tommy and Nancy's party. They got a right to invite whoever they want.' And obviously Rona, who was a gossip columnist, had done something wrong to not be invited. She had written that

Nancy Sr. was trying to make her daughters' lives miserable because her own life was miserable. So I said to him fuck you, I'm going to the party, with or without you. And I did. And he didn't go. That was very characteristic of Bobby."

THIS IS DARIN, Bobby's next album, was released in February 1960 and climbed higher than *That's All*, hitting No. 6 on the charts. The single "Clementine" reached No. 21. The new album, building upon Bobby's fresh and unpredictable renditions of pop standards in *That's All*, consolidated his reputation as a serious, indeed terrific singer. The album begins with an exuberant and irreverent Woody Harris version of "Clementine," so hot and vibrant that, as with "Mack," it's almost impossible to pay attention to the lyrics. You're just lifted off the ground listening to it. Here again, Bobby takes material that previously lay limp and tepid—sung around campfires—and transformed it almost beyond recognition. But that was only the beginning. Every song is given Bobby's unpredictable touch. Darin doesn't quite equal Sinatra or Garland on "The Gal That Got Away," but he's in the ballpark. There are genre-busting versions of the old chestnuts "My Gal Sal," "Have You Got Any Castles, Baby," and "Guys and Dolls," a lilting account of "Don't Dream of Anybody But Me," and two standouts arranged by Buddy Bregman, "All Nite Long" and "I Can't Give You Anything But Love." (The rest of the album was arranged by Richard Wess.) Bobby is almost a blues interpreter echoing Joe Williams and Big Joe Turner in "Nite." In these two songs his masculinity and sensuality predominate, but in "I Can't Give You Anything But Love," Bobby does something else as well: without in any way imitating Sinatra, and in a wholly original musical interpretation of the song, he brings a fire, energy, and passion that only Sinatra had previously achieved on recording. This song is the masterpiece of the album. It was not surprising that *Downbeat* wrote of *This Is Darin*: "Darin can sing and he can swing. He may even be the heir apparent to Sinatra's mantle." John S. Wilson in the *New York Times* had the same reaction: "Any doubts that Mr. Darin can stand up on his own are dissipated.

His musical personality comes across in electrifying fashion . . . This is a disk that belongs with the best work of such masters of the genre as Bing Crosby and Frank Sinatra."

Bobby went to London in March 1960 for his first foreign tour with a rock-and-roll show that included Duane Eddy and Clyde McPhatter. He became embroiled in controversy on opening night in Lewisham when he segued from his rock hits to a quiet rendition of "My Funny Valentine." The rock audience jeered him, and he baited them, saying, "I thought you people lived on the other side of town."

Dick Behrke, Steve Blauner, and Bobby discussed what to do for the next show that evening.

Behrke thought Bobby should cut "Valentine" from the show and give the audience what they wanted. Blauner, who still hated rock and would never change his mind about it, furiously disagreed. "Bobby lashed out at me," Blauner recalls, blaming him for booking him for the show. When Bobby seemed to side with Behrke, Blauner opened a valise with Bobby's shirts in it and dumped them on the floor, shouted he was quitting, and stormed out.

But characteristically, Steve Blauner didn't go far. He sat in the audience for the next show. Bobby opened with the same three numbers, and then did a spontaneous rock version of "Kansas City." Steve waited. Bobby went on to sing "My Funny Valentine." Steve sat there, crying softly. Bobby had apologized the way he usually did.

They hugged each other after the show and decided to continue with the tour.

The most prestigious jazz magazine in the country, *Downbeat*, featured Bobby on its cover on May 12, 1960, with an article entitled "Bobby Darin and the Turn from Junk Music." This was one of the most significant events in Bobby's career; it was recognition of a high order. Bobby was not only being recognized by an adult musical audience but by the most discerning, intelligent, and hip segment of that audience. The article was written by the magazine's editor, Gene Lees. A three-time winner of the ASCAP-Deems Taylor award for music writing, Lees would go on to become a prolific songwriter, leading jazz writer, critic, and author of many superb books about music, including *Meet Me at Jim and Andy's: Jazz Musicians and Their World, Singers and the Song, Jazz, Black and White*, and biographies of Woody Herman, Oscar Peterson, and Lerner and Lowe. This meant serious recognition of an almost unparalleled kind for a singer of popular music at such an early stage of his career.

Lees was the first music critic of real stature and insight to take Bobby seriously. His grasp of Bobby both as a singer and a person was perceptive and immediate. He wrote of him with acumen and sensitivity, identifying Bobby's gifts as an artist and his unusual personal qualities of integrity as well. Lees would never waver in his appreciation of Bobby; he would revisit the subject of Bobby's accomplishments long after Bobby's death, writing of him in 1998 and 2001 in his journal, *Jazzletter*. Each piece would reflect his ever-deepening perspective and appreciation of Bobby.

Lees's 1960 *Downbeat* article combined his personal interviews with Bobby and impressions of him with a critical assessment of his talent. He had flown from Chicago to St. Louis, where Bobby was appearing at the Chase Hotel, and had spent five days hanging with him and observing him in performance.

Bobby told Lees: "Fabian and all of them knew from the start that I wanted to progress beyond the [rock and roll] phase. I've been preparing for this all my life . . . Actually I never wanted to be a singer. I wanted to be an actor. And I still do. I was a songwriter, trying to get into the business."

Lees noted that Bobby's style was built on a "basic framework of Frank Sinatra, it involves elements of Tony Bennett (an odd kind of harshness in certain high notes), Bing Crosby (a loose-mouthed popping of the consonants 'B' and 'P'), . . . and occasional touches of rock-and-roll raunch."

Most important, Lees gave an assessment of Bobby that would be widely quoted. He would be the first critic to see qualities in Bobby that seemed to have the potential to eventually put him in the same league as Sinatra. "But there's one big extra: fire. Despite the faults of his singing, Darin today is unquestionably the only young male pop singer who handles standards with something approaching the polished intensity of Sinatra. To those who would offer the rejoinder that Darin does not have Sinatra's vocal finesse and musicianship, it should be adequate to point out that Sinatra is 42 while Darin is 23, and that Sinatra has been a professional singer for 21 years, while Darin has been singing for four.

"And Darin has an obvious capacity to learn and grow. . . . [He] is probably the most fascinating singer to watch on this side of the Atlantic. Darin once said that he wanted to be known as the singer who moved like a dancer . . . He has already reached this goal . . . he does indeed move like a dancer. He has a loose-limbed agility that permits him to intermix shuffles, Woody Herman–style kicks, and countless eccentric steps the semantics of which probably died with vaudeville . . . With this combination of excellent movement and intense, driving singing, Darin's is one of the most stimulating and vital acts in show business today."

Bobby has stayed with Lees over the years. In 2001 he wrote of him: "For all his pretense of assurance, it seems to me that Bobby Darin never really knew how good he was. And thinking about him sort of breaks my heart." In a 2004 interview, Lees still remembered how Bobby treated the teenage girls who besieged him that week in St. Louis with respect and kindness. "One afternoon he and I went for a walk in a park," he said. "A group of girls, carrying their schoolbooks, recognized him. He sat down on a park bench and chatted with them. None of them was what could be called pretty, but he treated them as if they were. There was a little giggling, and they got autographs, and thanked him gravely, and went on their way. I liked him for it. I liked him for a lot of things."

Writing of the ways Bobby had haunted him, Lees reflects, "I think of the guy I got to like in those days and nights in St. Louis. I think about the fine acting job he did in *Captain Newman, M.D.* I listen to his beautiful time and intonation and enunciation and phrasing, his musicality. Walden Robert Cassotto was a giant talent, still unfolding.

"Maybe he didn't get to do it all. But he came close . . .

"Oh could he sing."

It was also at the Chase Hotel in St. Louis, where Gene Lees met Bobby, that Bobby took one of his many repeated stands against racism. "Bobby would go crazy at racism," Steve Blauner recalls. "At the Chase we invited all the disc jockeys in to see the show and they weren't going to let the black disc jockeys in. So we said, well, then we're leaving. We were going to walk out in the middle of the show. So they finally let them in but sat them back in the kitchen. That was the first time blacks were ever in the Chase Hotel. Bobby did that. And the first black that ever opened at the Copa—George Kirby—Bobby did that. It was because of Bobby that it happened. And they did a bit in their act together. Taking Richard Pryor was Bobby's idea, not mine, and this was in 1960, when Pryor was doing warmed-over Bill Cosby. Bobby had the greatest eye and ear for talent that I've ever known. And he was right. Bobby took Flip Wilson to Vegas, first time he ever played there. Bobby almost always chose a black performer to open his show. He would tell the club owners: 'If the black kid don't open, the white kid don't close.'"

An incident in 1960 involving George Burns is deeply revealing, not only of how fiercely loyal Bobby was, but how much he needed and valued the father-son relationship he had with men like George Burns. The Sands Hotel offered Bobby a spectacular new 12-week deal over a three-year period that would pay him $25,000 a week. Burns wanted Bobby back as his opening act during the same period for a payment of $7,500 a week. Despite Steve Blauner's opposition, Bobby went with Burns. After signing with Burns, another conflict arose. Paramount, with whom Bobby had signed a seven-picture, million-dollar deal, wanted Bobby to play a supporting role in a new film, *Cry for Happy*. Bobby would be needed on the set at the same time he had committed to performing with Burns.

Having already shown his loyalty to Burns by turning down the Sands offer, Bobby assumed that Burns, realizing how important the film would be to his career, would let him off the hook for the Vegas engagement. He was shocked when Burns, who was not aware of the pay cut Bobby had taken to appear with him, refused to agree. Burns accused him of irresponsibility and pointed out how much more money he was offering him than he'd paid him initially. Bobby said, "I'm sorry, Mr. Burns. I won't do the film. You will have me in Vegas with you."

"All contracts we drew up had out clauses, in case of making a movie or a TV thing," says Steve Blauner. "But the contract had no bearing in this case: this is George Burns and Bobby. And Bobby reacts like George is his father. We get this role opposite Glenn Ford. This is the ring-a-ding guy, the stonemason, in the script. And George wouldn't let him out. George said, 'Well, how do you know it's going to be a good movie?' I said, 'I don't. But I know Bobby's going to be good in it 'cause he's gonna play the opposite guy from [bland] Glenn Ford. He's got the perfect foil in Ford.' So a comic actor got the role instead of Bobby. Later that year George came into the Copa and he held out his hand. I turned around and walked away."

Burns made up for it later. His 1989 memoir, *All My Best Friends*, is filled with the intimate presence of the giants of show business: Gracie Allen, Jolson, Durante, Benny, Garland, Jessel, Fannie Brice, Sophie Tucker—all of his peers from show business's golden age. Practically the only younger star to enter these elegiac pages is Bobby, and he fits in as naturally as he did—a 22-year-old going on 80—when he appeared in person with these great performers and seemed to effortlessly match them in both talent and personality, as if he had been on a bill with them at the Palace in 1932. Burns writes that he loved Bobby, and he writes of Gracie's death: "Bobby and I got very close. He was some kid. The day of Gracie's funeral he was worried about me staying alone in the house. So he stayed with me that night. Nobody asked him to, he just did it. That was very important to me."

"Bobby was alone with George," Steve Blauner recalls, "and then when he was leaving, George couldn't sleep. And he said to Bobby,

'Why don't you sleep in Gracie's bed tonight?' They had twin beds. And he did. And George slept."

"I was with George Burns at Caesar's Palace watching Sammy Davis Jr.," recalls Bruce Charet. "This was years after Bobby died. Sammy was the fucking end onstage. He finishes doing 'Birth of the Blues' and gets a standing ovation like you can't imagine, and George Burns just takes the cigar out of his mouth in his inimitable style and says, 'He's the greatest thing I've ever seen on a stage.' To which, I couldn't resist, and I said, 'George, is he greater than Jolson?' He thinks for a minute, takes another puff, and says, 'No, no. Jolson was greater.' And then I talked to him about Bobby Darin. He said again Jolson was the best. I asked him why. Very tough for him to explain. And he said, 'Jolson was crazy.' Not that he meant that Jolson was crazy as a human being. But onstage. What he really meant (and Burns wasn't that articulate) was there was a maniacal quality in Jolson. We talked about that too. Bobby had that too, manifested a little differently.

"Burns loved Darin. He said he was great. But if you look at Jolson's close-ups in *The Jazz Singer*, he's out of his mind! He has that quality, and Darin had it too. Darin had this kind of hotheaded little Italian kind of thing on stage: don't fuck with this guy because if you get him angry, you're going to have to kill him. He was 130 pounds and he had that rhythm about him. Bobby had warmth, but a lot of people have that. It's the other thing that makes you great. It's the evil side that makes you great, for lack of a better word. I have an Uncle Louis in Staten Island who runs a dry-cleaning store. He's warm, but I wouldn't want to put him onstage."

His forfeiture of the role in *Cry for Happy* put Bobby in a conflicted, depressed state. It was an aspect of his total honesty and inability that he could not feign an upbeat mood at his performance at his next engagement at the Three Rivers Inn in Syracuse. His first two shows were flat and repetitive, and he did more talking to the audience than singing. Confiding in Steve Blauner backstage, he said he was so discouraged he was thinking of quitting. He spoke of feeling isolated and alone after Polly's death and his sadness that he'd never gotten the chance to tell her how much he appreciated her, how he had wanted to thank her for "struggling for 22 years" and for giving him so much love. He felt let down by Burns's behavior and thought that Burns "couldn't care less about me." Yet he said he still loved Burns.

At the next, sparsely attended show, Bobby told the audience, "I did a bad thing. I drilled holes in the floor of the club, and it's slowly sinking." There was dead silence in the room. "It's rather disheartening for an entertainer to walk out to empty tables," he said. He concluded with a statement so honest and blunt it must have seemed unprecedented on a nightclub floor: "I would like to sing more for you tonight, but I just can't. I'm out of spirit. Perhaps you came in thinking, 'He's supposed to be a cocky kid.' Well, it isn't so. Any fool knows that bravado is always a cover-up for insecurity. That's the truth. And on that note, I'll say good night. God love you."

It was a momentary setback. Bobby always bounced back. In June 1960 he had his first triumphant opening at the Copacabana in New York. Making it at the Copa meant the biggest of the big time. It was one of the most famous nightclubs in the world. The Copa had been created by none other than Frank Costello and was named for the resort hotel in Rio de Janeiro. The 700-seat club's star roster included Sinatra, Sammy Davis Jr., Martin and Lewis, Sophie Tucker, Billy Daniels, Jimmy Roselli, and Lena Horne, among others.

The Copa was run since its inception in 1940 by Jules Podell, a former bootlegger with a police record, who fronted for Costello.

The Copa had been investigated in 1944 by Mayor LaGuardia for its ties to Costello. The investigation sought to prove that "there were known racketeers or gangsters frequenting the Copacabana," not to mention "persons interested or part owners who are disreputable persons engaged in unlawful enterprise." Hello. One had to hang around the Copa for five minutes to know that such individuals were Copa royalty and the heart and soul of the place. The Copa, while admitting to no relationship with Costello, eventually agreed to "terminate and sever" any connection that Costello may have had with the club. That termination and severance never took place.

Bobby performed "Mack," "Bill Bailey," "Some of These Days," "Clementine," Rodgers and Hammerstein's "I Have Dreamed," a medley of "Swing Low Sweet Chariot" and "Lonesome Road," Ray Charles's "I Got a Woman," and a few of his rock hits as if they were from the remote past: "Splish Splash" and "Dream Lover." The show was recorded for posterity on the album *Darin at the Copa*, which became Bobby's third Top Ten album, reaching No. 9 by the fall. There were raves from the entire New York press. New York went crazy. Bobby's apartment at the Hotel 14 was packed with celebrities, including Judy Garland with Liza Minelli. The crowds were so large that they filled the stage area, and Bobby was pressed up against the grand piano.

The late Nik Venet said that "Darin was one complete Broadway show posing as a nightclub act. He was a walking spotlight. The guy was like a grenade—he had a pin he would pull at a certain point, and he would just explode. I didn't know where he got it. You meet some other singers and they're the same onstage or off. But with Darin . . . Jesus Christ!"

Bobby's trademarks in performing were his fingers snapping, his shoulders hunching, his head bobbing, his legs kicking, his high-toned shuffles, his body whirling around. His limp body would bend and straighten, the elbows and knees moving in tandem, the neck undulating. He was brilliant on the piano, the vibraphone, the drums, the harmonica. He moved and glided to the music with elegance and panache; his dance steps were more like slides; he threw the microphone up and caught it. He was a cool and hot instrument of the music. He moved as the spirit moved him. This was a man whose life was at its peak when he performed.

He was a master at looking like everything just occurred to him. In one bit that he did, he took his guitar off the stand and suddenly looked round and noticed it. The guitar stand was kind of a wiry looking thing, with strings jutting out if it, and Bobby pretended to be surprised and said, 'Oh, if I was a grasshopper, I'd be in love.' He did that same bit at every show, always making it look like it was a throwaway line no matter how many times he did it. He was able to generate the sense of spontaneity each time. Even when he sang '"Mack the Knife," he always looked as if he was singing it for the first time. He never seemed stale. In reality, he was always picking up on what was going on around him.

Sex permeated Bobby's performance: hotheaded, aggressive, no-nonsense, assertive, masculine, explosive Italian sex. Bobby was the proud personification of it on stage.

One day Steve Blauner found out just how literally true this was. "I was sitting in the living room of his suite while he was in the bedroom, getting ready for the show," he recalls. "The valet came into the room, and he had something in his hand. And he opened his hand up and he showed it to me. And it's a condom. He then proceeded to tell me that Bobby wore a condom on stage every night. Because sometimes he actually came; he had an orgasm." Steve reflects on this. "Just think of it. The man's coming during the show. I mean there's nothing that tops that, baby. And that really tells you who the man is."

Terry Koenig, sister of Bobby's second wife, Andrea Darin, worked for Bobby in the early '70s after Andy DiDia left. She would lay out three condoms in a row for him before the show. "I used to steam Bobby's tuxes," she recalls. "Get him dressed. It was hysterical. One minute I was in graduate school at the University of Southern California, doing student teaching in the orange groves and strawberry patches of Orange County—Miss Bo Peep—the next I'm on the road steaming tuxes and putting out condoms for him. He would wear a condom during a performance because it was such a turn-on for him that sometimes he actually ejaculated. Well, I put it out, he put it on. Every performance."

Is there evidence on the videotapes of Bobby's performances of an ejaculation moment? There appears to be. The most extensive, sustained record of Bobby's performance is the 70-minute videotape of his great last TV show in 1973. Bobby had decided to scrap the format of the show to give a final concert. There is definitely a moment when he appears to almost go down on the microphone. He is very intense—even for Bobby—and it's clear that he's really turned on and almost gumming the microphone. It may be innocent, but it doesn't look like a platonic relationship.

"I remember Bobby before a show," Koenig continues. "He loved to go to museums, and he'd pick up women. And he had sex. He had all afternoon for that. He'd go and learn, and then he'd get them. He knew they'd be smart and he could talk to them. Oh, he loved sex. His heart did not slow him down.

"Bobby had an appetite for everything. He was just voracious. A Renaissance man. I've never met another man who had the ability to grasp details and connect them to a larger picture like that. He was the first man I ever met who really rose above business to the intellectual world of ideas. My personal opinion is that women fall in love through their ears. And he could talk that shit, my God! Women would want to come up to the hotel room and I just watched how all this went down. He used to say 'delicious' all the time. And he related a lot to just the pleasure of the mouth, the pleasure of touching.

"One time Bobby was sweating so much his toupee began to slip. Bobby had gotten some cockamamy hairpiece and made his own double tape. Steve shouted something in the back of the club. And Bobby did not stop performing. It didn't faze him. Bobby had four testicles."

Walter Winchell had become a Bobby groupie by this time. The old vaudevillian, still a popular columnist at that point but beginning to slip, went insane over Bobby, writing about him every day, following him from town to town. Winchell's help was inestimable; he remained a career maker and breaker at that point.

Comedian Bobby Ramsen, who would appear with Bobby many times, recalls that "Winchell started to mention Bobby's name in his column sometime in 1959. Somebody hipped Darin to Walter when Bobby was at the Crescendo in L.A. Winchell was so powerful, a star maker. He liked to make stars and break stars. As a result of Winchell's bombardment, all the stars came to see Bobby—Jack Benny, George Burns sitting ringside. Jesus, every star in Hollywood was there. So Bobby's coming into New York well heralded by Winchell's column. Winchell would come into the Copa for the second show every night and sit dead ringside. He had a table for two, but always waited until the opening comedy act was almost done and then he walked down the aisle, disrupting the poor comic. Now Bobby comes out and he is so cool, so arrogant, so self-possessed, so confident, standing out there like he owns the damn place. Winchell is sitting there, and Darin gets through. Now this happened every night: Winchell jumps up as Bobby is bowing, grabs ahold of Bobby, puts his arm around him, and says, 'Ladies and gentlemen. I've been a Broadway columnist. I've been a performer. I've been in show business for 50 years. I've seen everybody and everything. There's one thing that's important in show business and that's class. And here's a man who has the class that I'm talking about.'

"It was such a glowing tribute," Ramsen continues. "This was a send-off he was giving this young guy. And the amazing thing to me is: my eyes and Bobby's somehow met—I had never even met Bobby—Bobby's standing there, with a look on his face that says, 'Why is this old man carrying on like this?' He was so bored, it was such a pain in the ass to stand there for this long monologue. It was like he wanted to shake Winchell off and say, 'Get away from me, you nut.' So that's when Bobby and I first noticed each other. I was screaming inside. Anybody else would have killed for this."

"Bobby and I ran with Winchell toward the end of his career," Steve Blauner remembers. "One night at the Copa, Bobby got sick between shows. He could hardly walk. He had a pimple on his balls or something. We were trying to put together entertainment for the second show, with Louis Prima and Keely Smith. Winchell was going to emcee it. We were standing in the back of the Copa just before they announced Winchell, and he says, 'Here, Steve, hold this.' And he hands me his fucking gun. He had it in a little holster. I should hold this. At the Copa, if you took out a gun you were liable to find 20 others."

Bobby held a deep enmity for the Mafia, partly because of the way his "father," Sam Cassotto, had been neglected by Costello when he was in prison. "Bobby would cringe," Bobby Ramsen recalls, "when they would page his stepfather Charlie on the loudspeaker at casinos: '*Mister Maffia! Mister Charlie Maffia!*' Bobby didn't like low-class types. A guy once heckled him at the Copa: '*Ay Bobby—Attaway, sweetheart.*' And Bobby said, 'Ay! Ay! Someday you'll get to B! And then you'll be somebody!' He did have a thing about the Mafia. He had a hate on for them, no doubt about it."

During Bobby's next Copa engagement, Sam's old pal Frank Costello, silent owner of the Copa, had just gotten out of prison. "Bobby's attitude," explains Steve Blauner, "was that Sam had hidden Costello out when the police were looking for him, but that when Sam went to prison, Costello never took care of the Cassotto family." Blauner had become friendly with a reporter named John Jay Miller, who "wanted to be Winchell." Miller worked for Generoso Pope's tabloid, *The National Enquirer*. Now that Costello was home, Miller was on his way to see him at his apartment at the Majestic on Central Park West. With a snarling look in his eyes, Bobby conveyed a message for him to take to Costello: "Tell him Big Curly's son says hello."

When Miller gave the gangster the message, Costello said, "Who's Big Curly's son?" Miller said, "Bobby Darin." Costello's jaw dropped. "Bobby Darin!" He reached into his pocket and he took out a list. He said, "I was just checking the grosses from the Copa while I was in prison. And I see this Bobby Darin, and I was just about to call and see if they had him under contract to come back. He did great. Sam's son!"

For Costello, the mention of Bobby's father brought back fond memories. But Miller told Costello in a discreet way that Bobby didn't like him and why he didn't like him. Costello sighed and replied, "Leave it alone. What difference if one more person doesn't like me?

But to tell you the truth, I'm saddened. Let me tell you the facts; I really liked Bobby's father. In fact, when he got on the junk, we did everything we could. We kidnapped him." Costello offered to give Bobby the "personnel file" that detailed his efforts to rehabilitate Big Curly.

Steve Blauner explains, "This was long after Prohibition, but they were still bringing sugar in from Cuba to make illicit booze so they wouldn't have to pay the government tax. So they kidnapped Sam and put him on one of these sugar boats that came from Cuba to America. To try to cold turkey him, dry him out. But they couldn't cure him, so they had to cut him out. And then he got arrested. He was working with a gang that was stripping cars in Harlem. Costello said to Miller, 'I went to Polly. And I tried to give her money. Polly wouldn't accept it. But what's so ironic, I once gave them a present, which is probably how Bobby learned all his music. I gave them an upright piano.'"

On another occasion at the Copa, Blauner recalls, "it was after opening night, around 2 A.M. Julie Podell had a spread upstairs in the lounge in honor of Bobby, lox and bagels and sturgeon. And we're sitting there, and a short, nattily dressed guy comes up to Bobby. I knew he was a gangster. He said, 'You know, Bobby, I knew your father. We used to run together. Anything you need or want, just call me.' And Bobby says to him, 'Where were you when I needed you?'

"Now I get kicked under the table," Steve says, "by Podell's cousin, who was second in command, trying to let me know, warn me. 'What is he doing?' And I was such a brash son of a bitch. I said, 'Don't kick me under the table. Let Bobby say what he has to say.' And I had no fear, out of stupidity. I was in a rage. I shouted to the guy, 'If you want a piece of Bobby Darin, you'll have to kill two people to get it. And then you'll have nothing left.'"

Musician T. K. Kellman did not hear this conversation, but he remembers being summoned to the event. "Julie Podell had invited Bobby and all of us in the band to eat, but we didn't know, we thought only Bobby had been asked. It was 2 A.M. and the phone rings in our hotel room. It was Sal Sicari, the orchestra conductor. 'Where are youse guys?' he says. We said we didn't know we were invited. Sal says in the best English he can muster, 'I would strongly advise youse guys you got to get back here right away.' So we got dressed and went back. There's a long table with Julie Podell sitting at the head, Bobby beside him. Julie had his maître d's wearing these cutoff red waiters' outfits walking around: 'Want some stoygen?' trying to be as elegant as they knew how to be, not really pulling it off."

"Okay, so now the dinner ends," Steve Blauner recalls. "The band has gone back to the hotel. Bobby and I are left. We're calmed down, and Julie Podell's sitting with us. They'd kept me away from Podell because they figured I'd end up on a meat hook in the icebox, because of the way I was. Podell was a butcher up in the Bronx. He was given the license to run the Copa, he was put in to front it for Costello. And he was really one of these guys who talked out of the side of their mouth with a cigar sticking out. Now he says to Bobby, 'Look, I knew your father.' Then, like Costello, Podell offered to show Bobby the file. 'If you want to know more about him, I will put you in a hotel room and give you a dossier on him.'

"Now I remember Bobby and me leaving the Copa. And the sun was coming up. Podell came up to us, put his arm around Bobby, and said, 'Don't worry about nothing. Anyplace in the world that you are, if you need something, you call me.' In other words, if you're in trouble, I'll get you out of it. Because we extend all over the world.

"Then I walked Bobby to his hotel. I said, 'Bobby, why don't you leave it alone? You don't want to know anymore. Love this man [Sam Cassotto] for the fact that because of who he was, his example put you on the straight and narrow. That you are honest to a fault and won't cross the line.' So I have no idea if Bobby ever took Julie up on his offer. He never told me and I never asked."

There were other incidents.

"One time," says Blauner, "I'm at the Copa, and John Miller says to me, 'Do you see those two guys at the bar?' They were going down to Philadelphia where Bobby was playing at the Latin Casino, and they were going at the behest of Morris Levy. Why? The back story was that Keely Smith was still married to Louie Prima, but she was going out with Morris. Morris was the head of Roulette Records and he owned Birdland. And he was a sleazebag. Keely had been talking to Bobby about Levy. Bobby was aghast at this and said, 'Jesus, Keely, if you're going out with someone, at least go with someone who can take you into polite society.' She repeated this to Morris Levy.

"I said to John Miller, 'If one hair on Bobby's head is touched, he's a dead man. I'll kill him, and if I don't kill him, I'll hire somebody who will. And they won't miss him or mistake someone else for him.' I was referring to the fact that on another occasion wise guys were after Morris in Birdland and they knifed his brother by mistake. I continued: 'Now John, you brought me a message. I appreciate it. Now take the message back.'

"About a half hour later Julie Podell wants to see me at his booth in the corner. So I go over. 'What's goin' on?' He talked in a fast growl, and he'd pound a huge set of keys on the table. I said, 'Nothing. What's going on with you, Julie? You obviously called me over here to tell me something.'

"He said, 'Nobody's going to Philadelphia! I took care of everything! Leave it alone. It's over.' That's the end of that story. If Bobby hadn't been doing good business at the Copa, they would have gone to Philly. Matter of convenience."

"Everybody was scared to death of Jules Podell," remembers Dick Lord. "Bobby too. Waiters who'd worked there for 30 years would tremble—*tremble*—when he walked by. He had this big desk in the kitchen, higher than anybody else. And he would bang his ring on that table and he would bellow. If he had a couple of drinks, he would go crazy. The first time I played there, Bobby said, 'Whatever you do, don't talk to him. Don't look him in the eye, don't talk to him.' During performances, there were tiers at the Copa, over the floor. Podell would sit there, but he would not face the stage. He would face the wall! So when I performed, he never once looked at me. I think with the comics, he was counting the laughs to see how good they were."

"Two couples were sitting ringside," remembers bassist Bill Mc-

Cubbin. "They were inebriated. One of the guys kept interrupting, and Bobby said, 'Do I come to your office and interrupt you?' They got to be obnoxious. It was really disruptive to the show. Bobby was real cool. He would never get nasty with people. Bobby just glanced over at Carmine Fava, the bouncer in charge. Carmine and another bouncer went to the table. The guys were mouthing off to them now. Carmine and his associate, I swear to God, they picked up this one guy in his chair, walked him out through the audience back into the kitchen. The other guy followed him out and left the two women sitting there. Another bouncer came and took the table. Just lifted the table up, walked out with the table. The two women are sitting there in their chairs, facing each other with no table and no escorts anymore. They don't know what to do, and the audience is just howling.

"The band strikes up another tune and we kind of forgot about it. All of a sudden you hear the freight elevator bell ringing. They had taken these guys into the elevator, and you hear all this banging around. The bells going off, and boom! boom! Stopped halfway between the basement and the sidewalks."

Steve recalls the time it was Nina who came to Bobby's defense. In retrospect, knowing now that she was actually Bobby's real mother, he understands the ferocity with which Nina protected Bobby that day, that it was motherly instinct. "We were at the Three Rivers Inn in Syracuse," he says. "The dressing rooms were upstage. And I'm in the room after the show with Charlie Maffia, Nina, and Bobby. Obviously Bobby had told some people off during the show who were gangsters. They'd been noisy and rowdy. They pistol-whipped the guard downstairs and they came knocking at Bobby's door. Charlie starts to open it and they push it in. I remember Charlie was wearing glasses and he got cut above the eye. Now Bobby's going to run at them and take care of this. I grab Bobby and throw him across the room—almost throw him out a window. And now I start over to get these two guys. I remember seeing out of the corner of my eye Bobby trying to get up from where I threw him. And Nina was defending him. Holding him, protecting him, cradling him. And I kicked one guy all the way down the stairs. That was the end of them. And I understand now why Nina acted that way. If she had been Bobby's sister, she would have been too scared to do something like that."

T. K. Kellman worked in later Copa engagements with Bobby as his drummer. "Julie Podell was the most obnoxious character I ever met in my life," he remembers. "He'd sit by the cash register, which was high on a pedestal, pound his ring on this counter, bam bam bam, and yell. Somebody told me that one day Bobby was arguing with Julie, and Julie literally picked Bobby up and threw him across the room. Bobby slid halfway across the room on his ass. And then Bobby got up and kissed that old man on the mouth. We were all afraid of Podell. His boys were ever-present.

"Sunday night all the wise guys came to the Copa with their wives after Sunday dinner. They put on a show. They had their bodyguards with them and they sat at this long table. At the head of the table was Podell. At the other end were the bodyguards sitting in first position, then the relatives, maybe the wife, and finally the big guy. Bobby didn't like that Mafia kind of posturing.

"Bobby was performing, and this bodyguard in front did something real arrogant. It just struck Bobby the wrong way. So Bobby started bugging this guy. And the guy knew it. There was a bad vibe between them. He opened his jacket to show Bobby his gun. And that *infuriated* Bobby. I was pretty scared. I'm sitting behind Bobby and I'm thinking, Bobby's gonna duck and I'm gonna get shot. I'm right in the line of fire. There's no escaping if anything breaks out. So the guy in a conciliatory gesture reaches out to shake Bobby's hand. Bobby won't shake it. Bobby leaves the stage for a minute. Carmine warns him, 'You don't want to fool around with these guys.' Bobby says, 'I don't give a shit; they don't scare me.' Bobby comes back on stage, his jacket off. He sings 'When Your Lover Has Gone.' There's a real soft sensitive ending to it where he holds his hands out and a pin spot just shines on his hands. Everything is real quiet. But all of a sudden, there's another guy, a drunk guy, on the other side of the room, arguing with his wife. This guy yelled at the top of his lungs, 'Oh, fuck you!'

And the whole audience bursts out laughing. The lights go on. Two of Podell's boys somehow make their way through this packed two-inch corridor of people and tables. They go up to this guy and rip his table out from beneath him. They couldn't move him because the place was too packed. So they lifted him over their heads, literally lifted him up and carried him out lengthwise over the people, his wife following like some weird float. 'He's had too much to drink,' she's explaining to the crowd.

"So Bobby had to laugh. And everybody's cracking up and laughing. And it dissipated the tension in the room. The guy holds out his hand again to shake Bobby's, and Bobby goes over to shake it. The audience burst into applause, and the crisis was over."

Bobby did not suffer fools gladly. He held to what Estelle Changas of the *Los Angeles Times* once described as "the disquieting candor [he] refused to relinquish, an individualism which became increasingly visible."

AFTER CONCLUDING HIS TRIUMPHANT DEBUT at the Copa, Bobby was cast in his first major movie role in the summer of 1960. He was signed to appear with Rock Hudson, Gina Lollobrigida, and Sandra Dee in *Come September*. He would be playing the role of an American student vacationing in Rome who falls in love with another tourist, Sandra Dee.

When he arrived in Portofino, Bobby first became involved with an older woman: Sandra's mother, Mary Douvan. "Sandy's mother was even tinier than Sandy," remembers actress Carol Lynley. "She was like a little Kewpie doll. Pretty, perky, very personable, very up, but tiny, like bell skirts and bright colors and a little Pomeranian." Bobby soon shifted gears and infuriated Mary by courting her daughter.

In 1960 Sandra Dee was 16 and indisputably America's teen sweetheart. Producer Ross Hunter brought her, originally a 13-year-old model in New York, to Hollywood for a screen test opposite John Saxon. She signed a movie contract with Universal in 1957, at the age of 14, and appeared in her first film, *The Restless Years*. She made a great success in such films as *Imitation of Life*, *Gidget*, *A Summer Place*, *The Reluctant Debutante*, *Tammy Tell Me True*, and *Portrait in Black*. She was all wide-eyed innocence: white bread and apple pie, a saucy virgin, demure and vivacious, and beautiful. She became the exemplification of the pure American girl in the late '50s and early '60s, emerging as one of the biggest box-office attractions in the country. She was the only female actress to share every top-10 box-office poll with Doris Day and Elizabeth Taylor. She was surrounded by hairdressers, makeup men, publicity people, directors, reporters, and photographers.

"Bobby called me from Rome," Dick Lord recalls, "and said, 'You're not going to believe this. I'm marrying Sandra Dee.'" When they came back to America, they got off the plane and the first place they came to was my apartment in Brooklyn. The neighbors were going nuts: 'Sandra Dee's in the laundry room!' They were throwing themselves off balconies."

"She was a lovely, shy young girl who obviously had led a sheltered life, and this whole thing to her was brand new. She was used to going to the studio with her hairdresser and her mother, being pampered by the studio and groomed, and now she's in the real world, in Brooklyn."

"Oh yeah, America's sweetheart," Steve Blauner says. "It was that this ugly guy from the wrong side of the tracks—you know Bobby was always embarrassed by that stereotyped side of his Italian heritage, because he grew up seeing the guys in the underwear walking around. So he always went out there trying to prove how bright he was. You have to understand, Sandra Dee was when we really had movie stars. And this was—the prize. Sandra was the girl next door, this is what every girl wanted to be. Tammy, Bridget. Now I think Bobby felt he was in love with her, yeah, but look—he was dating the mother before Sandy."

The first time Bobby and Sandra met each other, Bobby was standing on the shore at Portofino, wearing a canary yellow suit with white shoes and waving at her, and Sandra was standing on a boat pulling in to dock. She looked up and thought, "Is that him? Oh my God!"

He called out to her, "Hi, I'm Bobby Darin. You're going to be my wife."

She replied, "Not today."

Bobby began by teasing her: "Sandra Dee has a flea," he'd shout across the room. She would get mad and say, "I can't stand that Bobby Darin."

He sent 18 yellow roses to her every day. On the surface, they were opposites. She seemed pristine, untouched, constantly chaperoned by her possessive mother. Sandra appeared to have had no private life or experience at all; she lived on movie sets, where she was treated like a fragile doll and a valuable studio commodity. Bobby was the Italian sharpie from the Bronx, sophisticated, brilliant, raunchy, brimming with experience of life. But there must have been an emotional undertow that helped to bring them together. She was the product of a dysfunctional past, secretly the victim of years of sexual abuse by her stepfather. Bobby was the unloved orphan, at least in his own mind, dispossessed and homeless. There was always a fierce cynical calculation in Bobby's moves, but there was genuine feeling on his part for her.

In a 1995 interview with Sandra by writer George Carpinone, he asked her, "How did you initially feel about Bobby?" Sandra replied, "I hated him! We spent four weeks in Portofino shooting, and I never said anything. He used to try to goad me just to get a response. He asked my mother, 'Why doesn't she give me a reaction?' And my mother replied, 'That's my daughter!' He took me on a carriage ride and he fell asleep. That started it, that one time. He shut his mouth and he lay in the carriage and his head was almost on my lap. I looked and thought, 'With his mouth shut, he's not as obnoxious.' He would do anything for a reaction. He [splashed me with water] in one scene and I had to be dried off. I thought the director was going to kill him."

Despite her mother's vigilant watchfulness, Bobby would find ways of getting Sandra alone every day. They would walk together through Rome or Portofino, witnessing scenes of poverty and hunger. Sandra was repulsed by it, but Bobby told her these were the underlying realities she needed to be aware of.

Carol Lynley remembers Sandra from the days the two of them modeled together in New York. "We were both child models," she says. "Sandy was personable, bouncy, cute. We were about the same age, and we were always surrounded by older people. Her stepfather, Gene, thought I would be very good for Sandy. He had money and took us out to wonderful restaurants. He would say to Sandy about me, 'Look at that girl eat.' [Sandra had eating problems with early childhood.] I never believed for a minute that he was a child molester.

"Sandy's mother was very pissed off about Bobby dating Sandra, because she had pretty tight control. Apparently she flew back to the States in a huff. And it took Bobby a day; Sandy was alone for the first time in her life, so she turned to Bobby. Good-bye Mary.

"Bobby really needed a passive type of lady. Sandy was absolutely catnip for a guy like Bobby. She was as cute as could be and helpless as a lamb. Could not have made it in the world alone. And Bobby never exploited Sandy. He certainly never took any money from her. He was basically very decent and caring; he liked women. I look at *Come September* now. It's all there. You could see her with him. She's 16; she's on the back of a motorbike with him. She's thinking, you can see it, 'What is this?' And Bobby just comes in and nails it and takes over."

"The marriage to Sandra," explains Rona Barrett, "was something that Bobby absolutely wanted more than life itself. When he went on to do *Come September*, where they were going to be together, I said to him, 'Shall we bet now on how long it's going to take you to get her or marry her?' And he laughed at me and said, 'Why are you always doing this to me?'

"So I knew from the beginning how crazy he was about her. But I also knew there was a rather strange relationship between him and Sandra's mother. On the outside Mary appeared to be one way; on the inside she was obviously another person and I believe inflicted a lot of pain on her daughter. I remember the late producer Ross Hunter telling me many years later about how he and Mary would bind Sandra's breasts up because they were getting so big, and they wanted her to appear to be flat-chested . . . So Mary in her own way inflicted her own damage on Sandra. Big time. I found this out many years later.

"Bobby was crazy about Sandra, but I believe it was a tormented marriage, with Mary hating him every step of the way. And the rumors were always there—which Bobby never admitted and never denied either—that perhaps there was a one- or two-night fling with the mother in order to get closer to the daughter. But Bobby was always attracted to older women. I think there was an attraction there. Bobby in all his romances, which were really nothing more than long rolls in the hay, were always with older women, except Sandra. She was the youngest person he ever went out with. It was more natural for all of us to believe that Bobby was having an affair with Mary than with Sandra. I think that Mary thought this was something for her and not for Sandra. And then Bobby turned his attention to Sandra, the person he had always wanted. And he wanted to marry a virgin; he was very hung up on that. That was part of the traditional Italian background. Bobby loved women. In his own way, he really loved them."

When the filming ended, Bobby flew home on November 14, but he met Sandra at the airport upon her return November 21 with a huge, six-carat emerald-cut diamond ring. Their engagement became worldwide news. "I'll tell you about that ring," says Steve Blauner. "When Bobby and I went out on the road, he'd leave money lying around. I'd grab it and steal it from him. One day I said to him, 'Sign this card.' It was a bank thing; he just signed it. He didn't care; he did whatever I told him. What I did was open this account. It was in his name, and only he could take it out. And I kept stealing money from him, stealing money from him. Now he's marrying Sandy; he wants a ring. My uncle was Baumgold and Brothers, the biggest diamond importers in the world. So I went to him and said, 'Bobby wants a perfect stone.' My uncle said, 'That's insane. Nobody can tell a perfect stone.' I said, 'Bobby wants a perfect stone,' so I got him this ring. It was going to cost ten thousand. I threw the bankbook at Bobby and I said, 'Here, you can pay for it this way. Take the money out of the bank.' He said, 'Where did this money come from?' I said, 'I'd steal it from you every night when you left money on the dresser.' So that's how he got the ring. It was six carats and it was a perfect stone. After that he was always waiting for another bankbook to surface. But I never did it again. But he always thought there was more coming."

At three o'clock in the morning on December 1, 1961, Bobby and Sandra were married in Newark, New Jersey. The party took place at Don Kirshner's apartment in Elizabeth. Nina, Charlie, Vee, Vana, Gary Walden, Don and Sheila Kirshner, and Richard and Mickey Behrke were there. Nina was Sandra's maid of honor, and Dick Behrke was Bobby's best man.

Hal Taines was part of Bobby's honeymoon in Florida. "Bobby had just married, and he was booked to play the Deauville Hotel," Taines recalls. "And Bobby and Sandra hadn't had a honeymoon. He brought her with him to Florida. He got very worried about her. He said to me and my wife, 'I'm afraid she's going to be alone up here at the hotel while I'm working. I don't know what to do. How about you and Suzie staying with us at the hotel? We have a two-bedroom suite. Sandra can be with you and Suzie.'

"So we moved in with him and Sandra," Taines continues. "She was adorable. A most wonderful, sweet, childlike woman. She was very, very withdrawn. You could see crowds would scare her. We would take her to see Bobby's second show, and then Bobby, Sandy, Suzie, and myself would go up to his suite and we'd stay with them.

"Bobby loved to listen to Ray Charles. He used to sit there for hours, until two o'clock in the morning. If Sandra was tired and went to bed early, even on the honeymoon, he'd sit there listening by himself through the night."

"One day Bobby and I were talking," remembers Rona Barrett, "about what it was like for him to fall in love with Sandra. I think a part of it was his reaching for the stars. He wanted to be married to the number one American dream, and he made that happen. He got to sing with Judy Garland, he got to perform with Sammy Davis Jr., he got to go with Durante, he got to be with George Burns, and he married America's sweetheart. It was like Eddie Fisher marrying Debbie Reynolds.

"In that conversation, we got to talking about virginity. He looked at me, just the two of us in the room, and said, 'Everybody thinks it was a great relationship. After we got married, I never went to bed with Sandra for the first three weeks. She wouldn't let me near her. I had to take it so slow.' And then he alluded to the fact that it was not an easy sexual relationship to have with her."

It was not Sandra's virginity or her real personality that made it so difficult for her and made her so difficult for Bobby. The years of sexual abuse by her stepfather, which Sandra told Dodd about many years later, had taken a critical toll.

Chapter Eight
THE GENIUS

BOBBY AND SANDRA WERE AMERICA'S NEWEST SWEETHEARTS, a perfect glow suffusing their lives that captured the attention of the country. Bobby's center of gravity shifted to the West, from New York to Los Angeles and Vegas, where he became one of the hottest and most talented stars. It was the American dream fulfilled: the swarthy, tough kid from the other side of the tracks capturing the heart of the most beautiful, captivating blonde movie queen. "Remember," says Steve Blauner, "here's a guy that the odds were would end up in prison before he'd end up anyplace. And he becomes a star: records, nightclubs, movies, marries the girl next door that everybody dreams of. Bobby *took* what he got. Bit into it and wouldn't let it go."

But in reality the marriage was troubled from the beginning. Sandra was ready for a glittering new screen role, not the sweaty complexities of a real marriage. Bobby and Sandra moved into a house on Stone Canyon Road in Bel Air. Sandra's hermetic, withdrawn personality was at odds with Bobby's outgoing vagabond life, the long nightclub hours, the evenings he liked to spend with his pals. "I worked with Bobby at the Three Rivers Inn in Syracuse," remembers Dick Lord. "He was there with Sandy. I felt sorry for her, because when he was onstage, people would watch him, but they would turn to see what Sandy's reaction was also. After the show, sometimes we would go for breakfast. She didn't want to go; she would very much resent this. She resented Steve Blauner, all of us. We were getting in the way of her marriage. She didn't want to share him. Sandy really didn't want anybody around.

"Backstage, she was like a shy person," Lord continues. "All these people coming to see Bobby were a little bit in awe of her. I think she felt like an outsider, and I really felt badly for her. She was a nice girl, and this was a gutsy world she knew nothing about."

"I saw a spoiled, petulant little girl," remembers Rona Barrett, "who adored this man but thought she should be married to a movie star and not a singing star. Hated nightclubs, never wanted to go, never wanted to be at his side. Could not understand why Bobby would be finished with some gig, come back to the house, and have maybe six or eight guys with him, and they would be shooting the breeze and staying up. So she went off on her own. These were two people who loved each other but couldn't live with each other. It went on until they finally ended."

"I would say to Bobby [at his house]," Steve Blauner recalls, "'if you want to talk business, come to the office. When I come here, I can see Sandy's eyes glaze over and it's not fair to her. I'll come over here, but I'm never talking business in front of Sandy again.' You have to understand, Sandy never really did anybody any harm. Think of a life where you grow up, your only friends are your mother, your hairdresser, and the makeup man. She never lived a normal life."

Bobby spoke of Sandra's childhood in later years to his second wife, Andrea. Andrea's sister, Terry Koenig, recalls that "Bobby explained Sandy to Andrea one day by saying, 'Mary so controlled Sandra's life as a young girl that if Mary decided they weren't going out that day, she just pulled down all the blinds and said, "It's raining. We're going to stay inside and not go to the studio."' She would totally manipulate this little girl into whatever she wanted. Sandy was an innocent victim of this harridan who used her for money and used her for power. Mary had always used Sandra. Now here comes Bobby and she can't do it anymore."

Mary Douvan was living in the house with Bobby and Sandra. She was always there or on the movie set with Sandra. "Mary would sit on the set and bask in the reflection of Sandy's glory," says Steve Blauner. "People would say to her, 'You must be Sandy's sister.' And she was basically, if you didn't know her, a nice person. But she was always there."

To Steve Blauner, Sandra was a helpless innocent. "Sandra was on an old seven-year contract with Universal," he remembers. "She may have been getting $750 a week. I went to her on her birthday and said, 'I'm going to give you a birthday present. I'm going to renegotiate your contract at Universal.' I said, 'I'm not going to be my normal self: I'm going to be sweet.' Sandra said, 'Oh no, you can't do that.' 'Why?' I said. She said, 'These are my friends.' 'Your friends?' I said. 'Three years from today, they'll say, Who is that girl we used to have on the lot? What are you, out of your mind?'"

At the same time, Bobby's relationship to Nina and Charlie, Vana, Vee, and Gary would be shot through with ambivalence throughout his life. As he became a star and his income skyrocketed, the family expected to benefit from his largesse. That never happened; on the contrary, Bobby seemed determined to keep them in the role of supplicants. Bobby gave and he took away, almost in the same breath. Dodd Darin relates in his memoir that Bobby's sister Vee told him, "Bobby always treated the family like shit. His attitude was always, 'Oh, they're just family. I could do anything and they will always stand behind me.'"

Hesh Wasser believes Bobby had a better motivation than that: he wanted his family to learn survival skills: "I was the one to whom Bobby confided his feelings about wanting his family to make it on their own," she recalls. "He wanted to believe that members of the family had the capacity of doing something for themselves. He saw them as basically a bunch of losers. We're not talking about one person who didn't make it; we're talking about the whole family. Their attitude was basically that they deserved whatever there was out there. They brought him up, they saved his life, they took care of him. They wanted to be supported. What family in the same situation wouldn't have asked for the same thing? They want a home, they want clothes."

"During his childhood," explains Hesh Wasser, "Bobby saw all these families around him with all kinds of successes: people making money here and there, growing, going to school. He never saw this in his own home. Whenever they wanted anything, they'd go to Bobby. In fact, just by his going to school, getting a scholarship, and doing what he did with his education, it really hurt him with his family. Because he surpassed them and probably, in his own way, acted as though he was better than they. When you're in a situation like Bobby's, everybody wants money. It's almost like winning the lottery. You want to run away. He was only 22 years old."

"Charlie and Nina loved Bobby," Bobby Rozario reflects. "But Bobby outgrew all those people. He educated himself. He literally outgrew them. He would never say that to them. But you could see it. He was a proud Italian, but he was not a *goomba*."

Whatever his motivations, Bobby's behavior toward Nina and the other members of his family could be interpreted as a slow and haphazard torture. This ambivalence was never the case in his relationship with Sandra and Dodd, nor with friends, or even strangers, with whom Bobby was very generous. Bobby gave surprise gifts of new cars to Dick Behrke and Dick Lord, and he was extraordinarily responsive to those in need, especially ill children.

Objective outsiders could meet Nina and Charlie and be touched by their boundless love and concern for Bobby. Nina and Charlie were not educated or sophisticated; they were simple, down-to-earth, hardly brilliant people without malevolence or calculation. "Charlie lived for eating, sleeping, and fucking," says Steve Blauner. "Nothing else ever crossed his mind." As for Nina, "Bobby couldn't stand her. She was embarrassing. She was big, fat, and loud." Charlie was a good provider but a cheating husband to Nina, but there wasn't a shred of disloyalty in his relationship to Bobby, whom he had carried around in his arms in Bobby's ill childhood. "Bobby was only alive because he had a good family who loved him," Hesh Wasser points out.

SANDRA BECAME PREGNANT in March 1961, and Dodd Mitchell Darin was born at Cedars of Lebanon hospital in Hollywood on December 16, 1961. Sandra pressured Bobby to quit performing now that they had a child.

But Bobby's successes continued to mount. Steve Blauner had negotiated a lucrative three-year deal for Bobby to play at the Flamingo Hotel for $2,000 a week. On January 31, Blauner was also executive producer of Bobby's one-hour TV special, *Bobby Darin and Friends*, which aired on NBC.

Bobby scored another knockout with his next brassy single, "Lazy River," which rose to No. 14 on the charts and No. 2 in England. Henry Mancini said of Bobby, "He has a way with a song that seems to be able to hit, because he's got an inherent sense of dramatics. It's in his singing, it's in his writing, and it's in his acting. Being around Bobby when he's performing or when he's getting ready to perform is like being in a buzz-saw factory, because he just has so much energy, energy and excitement, that he has to let it out—it's just that infectious."

"Lazy River" reflects all of the qualities Mancini alluded to. In the tradition of "Mack" and "Beyond the Sea," it's one of a series of Bobby's most inspired numbers, this time brilliantly arranged by Dick Behrke. Once again Bobby takes a tried-and-true number, turns it on its ear, and swings it like crazy, wreaks havoc with it, makes it shining and wild and new as if it has never been done before. And it hasn't—not this way. These are among the songs that are most frequently cited as belonging to Bobby's greatest period, extending from "Artificial Flowers" through "Mame" and beyond. Each is a milestone—it's never been done this way before and no one else will ever be able to do it this way again. Frenzy, abandon, joy, exhilaration, sex, you name it, it's here.

"Lazy River" builds from bass and acoustic guitar to an all-out swing assault. It's simply impossible to equate Bobby's capacity to swing with anyone's other than Sinatra's; that Italian fire and passion, the sense in which he flings you up that river with him and you are in for the ride and there's no way to get off—you are caught in that ecstasy, that constantly mounting flow of feeling. Whether anything in the record is actually spontaneous or whether this orgy is a planned one, it certainly springs out of deep joy and love of the music. From "Throw away your troubles, baby, dream a dream of me," to Bobby marking halfway by boldly declaring aloud "That halfway mark," to creatively borrowing a line from "River, Stay Away from My Door": "I ain't goin' your way—get out of my way," look out: Mack is back. As singer and drummer Grady Tate concisely describes Bobby's achievements: "That man swung his ass off . . . He was a little ahead of his time, or not quite up to his time, you didn't know what he was. He was a monster. An absolute monster. He took the Sinatra things someplace else, not allowing the swing to disappear, or the groove. And his civil-rights participation was about his own rights. See, he transcended all of those ethnic identifications. You didn't know what he was or who he was or what he looked like. His look kept changing. Bobby was a demon."

Come September opened to good reviews and consolidated Bobby and Sandra's standing as the movies' beautiful young couple. The film provides a genuine glimpse into Bobby and Sandra at the very moment they were falling in love. Bobby plays himself, or the self he was known for: brash, cocky, self-confident and yet, amid the fluff, still manages to inject a note of authenticity, flashes of the street kid that break through the Hollywood gauze. He sings a song he'd written for the film, "Multiplication," a good pop song that also injects some life into the proceedings and reached No. 30 on the charts.

Twist with Bobby Darin, his first rock-and-roll album, was released in December, and while it's a collage of old charts, it contains many real pleasures, including one of his best rock compositions, "Bullmoose," along with "Queen of the Hop," "Irresistible You," "Multiplication," his Rinky Dinks singles, and above all, his pounding rock-and-roll version of the venerable chestnut "You Must Have Been a Beautiful Baby." Those tremulous little voices like Rudy Vallee that sang with the big bands in the '30s were far from what Darin does with this number. It's another one-of-a-kind record in its magnetism and exhilarating freshness. When the record was released as a single, it shot to No. 5 in the United States and No. 10 in England.

It was during this period that Ahmet Ertegun had hired an unknown named Phil Spector at Atlantic and brought Spector to Bobby's house in Los Angeles to meet him.

"Bobby was quite temperamental," Ahmet recalls. "But I had my own way of handling him. His musical ideas were brilliant, but not always, and I tried to be very diplomatic with him. I had a notion that Phil, with his own inventive ideas, could help me produce Bobby's next record.

"The setting was terrific. On a tranquil Saturday afternoon, we pulled up at an imposing mansion. We were admitted by a butler who took us to a beautiful backyard, where Bobby and his wife, Sandra, were both in bathing suits, sipping cold drinks by the pool. I introduced Phil as my assistant. After some small talk, Bobby began singing us some songs he'd just written. I never liked to discourage Bobby. My policy was to listen to all his material and then praise those with the most commercial potential.

"'Good,' I said after the first song. 'Good,' I repeated after the second. 'Fine,' I commented after the third. 'Interesting,' I remarked after the fourth.

"'What?' Phil broke in. 'Are you fuckin' crazy or am I? He can't record these songs. These songs are pure shit!'

"'Who is this guy?' Bobby wanted to know. 'Get him the fuck out of here.'"

Sometime later, Bobby proposed making a record for Atlantic with the now-famous Spector as producer. He was astonished when Ertegun told him who Spector was.

Bobby's first movie of 1961 was *Too Late Blues*, a film directed by John Cassavetes and costarring Stella Stevens. The film, Cassavetes's first Hollywood feature, opened in the United States in January 1962. Cassavetes had already achieved acclaim for his independent film,

Shadows, and would go on in the future to make some vital and innovative films. *Too Late Blues* appears to be an aberration. Originally four hours in length, half of the footage was cut before the film appeared in theaters. It's perhaps unfair to assess this film on the basis of the truncated version that was ultimately released, but it's hard to believe it was much better than the inchoate mess it now appears to be. Bobby played John "Ghost" Wakefield, a pianist in a struggling jazz combo. Bobby is effective, but the film does not seem to have a plot or to go anywhere.

"Instinctively, Bobby was great," Martin Baum remembered. "He had that little extra something. Spirit. Something within himself. Desire to succeed. He needed to prove he could do things. John Cassavetes was like that also. He died too young. Bobby died too young. They had the same look. They were both short; they were both wiry. And they were both intensely dedicated to becoming artists. When they did *Too Late Blues* together, they were two peas in a pod."

Actor Stella Stevens recalls the days on the set working with Bobby. "I was a fan of Bobby's," she says. "I thought he was groovy. Cool and groovy, and also hot. There was a scene where I'm standing with my back to a wall in the hallway. And it's Bobby Darin and he looks great and he comes over to me and we kiss. Well, we had to try it one more time, and Bobby looked down and he had an enormous hard-on. The catwalk man up above and the lighting guys, they were all looking down and called out, 'Hey, check that out. Look at that woody!' Everybody on the whole set knew about it and laughed. Bobby had to walk it off for a while and then come back and try again. That was Bobby. Every time I think of Bobby, I think of that.

"Another time I was supposed to come out of the backlit bathroom wearing only a silk bathrobe and come over to him. He's sitting on the bed, and I take him and gently bring his head to my bosom. And he looked up just before our take and said, 'Don't mess up my hair.' He meant it, and I didn't. But it sure tempted me when he said that, but I know he didn't want this big ducktail sticking out of his hair if I fondled it the wrong way. So I did him the favor. He was self-conscious about his hair. It's too bad. If he were living today, he'd have a shaved head and still look very hot."

"I never wanted Bobby to make that movie," Steve Blauner explains. "I hated it. It was a terrible script. And I turned it down. Then Bobby and I got into a fight and I quit." But Blauner's quitting was short-lived, as it always would be, and he was soon back to battling on behalf of Bobby.

Blauner's assessment of Bobby as an actor is a reserved one. "I always thought Bobby was acting. If I walk into a theater and think somebody's acting, then they're not doing their job. I felt this way about most of the movies he was in. I never felt he had a real great director. I felt that, yes, you could get a performance out of him. He couldn't give it alone, not yet anyhow. He was great in *Happy Ending* where he played the Italian gigolo. Maybe in *Pressure Point*. There are parts of *Captain Newman, M.D.* that I don't believe."

SOME OF BOBBY'S FINEST ACHIEVEMENTS in 1961 were preserved on recording. Atco released *The Bobby Darin Story*, a compilation record of Bobby's 12 most popular singles. For the first time, "Lazy River," "Dream Lover," and "Queen of the Hop" were available on one album. The album was a hit from the start, reaching No. 18 on the charts and never going out of print over the years. Of special appeal on the CD are the brief narrations Bobby gives before each song, another idea hatched by Steve Blauner.

Then came *Two of a Kind*, Bobby's vocal collaboration with composer Johnny Mercer. Bobby's greatest recording triumph of the year would produce an album that has never lost its transcendent magic and never gone out of print (at a low point, it was one of only three Darin records that could be found in stores).

"It was very impromptu," Hesh Wasser remembers. "It was Steve's idea. They just went into the studio, Billy May did the charts, and it was a three-hour session. Mercer was delighted and flabbergasted at the idea. He was saying, 'You mean to tell me that you want Bobby

Darin to record with me?' This was fun, and there was the element of surprise. With all the albums Bobby did, that album probably did more to boost his career at the time than anything."

"There was just something about the two of them," Steve Blauner recalls. "Their voices are similar. So I went up to Bobby and suggested it. And we go and do the session, and they are having the greatest time. They were making mistakes and laughing, and we left it in.

"So they finished the album. They both come to me. 'We gotta do another album.' They're arguing. They're having too good a time. You can hear how good-natured it was. They're throwing lines out of left field. It was absolutely incredible; they had such a great time together." Bruce Charet comments, "That record is such a labor of love. It indicated where Bobby's heart was." According to Ronnie Zito, "Bobby was thrilled doing that album. He just had a ball with it. It was just so much fun."

Bobby never recorded an album more fresh and alive, more riotous, inspired, funny, and original than this. It's honky-tonk, riverboat, Dixieland music, and it feels as good as gospel. It's actually a lesson in the joy of music. Mercer and Darin wing it together, scatting, riffing, improvising, doing what's necessary. They are having a ball. They slide, they glide, they dance, they fly. The joy is palpable and infectious; they've created an ode to freedom. The timing and projection are impeccable. They take neglected Tin Pan Alley chestnuts, much in the same way that Bobby resurrected "Clementine" and "Lazy River," and infuse them with new life and a compelling rhythmic drive. The atmosphere is of an informal party, free and easy, ribald and raunchy. They've got conductor Billy May in their corner too. They interject puns, they interrupt each other, they banter back and forth. Bobby interjects the line "Roamin' in the gloamin'" to "Back Home in Indiana." Jerry Wexler had suggested including "Ace in the Hole," which is a gem. Bobby does Groucho, W. C. Fields, and Dean Martin on it, throwing in "Volare!" (just the one word) for good measure. He adds to "Two of a Kind" (an original new song by Darin and Mercer)—"Like the Tower of Pisa, I'm leanin' like he's-a inclined"; he throws in

Louie Armstrong too. There is wild suggestiveness in "Who Takes Care of the Caretaker's Daughter (While the Caretaker's Busy Taking Care)."

The impact of this album leads one to reflect more on Sinatra's observation that Bobby could best be appreciated on the nightclub floor. Really? This may be more of a subtle putdown than it seems at first. It's true that some fine singers do not fully translate their gifts to records; they are somewhat diminished in the process. Judy Garland, Michael Feinstein, Al Jolson, and the great Los Angeles blues and jazz singer Ernie Andrews are among a considerable number of artists whose gifts are sometimes muted on recording.

But this is not true of Bobby. Bobby, when he is at his best, is his best on recording as well.

This still leaves Sinatra in the number one spot, because that's where he deserves to be. But watch out: Like Mack the Knife, someone's "sneaking around the corner . . . Can it be our boy's done something rash?" When it comes to one ingredient, energy, listen to Sinatra and Darin and you'll score one for Mister D.

But the greatest triumph for Bobby and Sandra that year was the birth of Dodd. However erratic and tormented his life would become, and as driven as Bobby was in his career, his love for his son was paramount. His role as a loving father was one to which he would always give his heart and soul. And those were personal qualities that Bobby had in abundance.

As 1961 drew to a close, it is almost impossible to grasp the fact that Bobby Darin was only 25 years old. He never really had singing instruction, although he paid some visits to a singing teacher, Gian-Carlo Menotti. It was almost as if the greats were seated at a table one day: Sinatra, Benny, Burns and Allen, Dean Martin, Durante, Garland, Cantor, Louie Prima, and suddenly there popped up in their midst, fully hatched, seated right beside them: Bobby. And he fit right in.

Where the hell did he come from?

Some questions about the nature of genius can never really be answered or resolved.

Chapter Nine
THE CHAMELEON

IN JULY 1962, FRANK SINATRA WAS ON THE SET of the film *Sergeants Three* when he called Steve Blauner and asked to see him. When they met, Sinatra introduced him to Moe Austin and explained that he and Moe were forming a new label, Reprise Records. Sinatra said he was planning to sign Dean Martin and Sammy Davis Jr. for Reprise, and he wanted Bobby Darin on Reprise as well. Blauner said he wanted to think about it overnight and would get back to Frank in the morning. As soon as he left Sinatra, Steve ran over to Capitol Records and within hours Bobby had agreed to sign with Capitol, the label that he'd aspired to all along. Capitol, having lost not only Sinatra but Dino and Sammy, would pull out all the stops for Bobby and Nat King Cole. Bobby signed the three-year contract with Capitol on July 12, 1962.

"That was a big shock to me," says Ahmet Ertegun. "It could have been partly my fault, not to keep him closer to the funk, which is where he really came from. Because he had a real feel for that, just as he also had a real feel for the pure pop, swing pop. But Bobby also got influenced by his managers and by outside forces which were not always the best. They kept telling him, 'You shouldn't be on this funky little R&B label.' But we were doing the kind of job that made him a star. When his movie career started, he went to Hollywood, he met movie stars, and he became suddenly surrounded by movie agents and ambitious managers—all the glitter, all that we didn't really want to get involved with. And we haven't."

"At Atlantic, much of my interaction was with Ahmet, who I liked," Steve Blauner recalls. "Years after Bobby left Atlantic, Ahmet walked into a private club on the Sunset Strip, On the Rocks. 'Ahmet, how are ya?' and he just reams me out. Because I took Bobby away from him. Then his wife comes over and Ahmet says to her, 'I want you to meet one of my good friends, Steve Blauner.' I said, 'Ahmet, you're full of shit,' and I turned around and walked away from him. It didn't dawn on me then, but Atlantic had lost Ray Charles; they lost Bobby. They were in dire straits, I guess. I loved Ahmet. But I thought a major label would sell more records by accident than Atlantic at that time would on purpose.

"And Bobby loved Ahmet. The story about that is that Bobby's deal was up with Atlantic. They made no giant overtures. Didn't come around and kiss my ass, not that they had to. And then I got that call from Sinatra."

"Bobby reached the pinnacle at Atlantic with Dick Wess on those albums," Bruce Charet says. "When Bobby worked with Wess or when he did "Lazy River," he sounds like Bobby Darin, he's swinging his ass off. He doesn't sound anything like Sinatra. I think he left Atlantic because he was obsessed with Frank. He wanted to record in that studio at Capitol."

The late Milt Bernhardt was in the band the first time Bobby recorded at Capitol. "Bobby was pretty brash and usually would swagger in," he said in 2004. "It was an affectation. He'd been brought in from New York, and well, now he's in Hollywood. The first day that he came in the studio, he was about an hour late. And he looked around at the musicians and said, 'Are you sure this is the way Sinatra recorded it?' And we all made that same sound in response to that, we groaned. But he won us over."

The first part of 1962 was studded with missteps and stumbles for Bobby.

The rollercoaster year in film began with the release of *Too Late Blues*. Bobby could do little to redeem the film remake of Rodgers and Hammerstein's *State Fair*, in which he costarred with Ann-Margret, Pat Boone, and Alice Faye. Bobby's next movie, *Hell Is for Heroes*, was hardly a career-advancer either, although he received second billing to Steve McQueen. A sodden, slow-moving war drama in which little happens, Bobby is saddled with the comic relief character here, Private Corby, a black-marketer soldier, a role that contains the dimmest echo of Sinatra's Maggio in *From Here to Eternity*. Bobby does the best he can, but the film is lifeless, the role is stereotyped. Director Don Siegel strongly praised Bobby: "A fine actor, an underestimated actor." In fact, Bobby would ultimately make only two serious movies out of thirteen: *Pressure Point* and *Captain Newman, M.D.*

Bobby's final record for Atlantic issued that year was also questionable. "There were so many incarnations of Bobby Darin," says Bruce Charet. "He suddenly woke up one morning and decided to be Ray Charles." This was the farewell album for Atlantic, *Bobby Darin Sings Ray Charles*. Bobby not only sings Ray Charles; in many cases he follows Charles's arrangements with little deviation. There is no paucity of effort or passion, but the deepest reaction the album evokes is a desire to listen to Brother Ray himself. And the question it raises is: Why?

"It would have been very hard for Bobby to come up to the standard of Ray Charles," says Hesh Wasser. "Why would anybody want to do Ray Charles, especially some white kid? You're making a comparison between apples and oranges. I didn't hear anyone say it was a terrible album. Bobby took chances. That was part of what made him happen."

Wasser had taken the album to a major jazz critic, Leonard Feather, who had previously had no use for Darin's work. "Leonard Feather loved that album and wrote beautiful liner notes for it," she explains. "When I sat with Feather earlier, he told me he'd only heard Bobby's rock stuff and wasn't impressed. And I said to him, 'Well, give him a little time. I think you might change your mind.' Then Bobby goes in and records this Ray Charles album and Feather loves it. So that made me feel so proud."

"I'm proud to say," Bobby told Leonard Feather, "that I was on the Ray Charles bandwagon when it was just a baby carriage. In fact, two singers—Fats Domino and Ray Charles—opened up my ears to a whole new world, different from anything I'd heard until then. They both became major influences when I realized these are the roots."

Feather writes, "A friend of mine, noting the disparity in the Darin and Charles backgrounds and Bobby's victorious blockade of the gap, said, 'He may not have lived it,' said my friend, 'but he sure has loved it.'"

When everyone is on the side of the angels—Bobby, Hesh, Feather, Feather's friend—it's difficult to register dissent without feeling heartless. But good intentions—even love—are not enough to create a work of art, particularly when the original, real work of art was already done.

It is paradoxical that with all his feeling about Ray Charles, the record does not come out of Bobby's soul. He is not singing out of his own experience. He adds nothing new; it is almost an exact replica of the Ray Charles record without Charles's voice. Bobby keeps himself in a vise; he is enthralled by the original. What is most important to him, this noble reach he is making, comes through as ersatz and inauthentic.

Briefly, in the later part of "I Got A Woman," Bobby starts to liberate himself by the repetition of "She's all right," and moves into his own sound. He takes it and works with it, and the incantation comes alive: "I feel good . . . She's all right." But he soon reverts back to replication.

A more fitting act of homage would have been Bobby's reinterpreting Ray Charles's songs in his own original way, from the spirit. Yet that would likely have seemed to him an act of sacrilege. Ray did it first; he did it immortally, for all time. For almost the first time, Bobby sounds what he is: *young*, and he sounds out of his depth.

"Sometimes you don't get recognized in your own time," says Joel Dorn, who coproduced with Jimmy Scalia the monumental Darin CD-DVD *Aces Back to Back* in 2004. "The extreme examples are Van Gogh, photographers like Weegee, or composers like Charles Ives. In a strange way I rate Bobby on that level. I was a Darin fan but not a fanatic. I was a jazz disc jockey in Philadelphia. His Ray Charles record came out on Atlantic, which was my favorite record company in the world. I fell under Ray Charles's spell at the age of 14. So when Bobby's record came out, I had a three-hour Ray Charles show called *Night and Ray* every Friday night. That was when Ray was at the height of his powers, had his fastball, and was not joking. And I was *obsessed* with him, overcome. So I was on the air when Bobby's album came out and I said, 'You know, an album just came out that stinks, horrible, disgrace, blah blah.' And my remarks created a controversy.

"Now, coincidentally another guy at the station, Sid Mark, was and is the biggest Sinatra fan in the universe. So Sid hated Darin for his remark about wanting to best Sinatra. And Sid's on the air, and he's saying if you cut off his hands, Bobby couldn't sing, because he couldn't snap his fingers. So Darin picks up on it. He's got a jerk like him and a lunatic like me, and we're at the same radio station putting him down. Now he arranges to come to the station, and he's going on Sid's show to go head-to-head with Sid. So naturally I come by Sid's show. So in the middle of the interview with Sid and Darin, there's a break, the mike's off, and Bobby says to me, 'How you doing, young man? I understand you got a problem too.' As he became combative, he brought the Philly street out in me, so I was saying stuff like, 'The album stunk. Where do you get off? Who do you think you are?' And he's wailin', he's revvin' everybody up. So he and I just yelled at each other.

"Years pass. I'm following him, I'm digging him. I saw his show at the Latin Casino in Philly. He was the real thing. To me it was the sex. He lived for that thing. He was *there*; *that's what he did*. I'm sure he loved nailing broads, but I don't think there was a higher high for him than to nail an audience with his records, in person, in the movies, on TV, walkin' down the street. I had no idea he could do all that.

"So then I knew he was the real thing. Then I'd get together with people talking about who the greatest are. So I would be talking about John Coltrane, or the Dixie Hummingbirds, or Hank Williams. I would say for blown-away, full-scale entertainers, Darin. Guys would look at you funny. And I start to see that there's people who should have known better but don't really understand what a killer this guy is. I don't think the public ever got him as the complete artist he was. But now he's sneaking back in the game.

"You know, a lot of stuff he did was to me semirational. He never did anything gently. He became another person. When you look back at it, it's like a painter with different periods. I think in his neurotic whatever-it-was that drove him, there was a part of him that was flying out in a lot of directions at once, tuning in to things with an intensity, and then they would disappear."

Bobby became another person on the Ray Charles record, and then he returned to himself. There was a danger to Bobby's chameleon-like quality. It was a parlor trick, and he had to sit on himself to keep from being an impressionist all the time. In his attempts to grow, Bobby frequently strayed from his true gifts.

BOBBY'S RAY CHARLES RECORD sank like a pebble into a well. And then he soared again.

Stanley Kramer was one of the most socially conscious directors in Hollywood. He had recently completed *Judgment at Nuremberg*. He had chosen for his next project a screenplay that dealt with the relationship between a young black psychiatrist and a psychopathic young American Nazi imprisoned for sedition during World War II.

"Stanley Kramer was going to make this picture called *Pressure Point*," Steve Blauner says. "Hubert Cornfield was directing. The black psychiatrist would be played by Sidney Poitier. They were looking for a blue-eyed, Aryan-looking guy to play the Nazi. Steve Yates, the agent, kept badgering Kramer to just sit in a room with Bobby. Bobby and I go to see Stanley Kramer in his office. And they started to talk. Stanley zonked right into Bobby and vice versa. At some point in the conversation Kramer said, 'Excuse me for a minute.' He went out and down the hall into Hubert Cornfield's office and said, 'I found him.'

"Stanley Kramer and I saw a lot of Nazi types for that role in *Pressure Point*," Hubert Cornfield recalls. "And Paul Newman and Warren Beatty had passed on it. And then came Darin's agent, Steve Blauner. How he got ahold of that script, I don't know. He flipped over it and showed it to Bobby Darin. I told Stanley, 'To me, Darin looks like an Italian Jew. I don't think of him as a Nazi.' But Stanley told me we're not gonna do the film unless we have another star along with Sidney. Sidney at that point couldn't carry a picture by himself. Bobby was a singing star and he had done Cassavetes. So Stanley said to me, 'Look, the guy [Bobby] has such enthusiasm. Enthusiasm can move mountains.' I said, 'You know, Stanley, you're probably right.' I had no real problem with it. I had seen *Too Late Blues*. I thought Bobby was a good actor. As a person I thought he intellectually understood the role completely. I found him a very real, down-to-earth guy."

"The role had once been reserved for Marlon Brando," Steve Blauner says. "Not that Kramer was willing to compare the two. Kramer said that Bobby was reminiscent of a young Jimmy Cagney." Kramer later said, "Bobby intrigues me, the way he comes on. He's got that swagger, that strong personality, that dissatisfied, electric, catching-fire quality. I think he was a wonderful actor. I think he felt pain. And when you feel pain and frustration and some failure as well as success, which he had an inordinate amount of, I think those things [enhance] a person's talent. I can only say I think Bobby touched upon genius to be able to project his personality into an idea, and I'll always be grateful to him for that."

"There's a scene where Sidney is trying to hypnotize Bobby, and Bobby keeps waking up," Cornfield recalls. "I told Bobby, 'I don't want you to artificially mimic heavy breathing. I want you to run around the stage fast.' Bobby said, 'You know I have a heart problem.' I said, 'Don't give me that bullshit.' And he ran around. It could have killed him. I didn't know then. It shows the guy's a real pro."

Bobby's portrayal of the psychotic Nazi who is reluctantly forced to accept the help of the black psychiatrist because his nightmares are tormenting him is a nuanced and complex piece of acting. He manages to allow his loathsome character to dart in and out of sympathetic moments without ever crossing the line into bathos or sentimentality. It's a subtle balancing act. It was characteristic of Darin to take on such a challenging and uncommercial role. The part enabled him to engage artistically in a subject in which he was deeply interested: discrimination against blacks and Jews, the two ethnic groups in addition to Italians with whom he always felt the deepest identification.

"Hubert Cornfield, being a cinematographer, was more interested in the images he was getting and the reflection of the light off the windowpane, and gave no help to the actors," says Steve Blauner. "Of course, Sidney Poitier didn't need any help. Bobby needed all the help he could get. What would happen would be at night is, Sidney Poitier would come to Bobby's house on Rising Glen and they sat in the kitchen. Sidney would rehearse Bobby, go over his lines with him and coach him. When the picture was over, it was totally disjointed. So Bobby went to Kramer. And he said, look, we gotta do something about this. It won't cost you a dime, but let's fix this. So the beginning with Peter Falk and the ending with him were all shot after the picture had shut down. That's what Bobby did. They got Falk coming in for a cameo, providing sort of an explanation, and providing bookends for the picture."

Pressure Point did poorly at the box office. Nevertheless, from Bobby's perspective, it achieved a number of objectives. It advanced his reputation as a serious actor who was working with Hollywood's most respected actors and most acclaimed directors. The London *Observer* noted that Bobby's performance was "brilliant." In the spring of 1962 the Hollywood Foreign Press Association named Bobby the International Star of Tomorrow at the annual Golden Globe Awards.

As Bobby rose higher and higher in the entertainment world, he never forgot the streets where he came from. He reached out to mentor many aspiring performers if he felt they had genuine talent. Tony Orlando had met Bobby through Don Kirshner in New York in 1961 when he was 16, and the following year Bobby invited him for dinner at his house in Beverly Hills. Orlando recalls, "My first time in Beverly Hills at a superstar's house. Pull up in a yellow cab. I sit down and Sandy makes me mashed potatoes and gravy and pork chops. I want to slice the pork chop, and I'll never forget the embarrassment. Here I am: my pork chop slides off my plate and lands on Sandy's dress. And the gravy from the mashed potatoes was all over the napkins and the tablecloth. I covered my face. I was in tears.

"Suddenly Bobby grabbed my hand away and freaked out. He said, 'What's the matter with you? If you're gonna cry over mashed potatoes, you're in a lot of trouble. Mashed potatoes ain't crap.' So Bobby went and put his hand in the mashed potatoes and slammed it on his shirt. Boom! Then he opens up his shirt and slams it on his chest. Boom! He did it to make it even-steven. To make me feel good. Then he sat down with me and talked about learning to differentiate between important things and nonsense. Sandy went and changed her clothes. I tell you, when I walked out of there, I figured no matter what he said to make me feel better, this man will never talk to me again. But what happened was that that incident bonded me and Bobby forever."

The artistic impact of *Pressure Point* would far outweigh the three film duds Bobby had already made in 1962 and would counterbalance his next and fifth film, a lightweight comedy in which he costarred with Sandra, *If a Man Answers.* The film did not do well at the box office, but it advanced Bobby's movie-star status. The tension, contradiction, and pull between Bobby's artistic and commercial goals were all evident in 1961, with Bobby veering between movies about fascism and movies as profound as cotton candy, celebrating Ray Charles (honorably, if inadequately), and abandoning Atlantic for greener pastures at Capitol. Jeff Bleil wrote that a few nights before the opening of *If a Man Answers,* "Darin, Dee, and [Nik] Venet were taking a late-night cab drive down Broadway. The RKO Palace had just erected 30-foot-high cut-outs of Darin and Dee to hang above the marquee. Darin asked the cab driver to pull over just across the street. Darin and Venet got out. 'In the privacy of the night, we stood there in total awe,' Venet recalled. 'He said to me, "Can you believe this?"'

Whatever the future held, on that night Bobby was experiencing the full awareness of having made it. All the struggles had yielded him this. No matter what else happened, he had made a dent. He was up there in lights.

Chapter Ten
A HIGHER CALLING

On March 13, 1963, Bobby opened a successful engagement at Harrah's in Lake Tahoe. Bobby's country-pop song "You're the Reason I'm Living" reached No. 3 on the charts on March 23. But Bobby's personal life was not going well. The marriage had seemed to go downhill from the start. Sandra wanted Bobby for herself. She didn't want his old friends around. She didn't want him to perform in nightclubs.

"When Bobby married Sandra, I didn't get to see him much anymore," Frankie Avalon remembers. "We were like the Dead End Kids to her, especially Charlie Maffia. Charlie was at the house a lot. Charlie was a neighborhood guy, the guy who used to hang out at the candy store. And Nina—oh my God, she adored Bobby—was the kind of a chubby Italian woman that I knew so well. But Sandra wasn't a warm-up kind of a gal to any of us, even our wives."

"Sandra was a little bit of a basket case," says Al Kasha. "You could barely get to see Bobby. She had phobia problems. Alcohol. She was not helpful to his career, I'll tell you that. She was too needy. He married more of an image than a person."

Bobby was striving to keep the marriage together, and one of the things he did for Sandra was to isolate himself from his friends. "One day in 1963, I went to Bobby's office," says Dick Lord. "Bobby said, 'I can't be your friend anymore.' I thought he was joking. I said, 'Right, I don't blame you. I'm not much of a human being.' He said, 'No, I really can't. I have to make it right with Sandy. I don't know how to explain it, but I can't be friends anymore with a lot of people that I love. And that's it.' Then he said, 'Come back and talk to me when you have $80,000 in your pocket, okay?' And then Bobby and I didn't speak for a long time."

"It was annoying to Bobby that Sandy, who was a huge movie star and was treated like a queen, had these attitudes," says Bobby Ramsen. "When he was at the Flamingo Hotel in Vegas, he and Sandy were given a private house on the grounds. I don't care how much money you're making or what kind of star you are, in a club like that in order to get to the stage physically, you gotta walk through the kitchen. Everybody does, unless you want to walk through the audience. So Sandy would say to him, 'You're a big star. Why are you walking through the kitchen?' And it would kill him, her saying that. And Sandra wasn't making thirty thousand a week like Bobby, believe me. Bobby got mad: 'So what if I'm walking through the kitchen? Everybody walks through the kitchen.' Or she would say, 'You have to drive your own car. They send a limousine for me.'"

Just before Bobby would go on stage, Sandra would tell him that his hairpiece was crooked, and he would go charging back to his dressing room, only to find that it was perfectly in place. She would rile him in dozens of ways. She often goaded him about his relationship with Steve Blauner, accusing him of being Steve's "puppet." On one occasion, not getting a rise from Bobby, she turned on Steve. "I've signed 200 autographs today," she said. "How many do you think Bobby signed?" Steve replied furiously, "What you don't realize, Sandy, is that it's not a question of how many autographs you're signing today but how many you'll be signing five years from today." Blauner stormed out of the house.

When he left, the acrimony continued between Bobby and Sandra. She finally said that she thought Steve hung around because he was in love with Bobby. "If you ever insult one of my friends again," he warned her, "I don't know what will happen to us."

Sandra's alcoholism started early and it was a chronic problem between them. Bobby hid the problem from Steve Blauner. "Years later I bumped into a man who had been a friend of Bobby," Blauner recalls, "and he told me that Bobby would call him up late at night. He'd say that Sandy was gone, out drinking. They'd find her with her face down on a bar. And Bobby would say, 'Don't tell Steve.'"

The message to Sandra came in a phone call from Charlie, calling at Bobby's bidding. He said, "Bobby wants a divorce."

"One day Bobby and I were in the men's room," Dick Lord recalls, "and Bobby said to me, 'I think Sandy is in love with someone else.'" Bobby had seen Sandra talking to Warren Beatty at a party. He never mentioned his suspicion to Sandra. They reconciled four months later, with the understanding that Bobby would suspend his nightclub career by the end of the year. Giving up performing was something Bobby would have dreaded doing, but it was Sandra's pressure to have him at home more that was influencing him.

On July 23, 1963, Bobby was performing at Freedomland, an open-air theater in the Bronx. Although there was a pouring rain, Bobby had insisted on not using an umbrella. The audience had cheered him when he said that if they could stand in the rain to listen to him, he was not going to claim the privilege of staying dry while performing for them.

Bobby collapsed after the show, taking oxygen to still his erratic heartbeat. Carol Fellenstein, Bobby's secretary, remembers that night. "He had an oxygen tent: not a tank, but a tent. I remember the plastic. It was the first time I had seen it. His condition scared the hell out of me. He looked so little; he was slight in build."

Bobby was admitted to Mount Sinai Hospital in Los Angeles on July 31, 1963, for observation. The doctors told Bobby to rest for eight weeks and not engage in physical activity. In October, at the height of his career, he retired from performing. He made the announcement from the stage of the Flamingo in Vegas. Bobby had decided to concentrate on his songwriting and had already purchased Trinity Music from his former managers, Joe Csida and Ed Burton, in February 1963 and invested $500,000 in developing the business, which he renamed T. M. Music. Bobby installed Ed Burton as executive vice-president and general manager and moved the office to the Brill Building at Broadway and 49th Street. By October he had already gathered together a group of outstanding songwriters at T. M., including Arthur Reznick, Rudy Clark, Terry Melcher, Frank Gari, Debbie Stanley, and Kenny Young. Bobby installed Bobby Scott as manager.

"There were any number of reasons people have given as to why Bobby stopped performing," says Hesh Wasser. "I say it was because he was warned by his doctors that if he kept singing, he would be a dead man. That's one of the reasons he opened up the publishing house, because he couldn't keep going on tour. He was putting a lot of strain on himself by performing."

"I think Bobby was hiding behind why he was quitting," Steve Blauner says. "A lot of people thought it was his marriage. But I think that the real reason was empty seats, which he would never address. They were out of love with him, he thought, but what had happened was the nightclub business itself was slowly fading. With the advent of free TV, people didn't go out to clubs anymore. In Syracuse, at the Three Rivers Inn, I'd go out in the audience and pretend I was a waiter and drop trays.—Or, once when he came out on stage, I had a vase and I was trying to play it like a violin under my chin to crack him up—or anything to get him in the mood and take his mind off the sparse crowds. Then I realized it was the fear of failing. With an entertainer, you have to go out there, what if they don't laugh, what if there's silence, you're just naked all the time and have to deliver. The impact when they stop coming is devastating."

"Let's face it, he was really losing his career in 1963," says Darin archivist Jimmy Scalia, who has just produced a new compilation of songs from Bobby's later folk-rock period, *Lost Masters from Big Sur.* "Bobby went on hiatus, when he was doing the publishing. Then he comes back, over and over again. I mean if you were a prizefighter, how many hits could you take like that?"

"When Bobby decided to create some kind of a publishing company," Hesh Wasser says, "it was natural for him to come to New York because of Ed Burton, who was a father figure to Bobby and part of a three-way management team. T. M. Music was initially very successful, publishing Bobby's new hits, '18 Yellow Roses' and 'You're the Reason I'm Living.' Soon the songwriters in Bobby's stable at T. M. were producing hits of their own.

"Bobby was very committed to his own songwriting too," Wasser continues. "He wanted people to remember what he had to say, but he felt he could only do it fully if he did it with his own words. So he did what he felt he had to do at the time. Because of the way his life was laid out, what was really most important to him was the risk-taking. He always had the attitude that there's nothing you can't do if you really want to."

"It was a fun atmosphere at T. M. Music," remembers Carol Fellenstein, Bobby's secretary. "Pianos going—it was a hallway full of offices with pianos in them. Bobby's office was at the end. He also had a piano in there. We heard the songs being developed from beginning to end. Bobby abused his body. I made his coffee for him. He drank about 30 cups a day. He had this urn in his office, and he smoked incessantly. He was a hard driver, and he drove himself the hardest.

"Rudy Clark wrote 'The Shoop Shoop Song (It's In His Kiss)' while I was there, and it was enormous. And Rudy cowrote with Artie Resnick 'Good Lovin,' a number-one hit. The Drifters did 'Up on the Roof' by Artie Resnick and Kenny Young, Ben E. King did Artie's 'I've Got Sand in My Shoes,' and Artie also had 'Under the Boardwalk,' a huge hit for the Drifters. Bobby wrote tunes with Terry Melcher, including 'Hot Rod U.S.A.' for the Rip Chords. Two doors away were Lieber and Stoller. It was very exciting."

T. M. Music had also expanded into TV and record production. Bobby was an extraordinary talent spotter, and one of the first singers he spotted for his company was Wayne Newton. "Bobby calls me up in 1963 and says, 'Meet me at the Copa at midnight,'" Steve Blauner recalls. "I'm thinking. What the hell am I going to the Copa for at midnight? But I go up there. Bobby and I were sitting in Jules Podell's booth in the lounge and the conversation is boring me. I felt someone staring; out of the corner of my eye I see Bobby is staring at me. I thought, This is why I'm here. We went downstairs after the show and I signed Wayne Newton to a recording contract. And so Bobby was going to produce him.

"Wayne had that high-pitched voice. The publisher was freaked out because who the hell is Wayne Newton? They gave this exclusive because it was Bobby Darin. 'Mack the Knife' had happened. And this song, 'Danke Schoen,' was 'Mack the Knife' sideways, the tempo and everything. Anyhow, the result was a hit for Wayne Newton. And that was the beginning of that relationship."

"Bobby said that for 'Danke Schoen,' Wayne's voice would work," recalls Bobby's conductor, Bobby Rozario. "A high voice. He thought it was a girl singing in the lounge when he walked by, and when he looked up he saw a young man. And immediately Bobby's brain started clicking. And he says, 'I don't wanna do 'Danke Schoen.' I'll get this guy to do 'Danke Schoen.' They said, 'But we want you.' He said, 'Well, let's do it this way. I'll record him. If he gets a hit, fine, you'll be happy. If it's not a hit, then I'll do it.'"

"Bobby brought this guy to his office one time," remembers songwriter Rudy Clark, who worked for Bobby at T. M. Music. "He looked strange to me. He was big but he had a baby face. He had on these highwater pants that came way up above his ankles, and when I saw this guy I laughed. And Bobby took me aside and said, 'Don't laugh at this guy. This guy is going to be the biggest name in the music business. I'm taking him out to Vegas. Wayne Newton.'"

In his 1989 memoir, *Once Before I Go*, Wayne Newton expressed gratitude for the mentoring Bobby had given him and the chance to record "Danke Schoen." Newton offers a glimpse into Bobby's state of mind during that period.

> *I went to see Bobby at the Flamingo. I would visit him for inspiration. I went into his dressing room . . . He was sitting there with his head down, his hand on his forehead. I thought, What in the world could he be sad about? I stood behind him for a moment and finally, trying to break the depression that I could feel in the room, said, "What's bothering you?" He looked up in the mirror with tears in his eyes. "One day you'll understand," he said.*

He also recounted a traumatic story Bobby had shared with him about his childhood: "When he was a youngster, he shined shoes in New York City. A guy once gave him five bucks for a shoeshine that only cost ten cents. Bobby looked up and said, 'I don't have any change.' The guy looked down at this little kid and said, 'I'm not expecting any change. Take the money and get your face fixed.'"

Newton, of all people, understood that story of Bobby's. The story conjured up all the early embarrassments and humiliations he endured because of his appearance and high girlish voice. Newton went on to recount the first time he heard his recording of "Danke Schoen" on the radio.

"The disc jockey said, 'Here's a brand-new record that's an absolute smash, and it's supposedly being sung by a guy named Wayne Newton, but I happen to know it's Margaret Whiting recording under a different name.'" Newton wrote: "I had the number-one hit record in the country, I had Michael Jackson's voice . . . but back then all it brought me were attacks of vitriolic humor. I was the joke of the industry. But one man never laughed. He was a giant among men. He was Bobby Darin and he was my friend."

Meanwhile, things were jumping at T. M. Music as Bobby completed assembling his creative staff. Roger McGuinn of the Byrds, who was then Jim McGuinn, remembers meeting Bobby at Gene Norman's

Crescendo on Sunset Strip in Los Angeles, where Bobby had come to see Lenny Bruce. "I was playing with the Chad Mitchell Trio," McGuinn says. "Bobby saw my thing that I was doing. He came backstage and hired me to work with him on stage and to work for his publishing company. He said he wanted to add a folk segment to his show."

Bobby's country song "18 Yellow Roses" was a big hit at the time, shooting to No. 10 on the charts. "I played some sessions around the '18 Yellow Roses' period," McGuinn remembers. "Bobby would sing his hits for some 15 minutes, take off his tie, and bring me out. We'd share a spotlight in the middle of the stage and did three songs together—including Leadbelly's 'It Makes a Longtime Man Feel Bad' and Woody Guthrie's 'Alberta, Let Your Hair Down Low'—with the rhythm section and my 12-string guitar and harmony. After our stint, he'd do his standards. He was a great influence on me. He was from the vaudeville mentality of doing it professionally; he was like your shoes are polished, your suit is pressed, you're on time and in tune, and you hit the mark every time, instead of what I ran into later: rock and roll, where you're late and stoned and out of tune."

It was McGuinn who told Bobby about Bob Dylan. McGuinn would hang out in Greenwich Village at Gerde's Folk City and the Gaslight for hootenannies and jammed with Dave Van Ronk. Dylan, Woody Allen, and Bill Cosby would be there. "I told Bobby, 'There's a kid in the village calls himself Bob Dylan.' And Bobby laughed because he thought it was somebody trying to rip off his name. And soon he really got into Dylan, with the Levi jacket, and took his toupee off and really got down and funky. He was into what we used to call the ethnic folk music. I respected his integrity in selecting the songs he did and performing them with a kind of style that he did: Leadbelly, Woody Guthrie. The real stuff.

"He was a superman. Most people plug along at 30 percent of their capacity. He was going at 110. He didn't drink or do drugs. He'd have a black coffee with sugar before going onstage. Bobby was very confident, kind of brash. But he had a heart of gold. And the direction of the Byrds, the folk rock thing, was a direct result of working with Bobby. Because he told me, 'Rock and roll, get into rock and roll.' So while I was with him, I started combining the Beatles beat with folk music and I put together what they call folk rock. It was Bobby's idea basically.

"I love his rock. I love his Sinatra-style stuff and 'Mack.' Everything he did he did with his whole heart. He flew by the seat of his pants. He could think on his feet. And he was generous. One night after I got through, I leaned my guitar up against the piano after I got done while Bobby went out and did the rest of his set. In the middle of his set, he put his hand on the piano and it moved because it was on wheels. My guitar fell to the floor and cracked the neck off. The next day Bobby bought me a new guitar. He didn't just pay for it, he actually sent Charlie Maffia out to buy one at the music store and presented it to me."

"I was asked by Jeff Barry, who was a well-known songwriter, to sign with Bobby, who had purchased T. M. Music," recalls Arthur Resnick. "He was sharp, Bobby—and why not have your own songs and your own publishing and everything else? He was lonely. He'd come over to my house in Queens and my wife would make spaghetti. He would pick me up in a limousine and we would go trout fishing. Bobby had the funniest kind of laugh: *Er, er, er, er!* When he did his Robert Mitchum, it was wonderful. He'd move his head over to the left, with his chin in his chest, and stretch his face out a little bit, and he did look exactly like Mitchum."

Bobby's business acumen combined with his artistic instincts to make a great success out of T. M. Music. T. M.'s gross business rose from $321,000 in 1963, the initial year, to $450,000 in 1964. But with the arrival of the Beatles, the musical world was never the same again. The Beatles had 19 singles in the Top 40 of that year. By then some of the major singers, including Steve Lawrence and Eydie Gorme, Kay

Starr, Johnny Hartman, Tony Bennett, Della Reese, and Dakota Staton, among many others, no longer had major-label contracts.

JUST AS BOBBY HAD COMPLETED his transformation from rocker to a mature interpreter of standards, both ballads and swing, the ground again shifted under his feet. But the British invasion of rock was one development Bobby could not absorb into his many musical incarnations. It hurt all the American performers of standards, but more so with Bobby. After all, Bobby had walked away from being a rock-and-roll singer; he didn't want to return to that. His timing was off, but partly that was the consequence of the time pressure he was under. He would shift and shift again. In that dizzying process, his most valuable gift—his capacity for greatness—would suffer. In 1963 he was moving toward folk music.

Bobby was constantly in conflict. He was in revolt against himself. He was in revolt against materialism. He was in revolt against uncommercial art in that he wanted to get all the way to the top; he was an idealist but he would do anything to make it; he was in revolt against mendacity and slickness and glitz, and he was the personification of Las Vegas and Copacabana glitz. He was the best of it, and he was the last of it.

But there was also a sense in which there existed something precious and true in show-business glitz. It was a place where the Durantes and Sinatras and Dean Martins and Judy Garlands and Jolsons and Sophie Tuckers could shine; despite all its sheen and illusion, at its best it had a purity of heart, a simplicity, a truth, a universality, a genuineness. "How Bobby loved Sophie Tucker," Bobby Rozario recalls. "He did the first chorus of 'Some of These Days' like Sophie. He would rent old movies where she sang, he had her records, and Jolson's. He studied those great entertainers; he paid homage to them always. He'd see what they did right. He sang 'About a Quarter to Nine.' That was Jolson. He shared the bill with Durante when we performed at rallies for Bobby Kennedy. He loved them because they were great entertainers and knew how to reach the people. That's what he wanted to do. He came along that line. These were people who had to come on a stage cold without flashing lights and loud music. They had to stand there and entertain. There was no help from anybody. It was just them and the microphone and the audience."

According to pianist and composer Roger Kellaway, who arranged Bobby's great *Doctor Doolittle* album, the most authentic and vibrant performers Kellaway has ever encountered were vaudevillians and Dixieland performers—Bobby's progenitors, Bobby's roots and basis. Bobby was passionately drawn to two of the very greatest vaudevillians of all, George Burns and Jimmy Durante, and he utilized traditional Dixieland jazz greats like Nick Fatool and Eddie Miller in some of his greatest records, which were apparently lost in an Atlantic storehouse fire. Some of these recordings have recently been recovered and will undoubtedly be reissued in the future, including an incredibly smoking Dixieland record by Bobby, "Weeping Willow," that swings with the best he ever recorded. There is also an extant videotape of excerpts from these recording sessions on a 1966 documentary entitled *Return to the Coconut Grove* that has just been released to the public.

These talented musicians and entertainers were irreplaceable because every thing they did came from their souls. Pretense was unthinkable for them. Bobby melted at the sight of them; he loved them deeply. And he loved Nick Fatool and Eddie Miller so much because he was like them. And they loved him for the same reason. Yet he recoiled from being what he was, wanted to rise above it and become invulnerable, and yearned for the transcendent, the exotic, and even the pretentious. This was still the sickly street kid without an overcoat in winter, the self-conscious Bobby, shielded by the dictionary, who can be heard on some radio and TV interviews. Bobby desperately wanted to be taken seriously, not realizing just how serious—how immense—his innate talent and intelligence were.

Bobby was at heart a Broadway baby, son of Irving Berlin and Sammy Cahn and Jimmy McHugh and Rodgers and Hart and George M. Cohan, and he was ashamed of that fact. He wanted to be an intellectual and a truth-teller and a seer, but child of the slums that he was, with one semester of college to his credit, he was not schooled. He did not read deeply—he dipped into Allen Ginsberg's *Howl* and loved Jack Kerouac's *On the Road* and embraced the counterculture; it was an attitudinal thing. His intellectual attention span was really sustainable only for chess. He wanted so desperately to escape himself that he would soon remodel his image on Bob Dylan's, even change his name to Bob Darin, switch to denim and jeans, grow a moustache, and appear on an album cover looking like the shadow of Dylan.

"I always remember," says Al Kasha, "that I was fascinated when I met with Bobby at T. M. Music to find him smoking a pipe—suddenly he had a pipe in his mouth. Always changing his image. Bobby's whole career, which helped him and hurt him, is that on many records he was somebody else. On 'You're the Reason I'm Living' he's Ray Charles. He's partly Frankie Laine on 'Mack the Knife.' When he made 'Mack,' he told me, 'Everybody thinks I'm doing Sinatra. And I'm not. I really love Frankie Laine. I'm singing more like him than like Sinatra. And Bobby was right. If you listen to Laine sing 'Mule Train,' he's very clipped. And Bobby: 'I-can-only-give-you-love-that-lasts-forever' on 'That's All'—that's the Frankie Laine clipped phrasing, not the longer phrasing of Sinatra. I mean, it's Bobby, but he's influenced, he's affected.

"He achieved a firmly etched identity in the public's eye with 'Mack,' 'Beyond the Sea,' 'Clementine,' 'Lazy River.' That was the full image. He broke away from that foolishly. Those standards, that was really him. He did certain things that he owned. Bobby's transition to 'Mack the Knife' was an audience-pleaser; the transitions that came later were not. He said, 'I'm bigger than the audience.' He did what he wanted to do. You can't change on an audience; audiences don't like that. Even Sinatra, when he was fooling around with Ava Gardner and left his wife, with kids, he really lost. He had to disappear for a while, until he could come back with the swinging-lover image. It took four or five years."

Bobby could only be great when he was himself, and he never understood this. At the core of that misunderstanding was a lack of belief in himself. Picasso and Braque influenced each other, but they never gave up their own genius. Bobby did get lost in others. "Trying on so many musical hats," James Wolcott wrote, "he neglected the reason lesson Sinatra taught, which is: If you can't make a song distinctively yours, lose it; otherwise, you're just carrying someone else's baggage."

And the truth—as he understood it—did not set him free. It frayed his image. Bobby was beginning to be all over the map, and this diffused identity would take its toll on his popularity. It made him angry and poor and unable to obtain the hugely expensive medical care he needed to stay alive.

And, like most truth, it was not set in stone.

"UNIVERSAL WAS PLANNING A FILM called *Captain Newman, M.D.*," recalls Steve Blauner, "and I had read the book. I wanted Bobby to play the Labelwitz role opposite Gregory Peck. The part was perfect for Bobby. This Labelwitz was a wise guy. It would be especially great for Bobby going opposite Gregory Peck, who was like cement. A good actor, but very stiff. Bobby had a seven-picture deal with Universal; he also had one at Paramount. Peck was looking for help, box-office.

"We had offices at Universal. Right across the way was Tony Curtis. Tony would be in my office, I'd be in his office. Kibbitzing all day. I told Tony about this picture. He came into the office one day and said, 'Look, Steve, you were right about that picture and that part. And Lew Wasserman says that if I do this picture with Peck, he'll then make *Monsieur Cognac* with me, bup bup bup . . .'

"So they're taking Tony, who was a big star at that time, instead of Bobby. The book was episodic, about a shrink with episodes of what he had encountered in the Air Force. I pick up the phone and call the head of the studio. I said, 'Is the character Little Jim in the picture?' 'Yes.' 'Is he in it like in the book?' 'Yes.' 'I want Bobby to play the part.' 'Jesus, we can't afford Bobby.' I said, 'What's the price; what are you budgeted?' '$25,000.' I said, 'You got a deal, and it won't be part of our seven-picture contract either.' Then I said, 'We'll come up with a billing for Bobby; you can't bill him above the titles.' Well, they had never heard of this before. 'Why?' the guy said. I said, 'Look, you got Gregory Peck, you got Tony Curtis. You've got Angie Dickinson. Bobby's going to be in the picture 15, 20 minutes. It wouldn't be fair to his fans. We'll figure something out below the titles.'

"Well," Blauner continues, "that was not really my reason. If you were billed above the title, you had to qualify for best actor for the Academy Awards. If you were below the titles, you could only qualify for supporting actor.

"So I send Bobby the script. A few days later I get a phone call. 'Why am I doing this picture?' he says. He'd counted the pages he was in. If he walked away from this deal, I probably would have quit. I used to quit every other day anyhow. I said to him, 'I'll tell you why, Bobby. Because if you are one-tenth the actor I think you are, you will get an Academy Award nomination for this role. That's what this role will mean to you.' I said, 'Now about actually winning the Academy Award, I can't guarantee that, because it becomes a popularity contest. You've alienated enough people in this town. But the nomination you'll get.' 'Okay,' he says.

"Now when the nominations came out, I go over to his house to congratulate him. And I hug him. And he says into my ear, 'You were right.' Now that made me feel better than if I had gotten a ten-million-dollar check."

Directed by David Miller, *Captain Newman, M. D.* was an effective antiwar film in which Gregory Peck portrayed a psychiatrist attempting to patch up shell-shocked soldiers so that they can continue fighting in the war. Bobby played Corporal Jim Tompkins, a flyer who failed to rescue his friend from a burning plane and, consumed with guilt, was psychologically self-destructing. In Bobby's major, electrifying scene, Corporal Tompkins was given sodium pentothal by Captain Newman (Peck), broke down, and confronted his traumatic memories of his last mission. In one take, Bobby brilliantly captured

Tompkins's reliving the terrible experience and dissolving into spasmodic sobs.

He would never have such a challenging film role again.

OH! LOOK AT ME NOW was Bobby's first album of standards for Capitol, and it's an unalloyed delight. Working for the first time with Billy May's big band, this is one of the albums that showcases Bobby at his height, the essential Bobby, caressing the standards he loved, rendering them in new and totally unexpected ways. There's a lot of Irving Berlin here—magnificent, swinging versions of "Always," "All By Myself," and "Blue Skies"; a haunting version of Donaldson and Kahn's "My Buddy"; knockout upside-down takes on "Roses of Picardy" and "A Nightingale Sang in Berkeley Square" with a terrific brass arrangement; achingly vulnerable renditions of "You'll Never Know," "You Made Me Love You," and "The Party's Over"; a vibrant homage to Jolson in "There's a Rainbow 'Round My Shoulder"; and romping versions of the title track and "I'm Beginning to See the Light."

The album did not do well. Bobby had walked away from rock just as the Beatles would give it a whole new vital spin, and he was bucking a tide that overtook the music industry. He could not survive with the standards alone. He chose another alternative. Folk music had become a stronghold of popular music by late 1962, and Bobby had been moving in that direction for some time with the incorporation of a folk segment into his act with Roger McGuinn. Bobby had long been a fan of Cisco Houston and Tom Paxton, and he had a genuine feeling for the music. But did he love it? Well, perhaps he loved himself for doing it.

Bobby's next albums for Capitol were two folk-music forays. *Earthy* contained spirituals, prison and chain-gang songs, talking blues, and a Haitian song. Bobby recruited a friend from Bronx Science, Walter Raim, who had been working with Harry Belafonte, to arrange and conduct the album. "Bobby saw in folk music a sophistication of some kind," Raim recalls, "a higher calling. He had in his mind that he was doing something more important than singing Las Vegas standards. He was attracted to the realness, the down-to-earth thing."

There are few surprises here, unlike Bobby's creative interpretation of the standards or his rock songs. The character Bobby creates is not himself, and he doesn't sound like himself. Even while he masters these songs technically, and despite the poignant subject matter, he doesn't bring total conviction to them. There is something cerebral and distant about the entire undertaking, even though the prison songs, "Long Time Man" and Oscar Brown Jr. and Nat Adderly's "Work Song"—backed by bass and drums—are superbly done.

Golden Folk Hits contains many of the same virtues and shortcomings of Bobby's first folk album. Darin does more contemporary folk here, including strong versions of "Don't Think Twice" and "Blowin' in the Wind" (Dylan), "Where Have All the Flowers Gone?" (Seeger) and "If I Had a Hammer" (Hays and Seeger), and traditional spirituals including "Mary Don't You Weep" and "Michael Row the Boat Ashore." "Abilene," a flowing soft-folk number done with uncharacteristic ease and naturalness is simply wonderful, the standout on the album. Overall: serious, well-meaning, conscientious, well-sung, loaded with integrity, but they seem almost like reverential museum pieces. Bobby is somehow lost in the mix. Walter Raim told Bleil, "Although he wanted to do this very much, it was not who he was."

Bobby had a deeply political side to him, and the events of the 1960s conjoined to move him toward both a more activist role in the civil-rights movement and a different way of expressing himself musically and artistically. "Darin thought the civil-rights movement was the great revolution of the 20th century," Nik Venet told Jeff Bleil. "The man was civil rights conscious long before it became radical chic. It was a passion of his . . . You didn't have your younger entertainers at that time going on campaigns about civil rights. The mainstream entertainment industry was hands-off that subject. Talking about it now seems mild, but at the time, Darin put his whole career, and the possibility of getting blacklisted, on the line."

He took part in civil-rights marches anonymously. Bobby took part in the March on Washington in 1963 and many other demonstrations.

"Bobby didn't feel the kind of music he was performing was enough," says Hesh Wasser. "There had to be more said about the world, about what was going on. He was very much a person of his time. He wasn't looking to be some 20-year-old living in this show-business world of 50-year-olds."

Bobby had been a supporter and admirer of John F. Kennedy from the start. He was in rehearsal on the set of Judy Garland's TV show on November 23, 1963, when the news of JFK's assassination reached the studio. Bobby's radicalization intensified on that day.

The downward spiral of assassinations had only begun. The sense of joyful commonality generated in the first protest years of the 1960s would give way to a mood of darkening violence and pessimism in the United States about the possibilities of genuine social change.

"Darin got caught in the world's biggest music transition—from what it was to what it was going to become," Nik Venet told *Goldmine*. "He bridged the gap, that chasm, successfully, but at the same time, honestly. Darin could talk about Louis Armstrong and also about Elvis Presley, and understand both of them, and their success, and their music, and their styles. And *appreciate* both of them. He didn't [bridge any gap] because it was happening; he did it because it was him."

"Bobby Darin was drawn to what he did by the right instincts," reflected Bruce Charet. "His own experience is a metaphor for the whole conflict of that period of the sixties. Because you have Bobby with one foot in one generation and one foot in the other, and it's ripping him apart. And that was what America was going through.

"A friend in Vegas, a musician who worked all of Bobby's shows, told me that Bobby was the first act ever in Vegas to use two rhythm sections on the stage. He had the entire normal swing orchestra, and then he also had a rock rhythm section. That was emblematic of the conflict he had between generations. He was trying to be both."

"When Bobby decided to retire and break up the band," says Ronnie Zito, "I think he was floundering. I thought something was going on, either with his marriage or something else."

Whatever the extent of his "retirement" from nightclubs, Bobby was being battered by storms from within and without.

Bobby's last performance for 1963 was on *The Judy Garland Show* on December 29. It had actually been taped shortly after JFK's assassination in a studio atmosphere of sadness and grieving. Bobby dueted with Garland on a medley of perky, traditional show-business songs. Later on the program, however, he appeared by himself in a stark setting, no suit or tie, just a white shirt and slacks. He sang two spirituals from his new folk record: "Michael Row the Boat Ashore" and "I'm On My Way."

Caught between two worlds, he could not make up his mind.

Chapter Eleven

SLIP-SLIDING AWAY

On February 24, 1964, the Motion Picture Academy announced that Bobby had received a nomination for Best Supporting Actor for *Captain Newman, M. D.* Steve Blauner's prediction had come true.

Bobby rode to the Academy Award ceremony on April 7 in the Santa Monica Civic Auditorium in the Bobby Darin Dream Car, the automobile Andy DiDia had built. It looked fantastic: burgundy-over-ice and sparkling in sunlight, it was a glossy aluminum, glass, and chrome affair. Its fins flared like a bird's wings; headlights, windshield wipers, and door handles were hidden by its exterior. It looked like something Batman would drive. The car had a superpowered Ford engine and a Cadillac transmission. Its electrical system caused windows to drop, and headlights to pop open, and a T-roof to expose the stars.

The Dream Car encapsulated some of the glamour, magic, high velocity, and golden success associated with Bobby in those years—but also their precariousness: the car broke down almost instantly.

"I designed it in 1953," says DiDia. "When Bobby drove the car to the Academy Awards, I and Steve Blauner followed behind him in a limousine. The car had two fans and a switch that you had to turn on. Bobby didn't realize, so it heated up. All the magazines said the car caught fire, but it didn't."

"Andy was building that car for years," Steve Blauner recalls. "He had said he didn't know if the car would ride. I said, look, we'll put Bobby in the car a block or so away from the building, and we'll follow, so nothing happens. So Bobby gets in the car, and here comes this Rolls Royce, and who opens the window and leans out but Liz Taylor and Eddie Fisher. 'Where did you get that car?' And they're carrying on about the car, because there was nothing like it. It's in the National Museum of Transportation in St. Louis now. Well, all of a sudden, the car broke down and started to steam. Smoke was coming out of it. So we got Bobby in and dropped him off at the Civic Center."

Bobby was competing with John Huston, Hugh Griffith, Melvin Douglas, and Nick Adams for Best Supporting Actor, but he felt optimistic about his chances. The Oscar went to Melvin Douglas for his role in *Hud*. Bobby took the news hard. He never thought he would live beyond 30, and he was 28. Time was short. The loss was somewhat mitigated by his receiving the French Film Critics' Award for best foreign actor and a Foreign Press Golden Globe nomination.

Bobby was no longer performing in clubs in 1964, and his other activities were also more limited. Nineteen sixty-four was the year of the Beatles, and he didn't have a Top 40 hit for the first time since 1957. It seemed symbolic that his first single of the year for Capitol was a 1909 chestnut, "I Wonder Who's Kissing Her Now."

He began shooting his only film of the year, *That Funny Feeling*, with Sandra and Donald O'Connor on October 9. Richard Wess was collaborating with Bobby on the score, which included Bobby's composition, a lively and feisty number, as the title tune.

BOBBY'S MARRIAGE was an ongoing effort to maintain equilibrium. Sandra made no friends, and her isolation increased her dependence on alcohol. She did not have the language, the experience of life, to express what she felt to Bobby: the loneliness, the pressures of working all day on the set and trying to please Bobby as well, staying up all night with Bobby when he did a recording session or hung with his friends. The grueling schedule and her depression combined to make her sluggish and exhausted all the time. She became addicted to speed as well as alcohol. The speed brought her up; the alcohol brought her down.

Bobby found her increasingly oblivious and impossible to communicate with, her language slurred or feverishly animated, her physical appearance alarming, and on a hunch he took the pills in her drawer to the druggist. When he found out they were speed, he threw them all out.

But even when she was coherent and sober, they were worlds apart. Bobby had his pals, the guys he'd struggled with on the streets of New York, people to whom he was loyal and whom he loved. The affluent trappings of Hollywood, the status and celebrity, the swimming pool and valets, dropped lightly off him. Dick Lord recalls Bobby coming to his house and sleeping in his son's bed, enjoying the sound of his fish tank at night.

And there were many other consequential differences between them. Bobby loved the sparks of intellectual exchange and debate, of testing his wits against others and finding out new things and deepening his understanding. He wanted dialogue, openness, argument, communication. He had very little time; he didn't want to waste it. He needed to love what he did, and he was constantly searching for new ways of experiencing the high of creativity. If he was stuck in one groove, he felt calcified. Creativity came from watching, listening, feeling, reading, experimenting, and grooving with musicians and friends. And there was a suffering world out there that he connected to, the civil-rights revolution cracking the rock of segregation.

"I remember sitting in the chair in the middle of the room," recalls Steve Blauner, "and Bobby's sitting next to me. Sandy's there on the couch, and she's putting Bobby down through me. She says, 'If he tells you to bow, you bow.' It was vicious."

Bobby loved Sandra, but it was not working.

And it was not only an intellectual and emotional mismatch. "Bobby was into intergalactic sex," a friend of his says. "After a while he wasn't faithful as a husband. I went to a couple of orgies with him. He had enormous sexual energy, like everything else he did. My wife fell for him. It was one of those group sex things. You know, I still loved the guy, and I figured it was my fault. I was trying to be hip, part of that hipster thing. So I never had any resentment about that. My wife turned out to be a sex queen in Los Angeles. The marriage broke up right after that. I never held it against Bobby."

The spoken or unspoken assumption in all the accounts of Bobby and Sandra is that Sandra was the unstable one and the cause of the marriage's failure. All interpretations begin from that point. It is likely to stay that way, since Sandra has never been able to articulate how she saw the marriage and what really happened, and she grants no book interviews. In her March 18, 1991, article for *People* magazine, she did offer some cogent and moving explanations for the problems in the marriage. But her disclosure of her stepfather's sexual abuse and of her own addiction problems were what caught national attention and have only tended to underscore a public perception of her as a dysfunctional—although essentially decent and loving—wife and mother, a victim of her childhood.

Sandra went on to write of her anorexia during her early years working in Hollywood and that after she married, she suffered six miscarriages. "A doctor later told me they were due to the horrible way I treated my body," she wrote. She described her wedding night: "I thought I had blocked out the abuse, but on my wedding night, it all came back. I was scared. I sat on the couch for 12 hours in my coat. Bobby finally went to bed. I didn't tell him about my stepfather until after we were divorced. I didn't want him to look at me as if I were dirty. He didn't. When I told him, he cried."

She also underscored her own dysfunctionality by writing that at the time of her mother's death in 1988, "I died too. I couldn't function. I didn't know how to write a check. I didn't know where the phone company was. I'd been sheltered beyond belief. All the people

I loved were now gone . . . So I drank. I could put away a quart and a half a day easy."

Despite Sandra's resentment toward the time Bobby spent with his friends, he remained loyal to them. "When Bobby first came on *American Bandstand*," Dick Clark remembers, "he was very brash, very bold, in control, even though he'd had no success to warrant that. He had a hard edge in public, full of bravado. But I used to laugh when people told me Bobby was an arrogant little S.O.B. If you knew him, he was the kindest, most generous person. When I needed something, he was there at my beck and call. On one occasion, after my first wife and I had split, I had fallen on some rather bad times. I was drinking a little more than I should have. And Bobby was there to encourage me and help me and say get over it and move on with your life."

"I was just starting out as a comic," Dick Lord says. "Bobby had asked me to come to the recording studio where he was doing a session. So now I'm leaving. Bobby says, 'Where you going? Wait a minute.' And he takes a check out of his pocket and he says, 'Buy a car. You have a child. You ride around in that piece of shit. It's dangerous.'"

"Bobby was very supportive of me," remembers Carol Lynley, who had a lifetime friendship with Bobby. "I was very young and bringing up a child alone, working to support her; I had no child support at all. So I was a little fragile myself. Bobby lived nearby in Malibu. He had left Sandra. I used to take him horseback riding. You thought of him as an urban guy, but he was excellent on a horse. We used to go through trails and waterfalls. When Bobby came over to the house with Dodd, he would sit at the head of the table, he would be the man for the kids, he did what an Italian daddy would do. It was very helpful for me. He was very caring. He was very paternal, in a lightweight way. Just by being there. Not running away. A lot of people would react like, 'Sorry, that's nice, you with the kid, but I don't want to know about you.' Bobby was quite the opposite. Bobby wanted the responsibility. And he did it in such a graceful way.

"Bobby was like a cyclone hit me, and he was very determined. So that if he wanted to be your friend, you were his friend, don't even think about it. You still feel the presence even now. And of course when I see Dodd, I lose it. Because not only does he look like Bobby, he sounds like Bobby. He's got the same voice, and he's around the same age that Bobby was when I last saw him. I know how much Bobby loved him. And he was a very good father. He was the kind of guy that people thought, oh you know, Las Vegas, and all that. But he was a very good family man.

"He had a rhythm and a speech pattern that was very quick and quite musical. And darting. He'd go jump jump jump. And he could take you with him when he jumped, because he was so articulate. And his eyes took in everything. They stayed with you. He could verbalize what he felt, what he felt you felt. Bobby focused on other things besides himself. He had wonderful focus."

BOBBY WAS BACK with arranger Richard Wess for his new Capitol album, *Hello Dolly to Goodbye Charlie*. Darin and Wess create magic together. Bobby was at the top, the peak of his game here, offering the most beautiful versions of these songs ever done by an American singer. Wess brought out Darin's most extraordinary singing, and this album is a keeper. Almost every song sounds like a surprise, transcendent, in the hands of a vocal genius. "Hello Dolly" had been done not only by Louis Armstrong, but by just about everyone—in fact, done to death. It was a creaky piece to begin with. Bobby not only resurrects it but breathes a whole new life into it. The arrangement begins with the "Mack" bass line, and it feels initially as if it's going to be simply a reprise of the "Mack" style. The song keeps rising in the spirit of "Mack," and why not? Bobby's happy here, and the joyousness is contagious.

Here's where the comparisons to Sinatra are inevitable: the passion, the drive, and the energy are absolutely overwhelming. Bobby flies, and when he sings, "It's so nice to have you back where you belong," it's really Bobby who seems back, in his own element, Broadway alight, doing what he does best. It's a risk to end with an echo of "Mack":

"Look out, old Dolly is back!" and it would have been disastrous if Bobby had not outdone himself here.

The pace keeps building with "Call Me Irresponsible" with Bobby swinging this one to death, unlike the way anyone else could ever have dreamed of doing it. Here again the music builds and builds. Bobby chews and bites the lyrics; he's never sounded more potent or more sensual. You can't stand still to this. He growls his way through a brilliant "Once in a Lifetime," particularly on the word "moment"—and you know this is instilling a lyric with true depth and understanding.

"Days of Wine and Roses" is the first ballad on the album, and Bobby sings his heart out, his rendition so smooth, full-throated, and flowing, the words drawn out languorously, passionate, and strong. It's a beautiful, haunting interpretation. "More," which Ann-Margret, Jack Lemmon, and Walter Matthau danced to at the conclusion of *Grumpier Old Men*, is undeniable and smashing, a pulsating triumph. Bobby sings, "No one else could love you *more*"—he shouts the word, imbuing it with its real meaning of something beyond.

In each of the songs on this album, Bobby illustrates the meaning of Al Kasha's description of his "sounding like the words . . . you say 'hush,' it sounds like *hush*; 'loud' it's *loud* . . . 'soft' it's *soft*." Listen to the word "more" on the song and "moment" on "Once in a Lifetime," and you will understand what he means.

"When Bobby worked with Richard Wess," says Bruce Charet, "he sounded like Bobby Darin [alone]. There was a creative integrity to the sound. Listen to 'New York on Sunday.' That's perfect fucking Bobby Darin."

EARLY IN 1965, T. M. Music was ranked 18th on the list of BMI's hundred affiliates and received the sixth BMI Award for records that had reached the Top Ten. Bobby received the award for his recording of his own song, "I'll Be There." Previously he had won five awards for "18 Yellow Roses," "The Shoop Shoop Song (It's in His Kiss)," "Hey Little Cobra," "You're the Reason I'm Living," and "Under the Boardwalk."

Meanwhile, Bobby was becoming more deeply committed to the civil-rights movement. He was one of the founders of the Artists' Civil Rights Assistance Fund early that year. Show business seemed divorced from the storms that were buffeting the nation. The more he confronted those realities, the more he tried to determine what role he could play as an artist to contribute meaningfully to the struggles he passionately identified with. He began to feel that he was split in two.

But Bobby's "retirement" from nightclub performing was eroding his career. The steady, electric momentum of his early years had been slowed to a crawl. His records were not selling, even the great album he had just made for Capitol. Bobby was no longer a wunderkind; he was a major nightclub performer who was no longer doing what he did best. He made just two nightclub engagements in 1965, both at the Flamingo Hotel in Las Vegas, in January and in June. And he had gradually begun to disperse his singing identity, which was confusing the Vegas audiences that loved him. Steve Blauner had to exit from the scene as well, since there was simply not enough for him to do for Bobby. He was replaced by David Gershenson. The loss of the tremendous support and fraternity that Blauner had given him was a major blow.

Blauner had been very careful when he left Bobby to make sure Bobby would remain solvent. "When I left," he recalls, "I had him in oil wells that were pumping, all kinds of oil deals because it was a tax write-off if you lost the money. And then I bought Bobby some stock in Xerox. And I said to him, 'This is your going-away money. This stock will double every two years for the next eight or nine years, and don't ever touch it.' Then, when he got the divorce, he gave Sandra everything because he wanted to keep the publishing company. And he got screwed with that."

Bobby was also experiencing the ongoing strains of his marriage with Sandra and his relationship with Nina, Gary, and the other members of his family on the East Coast. Gary Walden feels anguish about the relationship to this day.

Bobby and Atlantic Records producer Jerry Wexler

Bobby and Sandra Dee in a scene from *Come September*

Sandy, Dodd, and Bobby on opening night at the Coconut Grove in Hollywood, March 1966

Bobby brought son Dodd, 8, to the Hollywood Stars' annual baseball game at Dodger Stadium.

A scene from the 1962 movie *Pressure Point*, in which Bobby starred opposite Sidney Poitier

Publicity still from *Hell Is for Heroes*: (left to right) Nick Adam, Fess Parker, Steve McQueen, and Bobby

Bobby loved to relax by playing the piano. Here he is seen at the Harwyn Club in Manhattan, a favorite party spot of celebrities during the early 1960s.

Joyce Becker, Bobby, and Joanne Campbell

Bobby in his protest-song phase, with singer
Errol Dante at the Copacabana in 1969

"We didn't see Bobby much," Walden says. "Mainly we saw him when he was performing on stage. Anytime we [Gary, Nina, Vana, and Vee] got to see him perform was always a joyous time. But otherwise—I guess we weren't good enough. We weren't presentable in his eyes.

"My family, especially my mother, Nina, was mistreated by Bobby beyond anyone's wildest imagination. Nina wasn't thin, granted. Did she have a New York accent? Yes. Did she have a crooked smile? Yes. Was she a whore? No. Was she illiterate? No. Was she dumb? No. Those protest albums, *Commitment* and *Walden Robert Cassotto*, that he made toward the end, I mean that's his heart; he was compassionate about that and really felt it. But when it came to his own family, where was any of that?

"Now it's only the joy of the performer that I think about and relate to my kids. I haven't let my daughter read anything about Bobby."

In May 1965, Capitol released another good album by Bobby, *Venice Blue*, with arrangements by Richard Wess and Ernie Freeman. "Venice Blue" had first been released as a single, where it charted poorly at No. 133, but Bobby had an unaccountable enthusiasm for the song. The French import had saccharine lyrics and a mediocre melody; for one of the first times, Bobby's judgment was shaky. Nevertheless, Bobby wreaks havoc, magic, and glory with "I Wanna Be Around" and "The Good Life." As frequently as they were recorded, he does them mint-fresh and totally unexpected. Once again on this album, Bobby makes music that was never done this brilliantly before and may never be done that way again—unless some cocky little bastard genius comes along to make it new all over again. Until that day, we have Bobby. After that day, there may be someone else, but there will never be another Bobby.

MEANWHILE, in the real world, racial antagonism had burst through to the surface. Six days of horrific rioting occurred in the Watts section of Los Angeles in the summer of 1964.

Rudy Clark, the only black songwriter at T. M. Music, remembers: "When they had the riots in Watts, Bobby was preparing to go there and see if he could talk sense to the rioters and calm them down. He really wanted to go. Jesse Jackson went out there and they booed him. Those people didn't want to hear nothing. I felt Bobby's commitment would have gotten him hurt. He was a little bit too committed. I don't think he had a true bead on himself concerning black people.

"He would always question me about whether blacks were buying his records, and I told him they were. There were a few white artists that black people would buy. Elvis Presley was not one of them. Bobby was. So was Tony Bennett, Sinatra, The Four Seasons. Nobody knew why this was so. So I told him the truth; they were buying 'Mack the Knife' and 'Splish Splash.' But because of that, he thought that he might have an influential voice in Watts. And I told him it would be a big mistake.

"Being compassionate toward oppressed people and wanting to reach out to them is one thing," Clark continues, "but you're not their leader; they're not going to listen to you, man. Particularly at a time like that. Things were getting violent. You had the Black Panthers. The black commnity was saying enough is enough. They were desperate. So I felt it was dangerous for Bobby to go to Watts.

"Bobby reacted very angrily when I talked to him this way. And it became very heated. We went back and forth. Part of his plan was to do the Copa and then fly out to Watts. So when he left, I took his tuxedos and stuff and locked them in my room, and I went out to eat.

"I came back two hours later. He was very mad. I said, 'Hey, look, I didn't know, I just pulled the door to, what do you want me to do, man?' He said I did it deliberately. He was pretty bitter. It became a little violent. It turned into a pushing and shoving match. Some name-calling and stuff like that. I wanted to call his family in California and have somebody talk him out of it, but I had no numbers. Because he was about to get himself hurt.

"But it boiled over, and he left. He did not go. After a while it cooled off. I always knew he wanted to resolve a dispute when he asked me did I want to play darts. So we wound up throwing darts at the wall. That's the only way Bobby relaxed, the dartboard.

"At that point in his life, Bobby wanted to stretch out into something. He had mentioned going into politics a couple of times. He was like searching, torn between three directions. One was to be a dropout type of person on the order of Peter, Paul and Mary, the type who wears dungarees. He wanted to live in the woods or just go completely folkish. The other direction was to go into the civil-rights movement as a leader like Jesse Jackson. And the third direction was politics. So he was talking a lot about working with Bobby Kennedy, who he loved.

"So I tried to explain to him that emotions were too hot for a white person at that time to go into the civil-rights movement. But you don't explain nothing to Bobby. He gets an idea in his head. And he thought he had a time limit on his life, that he was supposed to be dead at 30. I learned this later. I didn't know then why he was rushing and always pushing. He was moving too fast and spreading himself out too thin.

"Bobby really had a special rapport for black music and for black people. A lot of times he had me bring my wife down. It got to the point where I had to say, 'Hey, Bobby, hold it, man. This is my *wife*, man.' He'd be pullin' on her, 'Come on, we're gonna go someplace else.' Trying to hang out. He'd want my wife to bring some of her friends. Bobby had this thing for beautiful black women.

"Bobby would always come to me and say, 'Hey man, next Saturday we goin' wenchin'.' That was his word. 'We gonna go up to Harlem, to Small's and stuff.' And one day I said, 'Hey, Bobby, listen. Whenever you get this notion that you want to go wenchin', man, why is it always we going to the black community? Why don't you one time tell me we goin' wenchin', man, and let's go into a white community?' Bobby apologized. He wasn't aware that he'd been doing that."

Bobby's contract with Capitol expired in the summer, and he moved back home: to Atlantic, Ahmet Ertegun, and Jerry Wexler. His three-year span at Capitol had been a disappointment for him. With the exception of two Top Ten singles, "You're the Reason I'm Living" and "18 Yellow Roses," his recording efforts, including five albums—two great ones—yielded negligible results.

In November 1965, Bobby experienced another debilitating heart crisis, the worst since his collapse at Freedomland. He had been in New York taping *The Steve Lawrence Show* and working at the T. M. office. He had begun to run a high fever several days before the taping. After the show was taped, he prepared to return to California. He called Sandra and asked her to meet him at the airport and to bring some blankets. Bobby arrived at L.A. International ashen, his face swollen to the point that he was almost unrecognizable. He was shivering and could hardly talk. He had lost 20 pounds and was running a 103-degree temperature.

Dr. Levy, Bobby's cardiologist, warned Sandra that if his fever remained that high, he might contract pneumonia and that it could be fatal in his condition.

The next day, Bobby was taken by ambulance to Mount Sinai Hospital. His condition was precarious. Dr. Levy disclosed that eight of the ten lobes of Bobby's lungs were filled with phlegm. He had pneumonia.

He was 29, a year before the year he had long expected to be his last.

Sandra stayed with him through the night. Dr. Levy did not expect Bobby to survive. On the second night, however, his fever broke. By the following day he was on the road to recovery.

But Bobby's heart condition had begun him on a downward spiral, one that filled him with fear and dread that took up more and more of his time and would eventually drain him of hope.

Says Steve Metz: "Every day, Bobby thought he was going to die."

Chapter Twelve
THE
LOST
CHORD

BOBBY WAS APPROACHING HIS 30TH BIRTHDAY in May 1966. "As Bobby got older," Hesh Wasser says, "his awareness of death took its toll on him. He had been living all along with the knowledge that he was supposed to die by then. And then the time does come. And it changes your whole way of thinking and being."

Bobby told a reporter, "My philosophy is to take one day at a time. Tomorrow is even out of sight for me. Each morning, I say to myself, 'Well, here I am again! Let's go!'"

Despite his condition, Bobby returned to nightclub performing in January at the Flamingo in Vegas after an absence of over two years. Bobby scored an absolute triumph. He added some of his finest songs: a half-spoken Depression lament, "Brother Can You Spare a Dime" by E. Y. Harburg, and the profoundly moving finale number by Sol Weinstein, "The Curtain Falls." It was a song that seemed to presage Bobby's fate. Even though it hadn't been expressly written for him, it was a show-business saga about a singer who loved what he was doing so much, he expressed wonderment "that I get paid for this." Bobby brought depth and tenderness to it.

There was no way of denying the frightening realities of his condition, for he experienced it constantly under his skin. Bobby kept an oxygen tank and mask backstage at all his performances, and he made frequent use of them. He was constantly drained by a racing erratic heartbeat, and he would spend hours recovering after a performance.

Another sign of Bobby's lowered expectations was his landing a television series. He appeared with Eve Arden in "The Sweet Years," a TV pilot that ran as an episode of the program *Run for Your Life*.

While most of these events seemed mired in mediocrity, Bobby, as always, was about to bounce back in a spectacular way. "Bobby called me up in 1966," Bobby Ramsen recalls, "and said, 'I want you to come with me. Here's what we're going to do: I'm gonna hire a private car to attach to a train to take us to Florida, Vegas, and L.A.'

"On the train," continues Ramsen, "were Bobby, me and my wife, Sandra, Sandra's mother, Mary, Charlie Maffia, Helen Turpin, Sandy's hairdresser, David Gershenson, Bobby's assistant, Tommy Culla, our own private cook, and of course Dodd, who was four at the time. We left from Vegas after the last show on closing night at the Flamingo. All the papers covered the train; it cost a lot of money and got a lot of press. It was referred to as 'Bobby Darin's Comeback.' They brought in champagne and caviar and pounds and pounds of Chasen's chili. It was all very exciting, a five-day trip.

"Something jarring happened on the trip. Bobby had done the TV pilot for *Run for Your Life*. He was all excited because they were talking about a spin-off for his own TV show. So he's waiting to hear. We were having the best time on the train. We were laughing and singing and playing Monopoly and a dice game. The food kept coming. In Chicago, Bobby rented two rooms at one of the big hotels and we were laid over for a few hours.

"When we got back to the train, it was an entirely different Bobby. He was very down, very upset. He had a book that was hot at the time,

Truman Capote's noirish *In Cold Blood*, went into his cabin, and we hardly saw him for the next two days. I know what happened. He called California and he heard the TV spin-off from *Run for Your Life* was not gonna happen. So he was very brought down. Very unhappy. He wanted it bad. So he stayed in his room. Then we pulled into Miami and the owner of the Deauville Hotel, Morris Landsberg, was there to greet Bobby. The Deauville was a successful engagement. Then back to California and the Coconut Grove."

Bobby's March 9 opening at the Coconut Grove was one of the greatest moments in his entire career. Hollywood royalty turned out: Jack Benny, George Burns, Johnny Mercer, Gregory Peck, Henry Mancini, Mia Farrow, Juliet Prowse, Michael Caine, Edward G. Robinson, Steve Lawrence, Eddie Fisher, Ben Gazzara, Carol Lynley, Nancy Sinatra Sr., Anthony Newley, Frankie Avalon, and Andy Williams flowed through the entrance. It was clear testimony to the extraordinary esteem in which Bobby was held by the most talented and celebrated performers in Hollywood.

Sandra sat front and center, wearing an emerald-green gown, a white mink, and emerald earrings. She held Dodd, who was wearing a custom-made tuxedo to match his daddy's, on her lap.

There is a surviving record of parts of Bobby's Coconut Grove performance on videotape, with the spoken reactions of many of the celebrities. The documentary also contains substantial glimpses of Bobby on the train ride that Bobby Ramsen described: Bobby with Sandra (it was in the final year of their marriage), deeply affectionate moments with him and Dodd, telling excerpts from his studio recording sessions, and Bobby speaking in voiceovers very frankly about his feelings of fear and about his career. He is seen in private relaxed moments, not dressed up, and it is clear that he was unprepossessing, with a receding chin, a small frame, and narrow shoulders. Once he begins singing, of course, he soars and becomes handsome and mighty.

This is a precious record. Anything but a glossy P.R. product, it straightforwardly records the reality of what was happening. It is technically imperfect and grainy, but it stops time: it fully captures Bobby's greatness. Bobby is fully here—his love of singing; moments of his great performance on stage; his mastery of every detail in the recording studio where he produces and directs as well as sings; his loving relationship with Dodd. "I let my little boy have something that I know I wanted when I was his age," he says, "a big kick, a father. Somebody to be quiet, somebody to make noise, somebody to laugh, somebody that can put their hands together." Seated on Bobby's lap or hovering right behind him, having a wonderful time, Dodd is grinning and reaching to strum the guitar. Bobby encourages him and Dodd plucks a string mischievously. Bobby says, "You phony baloney, stick of macaroni," and hugs his son. It is a very loving relationship.

Bobby does great versions of songs he hadn't recorded: "I've Got the World on a String," Durante's "One of Those Songs." There are glimpses of his spontaneous creativity. He is almost always seated with his guitar and at one point at the breakfast table bursts into an improvised new song, made up on the spot, about the little houses by the railroad tracks he's seen from the window of the train 20 miles from San Bernardino, of poor people struggling to survive. He sings, "Guess what? They look just like you and like me." As he finishes, he grins, satisfied, at the person seated opposite him as if to say, "Wasn't that fun, and it was good too." And it really was.

This was not a person of one dimension; there was searching, and caring, and keen understanding. And there was kindness.

"Bobby's personality was not just a flat screen," says Ed Blau, his lawyer. "There was a lot of depth, a lot of color. A richness.

"Bobby spoke of his approaching 30th birthday. 'I am very, very concerned,' he said, 'that I'll be 30 in a couple of months. Walden Robert Cassotto didn't expect to live to 30. Just the idea of being alive and chronologically arriving at 30, Bobby Darin has done an awful lot. I don't mean to say that he's already a success and therefore the world is over for him. You can only do those things if you're alive. One of the terrible dawns that hit you.'"

The documentary contains overwhelming praise of Bobby from his peers. Gregory Peck said, "Bobby was already one of the great showmen, and it was certainly no surprise to me that he could act and bring the same exciting qualities to his acting that he had been bringing to his singing and to his performances in clubs. He goes all out. He has lots of courage, takes chances, gives all of himself... [he] conveys pathos. Bobby, in his work, is touching, he's moving."

George Burns is the adoring father figure whose presence casts a glow over the entire proceedings. "I love Bobby." He adds mischievously, "I wanted to adopt Bobby. He said no. I would have made a fortune with him."

There are scenes showing Bobby's total mastery in the studio, conducting rehearsals as he goes over two of his greatest songs, the unreleased "Weeping Willow" (which he did not write) and his own song, "Rainin'," probably the finest song he ever wrote. The "Weeping Willow" footage is particularly invaluable, since the record has never been released. Watch this session and try to sit still; it is impossible.

The scene for "Rainin'" shows Bobby creating and conducting the song as he goes. The song is a haunting one, full of sadness and lament, yet it swings gently and beautifully.

ON MAY 1, 1966, less than two weeks before his 30th birthday, Bobby informed Sandra he wanted a divorce. He didn't actually tell her himself. Once again, he had someone else call her: Dr. Dick Goodwin. Prior to that, Charlie Maffia had called her, and so had Ed Blau, Bobby's lawyer. It was understandable that Sandra would need to be convinced. Bobby had returned to be with her again and again. In a sense, he never really left her until that final call in May 1966. She now agreed to file for divorce. Even after the divorce, Bobby would often visit Dodd and wind up staying overnight with Sandra.

Despite the enormous publicity generated by the train tour and Bobby's smash comeback at the Coconut Grove, it was clear that his career was no longer on the upward trajectory it had been on for almost ten years. Choice acting roles were not forthcoming. Bobby was king of the nightclubs again, but the nightclubs themselves were closing or in decline. He was back to the standards, but the public had moved elsewhere, to the Beatles, to rock, and to folk music. He hadn't had a hit record in three years.

Bobby reached 30 on May 14. From now on it was borrowed time. He would reach out more desperately than ever to catch the golden crown that always seemed so close, but it would become more elusive with each passing month.

On August 12, Sandra filed for divorce in Los Angeles Superior Court. She charged extreme cruelty and mental suffering and sought custody of Dodd.

Three days later, Bobby recorded two folk songs written by Tim Hardin: "Reason to Believe" and "If I Were a Carpenter."

Once again—perhaps for the last time—Bobby got the public's musical mood right. "If I Were a Carpenter" was a tough sell at the beginning. In the era of the Beatles, Bobby's track record as a pop and adult performer tracing back to the fifties created an initial resistance to the song by both disc jockeys and the public. But in time, the paradoxical result was that "easy listening" stations that had played Bobby regularly now rejected "If I Were a Carpenter," while Top 40 Radio dug it. The record began to move up the charts by October and shortly reached No. 8.

Bobby had again wrested triumph from a state of decline, and he had done so by boldly gambling with his image and trusting his instincts. His recording was a great achievement, one that has stood the test of time. It is now considered a folk classic. Bobby earned a Grammy nomination for Best Contemporary (Rock and Roll) Solo Vocal Performance. The winner would be Paul McCartney for "Eleanor Rigby," but Bobby was in good company. He had achieved relevance again.

Bobby now planned his next album, which would also be titled *If I Were a Carpenter*, and it would be a full-fledged folk-rock recording. This about-face was not a gimmick for him; it began with *Earthy* and *Golden Folk Hits* in 1963. His look began to change from tuxes to jeans and boots, but it was more than a cosmetic changeover. Bobby felt closely aligned with the counterculture and the music that reflected it. Fighting death every day, he wasn't about to allow himself to be mummified in his singing or performing. He wiggled out of every pigeonhole. He did it so well that no other singer has become *more* alive after his death and is making the biggest comeback of his career 30-odd years later.

Nevertheless, this transformation posed major risks at the time. He was puzzling his bedrock nightclub audience, and the youth audience of folk rock did not know what to make of a new Bobby. He would never be on the cusp of the folk movement like Dylan, Peter Paul and Mary, and Tim Hardin; his crossover appeal would be limited. Wasn't this the finger-snapping wiseass from Vegas in a hairpiece and tux cashing in on the latest craze? But he had probably been the first singer to perform Dylan in major nightclubs.

Then came *Inside Out*, released in May 1967. Darin's new album was not a replica of what he had done before in folk music. There were the Tim Hardin songs, but there was also "I Am," a song of self-exploration Bobby wrote that was far more contemporary in theme. The songs on the album were not the elegant artifacts of his 1962–63 folk period. There were fine new songs by Hardin, John Sebastian, Randy Newman, and the Rolling Stones. But "I Am" was fresh material wrung out of Bobby's own soul and experience. This was a new language of his own, and there was no way it could be construed as a rip-off of anyone else's work or sensibility. It expressed Bobby's concerns and obsessions and was a harbinger of the direction Bobby would be taking next.

Inside Out was a dismal commercial failure. The second phase of Bobby's folk period had ended. But Bobby was not through changing. He never would be.

On March 7, 1967, Sandra and Bobby arrived at a divorce settlement. Sandra received custody of Dodd, their home, several oil wells in Texas, and a $2,000-a-month award for child support.

Bobby maintained his show-business image on TV and on stage. When he appeared at the Copacabana in March, *Billboard* wrote, "As a singer, mimic and purveyor of light banter, Darin goes to the head of the class. He's all showman."

"Dr. Martin Luther King Jr. came to the Copa with a whole bunch of people to see Bobby perform that March," remembers Bobby Rozario. "They sat in the back. Halfway through the show, Bobby was singing his message songs, and he stops and introduces Dr. King. And there's like dead silence in the room. No applause. So Bobby went into his next song. And the next thing I see is that Dr. King's bodyguards are taking him out of the place because they could feel the audience didn't like them. So they left. Bobby felt terrible. He was very disappointed. But he appreciated that Martin Luther King came, thought enough about him to come. But he couldn't stay; it was just too negative. And so the audience started like being angry at Bobby. Like what is he doing? This is not what we paid our money for."

Bobby performed at Princess Grace's annual Red Cross Gala in Monte Carlo on August 25. He was on the front page of the August 29 *New York Post* dancing with the Princess.

But Bobby's socializing was not filling the void in his life. "Bobby was very political," says Hesh Wasser, "although he rarely discussed his politics on the outside. The only time that politics really became a topic of discussion for him was during the Vietnam War. He was a staunch Democrat. He was at the inauguration of Lyndon Johnson. He was very anti-Nixon. He loved Laura Nyro and her song, 'Save the Country.' He sang that song all the time."

Bobby adulated Robert F. Kennedy, Al Kasha says. "He was like Sinatra in that regard: the New York Italian boy who saw that immigrants were helped by Democrats. He saw that in the Kennedy brothers. He wanted to hang with them."

Jack Newfield, RFK's biographer, wrote: "RFK remains the lost chord of American politics: the missing unifying link between blacks and working-class whites. He was the blues note that touched all the people of no property and no power regardless of color."

By January 1968, Bobby was actively involved in Democratic Party politics. He joined his beloved Jimmy Durante in Indiana to entertain at a Democratic rally for Senator Birch Bayh. Durante—Italian son of a Brooklyn barber who listened to opera all day on an old Victrola in the shop—and Bobby, Italian boy from the Bronx whose father would always be unknown to him. Two of the greatest entertainers of all time, both men of uncommon humanity, were there to testify that you could not always "start off each day with a song."

On April 4, 1968, Dr. Martin Luther King Jr., America's prophet, was assassinated. In May, Bobby announced his support for Robert F. Kennedy for the presidency of the United States.

Bobby had been traveling with Kennedy for about ten days. He warmed up the crowd in advance of Kennedy's appearance by singing "This Man Is Your Man," his version of Woody Guthrie's "This Land Is Your Land."

Bobby was with Kennedy in Oregon and RFK had invited him to join him on the plane ride to Los Angeles. During the flight, RFK had asked Bobby to sing "Blowin' in the Wind." Bobby did, and Kennedy liked it so much he asked Bobby to sing it three more times. It became his favorite song. Bobby accomplished what Jack Newfield had been unable to do: turn RFK on to the music of Bob Dylan. Newfield wrote in his biography that RFK "said he couldn't stand Dylan's whining voice, and felt most of the songs were 'too depressing.'" One day in June 1968, Kennedy told him, "Bobby Darin sang 'Blowin' in the Wind' for me. I really liked it. Especially that line, 'How many years can some people exist, before they're allowed to be free?'"

Bobby Rozario, who had become Bobby's new conductor, recalls, "Bobby took a job at Mister D's in San Francisco before doing the convention at the Cow Palace for Robert Kennedy. Kennedy had said onward to Los Angeles, but we were still working in Frisco; we had to finish the engagement. So Kennedy went to L.A. and we were on stage working, and the road manager came up to me and he said, 'Don't say anything right now. But they've just shot Robert Kennedy. Let Bobby finish the show.' So Bobby finished, and I walked backstage. I could hear him: he was throwing things and ranting and raving. And he said, 'That's it. Cancel the job.' So we all packed up and left."

"Bobby left San Francisco," remembers Steve Blauner, "and went to Washington to the gravesite. He didn't go to Saint Patrick's Cathedral. After the ceremony at Saint Patrick's, they put Kennedy's body on a train to Washington. And there were people all along the tracks. So the train was very late. The press at the gravesite wanted to interview Bobby, but he wouldn't talk to them. He went over to Resurrection City, where the blacks were marching. There was a lot of rain and mud, and he sat and played for them. Finally the coffin arrived at Arlington with the Kennedy family and it was very dark by then. Thousands of mourners held candles in the night. Bobby wept. When the ceremony was over, it was too late—they weren't going to cover the coffin until the next morning. So Bobby slept at the coffin. He was alone there all night. He lit a candle. He would not leave it until it was covered. In the morning the workmen arrived to complete the grave. Bobby stood watching in the dawn light while the men lowered Kennedy's casket into the ground and covered it."

"RFK's murder, that destroyed him," says Dick Clark.

"I think his greatest sadness was when Bobby Kennedy died," recalls Carol Lynley.

In July 1969, Bobby was on the cover of *Beyond* magazine. The headline read: "Bobby Darin Tells of Mystic Revelation at the Grave of Robert Kennedy." Bobby told the reporter that the spiritual force of Kennedy had reached out toward him with such strength that it enabled him to "see things with a peace and calm I had never seen before. It was as though all my hostilities, anxieties, and conflicts were in one ball. That ball was flying away from me into space."

The reporter noted that when Bobby resurfaced on nightclub floors, instead of the flashy costumes Bobby had worn before, he was clad in simple denims, and he was no longer wearing his hairpiece. He felt "reborn." Bobby told the reporter, "I'm just glad to have a second beginning with my life."

The changes in Bobby took place gradually, but they were volatile, and audiences and nightclub managers did not understand what was happening to him. He was gaining a reputation for being difficult to handle. Within a month of the assassination, Bobby was back at the Frontier in Las Vegas. Bobby Rozario recalls, "Something upset Bobby, triggered him, and he decided to walk off the stage. He had only done like three or four tunes that night.

"So he walks off, right into the casino, out to the front, out the door, straight to the airport, and then back home. That was the first time he ever did that when I worked with him. I was shocked, because here the audience was looking up at us on the stage. Only the musicians were left. I remember that it took forever for the curtains to come down. Just sitting there with egg on your face. So we just kept playing playoff music until the curtain finally came down."

"I was visiting him in Vegas," Dick Lord recalls. "I had gone to sleep in my hotel room, and he called me and woke me up. Bobby said, 'I just spoke to Robert Kennedy.'

"I said, 'Robert Kennedy is dead.'"

"Bobby said, 'Yeah, but he told me what I had to do.' That's when Bobby got involved in planning to run for political office."

Chapter Thirteen
WHIRLING DERVISH

WHEN NINA THOUGHT THAT BOBBY was giving serious consideration to carrying on RFK's legacy by running for office himself in 1968, she became frightened that Bobby's opponents would find out the truth about his birth and exploit the information to destroy him. She called Bobby at the Latin Casino in Cherry Hill, New Jersey, where he was appearing, and told him there was something of urgent importance that she had to tell him in person. Nina and Vee drove to meet Bobby at the Barclay Hotel in Philadelphia. Nina went up to his room, while Vee waited in the lobby. Bobby met her at the door, Nina with her rasping voice and sagging hose, 51 now, very obese, almost popping out of her baggy flower-print dress. That was how Bobby saw her.

She began by asking Bobby whether it was true that he was seriously considering going into politics. There was a long silence. "Why are you asking me these things?" he said.

She finally told him the truth. "Bobby," she said, "I'm not your sister."

"What are you talking about?"

She was crying. "Polly never wanted you to know," she said. "She thought you'd never grow up right if we told you. I'm your mother."

He didn't seem to hear it. "What is this bullshit? What are you telling me?"

"Sweetheart, I just told you. You're not Polly's son. You're mine. Bobby, I'm your mother."

He sat down on the couch and stared at her. His legs were weak and his heart was pounding.

"Then who's my father? Charlie? Who's my father?"

She refused to tell him. She explained that his father never knew that she was pregnant.

He was falling into space. He wanted to hold up his hands to stop the fall.

"Why are you telling me now?" he said.

"I'm not a young woman anymore, Bobby. I have to tell you."

"Why? What for? For spite, money, ego, what the fuck was it?" He was crying. "You must be the strongest person in the world," he said.

"You're my baby," she cried out. "Don't you know what that means; how much I love you?"

"No," he said. "I don't want to know. My whole life has been a lie."

BOBBY WAS REELING. He was embittered and enraged.

"He came to my office," Steve Blauner remembers. "He was shattered. I didn't believe it. I went and got the birth certificate. It said that Nina was the mother and father unknown. He was the most honest person in the world. The woman he loved, Polly, had drilled into him that you don't lie. Now he found out his whole life had been a lie. He found out the woman he couldn't stand was his mother. He was beaten down. RFK's murder started it. But he would have recovered from that. Finding out about his mother was a mind-blower."

According to Shirley Jones, Bobby called her one evening and asked her if she could come over to his house. He said, "I have to tell you something."

"I went over there," Shirley Jones recalls. "He said, 'You're not going to believe this, Shirley. You're just not going to believe this.' That's when he told me that the woman he thought was his mother was his grandmother and that his sister was his mother.

"He was stunned, and I was stunned. He was just so angry. He said, 'I'll never get over this.' Then he said, 'And I don't know how much longer I have to live.' And he talked about his heart. I hadn't known about that either.

"It was Nina that he felt more betrayed by than his grandmother. He said, 'I'll never feel for her [Nina] what I felt for my grandmother.' And he was very sad. I sat with him quite a while. It was very traumatic for him. He didn't know how to trust after that. He didn't want anybody to enter into his little area anymore.

"This was a death sentence for him somehow. I called and left messages. I never heard from him after that."

The woman who symbolized to him all he had repudiated in his life, all that he had run away from, was his mother. He could not stand the sight of her.

But how could he not have known all along?

One person had known about it. Who else? Hesh Wasser. A young girl told Hesh that Nina was in fact Bobby's mother.

"A little girl of 14 named Gail Leichter actually told me at Dick Clark's show in 1959 [her parents had told her], but I kept it to myself," Hesh says. "Bobby's family used to have a bungalow in Staten Island. They would go there in summer. And Gail Leichter's family lived next door. One of the reasons they went to Staten Island was for Nina to go into hiding when she was pregnant with Bobby. That's where she had the baby. Gail very nonchalantly said to me, 'By the way, do you know that Polly is not Bobby's mother; she's his grandmother?'"

Hesh never raised it with Bobby. "I don't know why. I guess I had the feeling it was a subject not to be touched. I felt it would interfere with the friendship. And I don't think I wanted to believe in my heart and soul that Nina was his mother. He was so proud of Polly. She really made him what he was.

"It's hard for me to believe that Bobby didn't know. Polly was already a pretty elderly woman; she was 46 when Bobby was born. It's possible Bobby was in denial about it. Knowing Bobby, I can't believe he hadn't considered that.

"Bobby may not have been as shaken up as he seemed when Nina finally told him," Wasser reflects. "This might all have been a put-on. Now he could act out his rage against Nina. And it wasn't only Nina that had lied to him. Polly had lied to him. And his hatred for Nina really came boiling out. He had been holding it in. Exactly why Bobby hated her that much, I have no way of knowing. She was very good to him."

"He never came to terms with finding out the truth in 1968 until the time he died," says Gary Walden. "He was betrayed and he was lied to. The ultimate lie.

"We still went to see him perform at clubs, but there was that tension between him and Nina. She immediately knew that her being anywhere near him would make him uncomfortable. So now she would just meld into the woodwork and sit far back in some other area of the nightclub so he wouldn't have to see her."

The truth about Nina set off another vortex in Bobby: wanting to know who his father was. He had assumed all along that Sam Cassotto was his father. Gary explained, "He loved Polly and he knew Polly was very talented and well known in the theater, and he knew it's gotta be in the blood. So he wanted to know now. And that drove him mad. It must be his father where he got everything from. Nina told him nothing. Whenever they were together, Bobby always asked her, 'Are you going to tell me who my father was?' She said, 'No, I'm sorry, sweetheart.' Bobby shouted, 'How can you not tell me?' Bobby spent a small fortune on investigators trying to uncover his father's identity."

By 1968, Bobby was falling apart. King and Kennedy were murdered. His career was breaking up. Nina's disclosure was one more blow.

"And then Bobby lost his publishing company," says Steve Blauner. "Don't forget that when he wanted me to manage him, he gave up part of his birthright. He had agreed that anything that he sang or wrote, the publishing company would publish until the $100,000 figure, and they would still own those copyrights forever. Then he had the balls to turn around and buy them back, so that he retained them all. He bought back his soul. Then he called me up one day and told me he sold his publishing company to Commonwealth United Corporation in August 1968 for $1,300,000. Bobby received $1 million in Commonwealth United Stock," the balance going to his lawyer and to Ed Burton, who was vice-president and general manager of T. M. Music. CUC agreed to purchase exclusive publishing rights to all of the music Bobby wrote over the next five years.

"He called me up every day: 'It's a million one, it's a million two, it's a million four!' So immediately I went and checked out the company. And I called Bobby. And I told him to sell the stock instantly. He went, 'But it's a million—!!!' I said, 'I don't care what it is. It's just a matter of time until they go under. They're going into the motion picture business with nobody there who knows what a motion picture is.' I didn't know it was not registered stock and that he could not sell it anyway. And they did go under, and he lost everything. He lost the copyrights."

The Vietnam War was still raging, and America was in crisis. Now the changes in Bobby came with a vengeance. There was more to life than show business. He opened at the Coconut Grove in Los Angeles on October 30, 1968. Bobby began in traditional mode in a tuxedo, with a 21-piece orchestra and some of his standard hits, along with "Try a Little Tenderness," "Let the Good Times Roll," and "Talk to the Animals." For the latter part of the show, Bobby took off his tuxedo and put on a blue denim jacket. He returned with a four-piece combo and introduced a new song, "Long Line Rider." The intense rock number was based on an incident at an Arkansas prison where the bodies of dead prisoners were uncovered in the ground.

People were looking at each other, wondering what was going on. Bobby had changed his identity and moved from entertainment to social commentary. It was like giving an audience a dose of medicine they weren't expecting and didn't exactly relish. In fact, many were infuriated.

The changes kept coming. Bobby now refused to wear a regular tux at all. He wore a denim tux instead. He took off his hairpiece and grew a moustache and long sideburns. The overall look was not flattering; he appeared older, pallid, and sour.

In July, Bobby formed his own record label, Direction Records, in order to produce records in which he would be able to express his social concerns. He made two albums, *Born Walden Robert Cassotto* and *Commitment*. The first had on its cover a blurred picture of Bobby in a tuxedo to the left and a grainy childhood picture of Bobby on the right. It was a striking collage. Estelle Changas wrote accurately in the *Los Angeles Times* that "the feeling is of the artist searching for his origins, attempting to return to the most essential part of himself, an identity obscured and distorted by the slick superficiality of his celebrity image." Slickness was very much what Bobby was trying to discard. "When I put on my denims," Bobby told Al Aronowitz of the *New York Post*, "I was divesting myself of the slick and the sharp and the styled and the tailored."

"When Bobby decided to write message songs," Bobby Rozario remembers, "I helped him put the albums together. I thought they were very creative, but I knew instinctively that America wasn't ready for them. Because Bobby had already created this cool swinging image."

For the *Commitment* album, Bobby now called himself Bob Darin, and the picture of him on the album cover looked like the exact replica in shadow of Bob Dylan. Discussing the album at the time, Bobby said that "years ago I had the choice between ethnic and plastic, and I chose plastic. And twelve or thirteen years later, it dawned on me that I'd chosen the wrong one."

Jimmy Scalia has compiled much of Bobby's Direction material (some of it never released before) in a new album titled *The Lost Big Sur Masters*. "Take his song to Robert Kennedy, 'In Memoriam,'" Scalia says. "While he was waiting for them to put the coffin in the ground, he didn't want to be photographed. Because he was there for his friend. He was grieving. He stayed all night; the crowd dispersed; he stayed. The song is really written not about RFK when the train took him, but about what happened when nobody else saw. Bobby's were the only set of eyes left, and he's writing about the burial of his friend. Listen to the song. It's very low. He plucked the strings three times slowly, almost like a bell.

"Another song I unearthed for the *Big Sur* album is 'Long Time Movin'.' Bobby conveys to the listener the time he has left here on earth and what he will leave behind. It's a bit tongue in cheek, and the lyric doesn't have a bitter bite so it helps get his point of view across. He sings, 'I'll be a long time movin' before I'm home; I'll be a long time sleepin' when I'm gone.' You hear his whistling skipping across the rhythm of the guitar, and it sounds so much less threatening than what he is really saying."

"Bobby knew when he went into the protest thing," recalls Hesh Wasser, "that he wasn't going to get the same kind of acceptance. He would have loved everybody to jump up and down and say he's the best thing that ever happened and better than Bob Dylan. He knew that wasn't going to happen. He did it because he wanted to. His audience was the nightclub audience. Soon he couldn't get work in Vegas; they didn't want him. The hotel owners wanted the old Bobby Darin."

The two Directions albums constitute an autobiography of Bobby's state of mind during the late sixties. The songs are extremely varied in style, genre, and mood. Some are heavy and thematic, like "Long Line Rider;" some, like "Jive" and "Distractions," are there for the joy of it. Bobby's familiar singing style is largely absent. The arrangements are sparse, with guitar, bass, and drums. Rock, folk, bluegrass—a little of everything. The songs are filled with urgency and need, and they do not sound at all derivative of other composers or singers. They have a total integrity and painful honesty, and they are fresh and diverse in lyrics, melodies, and themes.

In the self-lacerating "Song for a Dollar," Bobby sang of himself as being a "flim-flam man" who lied to gain fortune and fame. This was a distorted and demeaning view of all he had achieved. He had committed the crime of entertaining, of being a clown and a showman when the streets were burning and children were starving. He saw it that way. He was unforgiving toward himself.

He could accept it when Ray Charles sang Berlin, Gershwin, or Sammy Cahn. Brother Ray did not always sing of pain and conflict, and he almost never conveyed messages. He did "Making Whoopee" and "Just for a Thrill" without a guilty conscience. Sometimes he sang about fornicating or sounded as if he was. Listen to his grunts and sighs on the glorious "All I Ever Need Is You" on *Volcanic Action of My Soul*. Sinatra swung his ass off; Little Richard, Sam Cooke, Dinah Washington, Louis Prima, Tony Bennett, Aretha Franklin, Joe Williams, Etta Jones, Carmen McRae, Ernie Andrews, Dean, and Sammy, they sang out of their souls. But Nina's revelation had pounded it into his soul that his whole life had been a lie. The first thing he had done was rip off the fucking hairpiece. Yet there'd been times when he could tip it at the door to the boys in the band; do a goof about it and have some fun.

THE TWO ALBUMS did receive belated critical praise, but disappeared down a well, almost never to be heard from again for some 30 years. Today they sound as fresh and alive as they were then. Estelle Changas would later write in the *Los Angeles Times* that "the songs convey an urgent sense of someone beginning absolutely fresh."

While working on the albums, Bobby found a new group of musicians with whom he was in sync and whom he would be close to for the rest of his life. "We were four funky R&B rock-and-roll guys from Nashville," Quitman Dennis remembers, "working on that album with Bobby: me, Tommy Amato, Billy Aikens, Bob Paythress, and Brent Maher, who was engineer.

"We just saw him as a guy who was going through a sort of midlife crisis and wanted to make a difference," Dennis continues. "I thought those political songs of his were a noble attempt, and I appreciated the fact that he wanted to do that. But I wasn't really sure who was going to be interested in listening to that. So he just grabbed topical issues: finding corpses in the dirt in Arkansas. It was a good try, but it wasn't a major-league success. There was a lack of patience in Bobby in his writing. Songwriting takes a bit more tenacity and willingness to go through a time-consuming process. He just cranked them out.

"I could see that Bobby resented the pull on him from the audience to do his historic act. That's why the people had come. He wanted to do the new things, which made him happy to express. He resented the audience for that pressure."

"After completing the *Commitment* album," Bobby Rozario remembers, "we got invited to do *The Jackie Gleason Show* in Florida. So Bobby and the band and myself flew to Florida to go on the show. So they asked Bobby what he was going to sing. And he says, 'I'm going to sing "Long Line Rider."' They said good. They said, 'Will you do "Mack the Knife"?' And Bobby said, 'I would rather not do "Mack the Knife." But they wanted Mack, so he said, 'All right, I'll compromise. I'll do "Mack," but I have to do "Long Line Rider" too. That's the song I want to do.' So they said fine.

"Now in television we have a run-through. The cameras can block, and they can see what kind of shot it is. So Bobby had to give them a copy of the lyrics. So we're all set up and we start doing the song. Well, I guess somebody ran up to the office with the lyrics and said, 'Listen to this: It's about dead bodies. It's about somewhere down South where they found these dead bodies of prisoners buried on the prison grounds. Is this really what you want in your show?' And I guess they talked to Jackie Gleason, who said, 'Absolutely not. He cannot do that song.' So the producers came down with the message that we couldn't do the song. We could do 'Mack' but not 'Rider.' So Bobby says, 'Well, it's a wrap, guys. Pack up and go home.' We walked out. As the audience was walking in, we were walking out with our instruments. They were coming one direction; we were fighting to get out."

Bobby and his band next went to the Copacabana and opened there on January 2, 1969. Bobby's makeover made Jules Podell furious, and it would be Bobby's last engagement there for years. "We're doing the same show with all the swing tunes," Bobby Rozario recalls, "but in the middle Bobby throws in all these message songs. Now I'm playing the opening number and I haven't seen this yet: Bobby comes on stage and he has a tuxedo jacket with the Levi pants. For the very first day. Podell is going, 'Oh my God, what is going on?'"

"It was fun at first," says Bobby Rozario, "but then I began enjoying it less, because the audience was so negative about it. They were walking out. Bobby didn't seem to care. At that point I decided that I was going to find something else to do. I just said, 'Bobby, it's really not me.'

"I thought it was wrong for him. Because he had already created that one image that was so strong in the audience's mind. I just felt awful that people were walking out."

Dick Clark saw the act and told him, "You're Bobby Darin, not Bob Dylan. You're a different kind of dog. Go back and put on the tuxedo. Do what the people expect of you. They don't want to see a balding hippie sitting on a stage."

"Becoming Bob Darin was an ill-conceived attempt to shed the Bobby as in Bubblegum image," says Mimi Greenberg, now a retired clinical psychologist in Los Angeles. "He had become a shadow of someone else. That's the dark side of him. He would get very caught up in fantasy and live it like a reality. He wanted to be Bob Darin because he thought he would be taken seriously. As Bobby, he was always going to be the kid."

"I said to Bobby, 'What the hell are you doing?'" Steve Lawrence remembers. "He said, 'This is what I'm feeling now.' He just went that way because that's where his head was. His passion led him there. The audience didn't follow him."

But Bobby made his brother Gary very happy one night of that engagement at the Copa. "Bobby had such admiration for the Jewish people," says Gary Walden. "He saw them as having been beaten down time after time and having had the resilience to always come back. He loved them. We went to the Copa to see him on January 6, 1969, my birthday. Bobby had distributed lighters to everyone in the audience. He announced, 'Gary is 13 today," and right then and there the spotlight shined on me. The houselights went out, and everybody lit the lighters. They killed the light on Bobby, it was only on me. Wherever I looked, in whatever direction, there were just the lights from the cigarette lighters. Bobby said he was very proud of me now that I was officially a man. This was my Bar Mitzvah. He explained how in Jewish ritual 13 was the age of becoming a man. And I bowed and I was thrilled and they sang 'Happy Birthday' to me and it was an absolutely great moment. So many years ago."

Gary says ruefully, "That was a moment that no one could steal from me."

BOBBY OFFICIALLY JOINED THE FOLK-SONG CIRCUIT in May 1969 by opening at the Troubadour, Los Angeles' premiere folk-song club.

Jack Gilardi saw him at the Troubadour. "I was hurt," he recalls. "Believing Bobby was so talented, believing Bobby was that inventive, that creative, and to be down there—you almost wanted to cry. That this talent, this brilliant young man, was a wasted thing and not giving what the people should have from him. Singing there with the long hair and the beard: he didn't look good. And playing the guitar. When you've seen the rise of a talented young man, my God, the drive, and the people starting to clamor and wanting to be with him, and all the way to the top. Nominated for the Academy Award, playing wherever he wanted, and looking good. And all of a sudden, downhill. He didn't give a goddamn. Like he was punishing himself."

George Burns saw Bobby there too and told Dodd Darin: "I went backstage and I said to Bobby, 'You're doing it all wrong, kid. In the first place, you're not gonna bring back Bobby Kennedy. He's gone.

People exit different ways. That was his finish . . . But if you want to do something for Bobby Kennedy, put on your toupee and your tuxedo . . . Play Vegas and all the great nightclubs and make as much money as you possibly can and give it to the Kennedy charities. Then you're doing something. You're doing nothing for Kennedy now.' He did it eventually. I don't say he did it the next week, 'cause he had a mind of his own. And I loved him very, very much."

"I do think Bobby made it work," says Paul Anka. "Unfortunately, the infrastructure of our business is such that people don't allow you to make that radical a change. He was believable. But you start changing—the sideburns, moustache, the jeans—you've got agents who used to book you but can't now, so they put a rap on you. The business wants the easy way, the easy money."

On July 23, 1969, "Bob Darin" introduced one of his most enduring folk songs, "Simple Song of Freedom," at the Bonanza Hotel Opera House in Las Vegas. Once again, in the midst of the bizarre, high-voltage, chintzy environment of Vegas show business, facing the crowd—mink-draped, diamond-bedecked women and their high-roller husbands and boyfriends taking a break from the casino tables, broads, booze, and dope—Bobby injected a note of compassion and realism that rattled, shook, and somehow moved his audience. "That was probably the best piece that came out of Bobby's folk period," says Quitman Dennis. "Even though it was topical and current politically, it still had validity when you removed those things."

Once again, Bobby had wrested triumph out of defeat with this song. It was not a great song, but in its modest and moving way it cast light on an entire generation. Was he soaring, or was he crashing to defeat? With Bobby, it was often both at once. All that was certain was that in the midst of great turmoil, suffering, and change, he had carved out this small glistening diamond.

BOBBY WOULD TURN THE SCREWS on Nina and his family one more time in 1969. "Bobby was living in an exclusive section of Malibu called the Colony," Gary Walden says. "He had decided he was going to give my mother a car as a present. He let her pick whatever car she wanted. So my mother, being a practical individual, picked a station wagon, a Chevy Kingswood Estate.

"So they delivered the car. My mother was thrilled. It was the first car we ever owned that had air-conditioning, power windows, and power seats. It was gorgeous. Bobby said, 'Come out for the summer.' Fine. So we drove across country. We get to the house. There's the maid's quarters, with a two-car garage, double doors. There's a regulation-size tennis court fully fenced. And then we reach the house. It was empty. The only things that were in it were oriental rugs in the living and dining rooms.

"Out by the pool, the fence was a glass wall. You went out this door and you were right on the ocean. A four-bedroom house. In each one of the bedrooms was a mattress: no box spring, nothing. The house had the rugs and the mattresses. And that was it. Bobby rented this house unfurnished for ten thousand dollars a month for June, July, and August. No silverware, no pots.

"So we get out there and: now, how are you going to cook? What are you going to eat on? Even if you get paper plates and plastic forks and knives, you try to find that stuff in Malibu. Forget it.

"Bobby had mailed us the keys and the directions. He was living on Rodeo Drive. My mother called Bobby and said, 'Sweetheart, there's nothing in the house.' He said, 'What do you mean?' She explained. 'Yeah,' he said, 'I rented it unfurnished.' At the beginning of the third month, August, Bobby drops the bomb on Nina: 'I'm selling everything and moving to Big Sur. You're fired. You have to return the car to Jersey.'

"When Bobby told us, Nina said, 'But sweetheart, we came all the way out here, we spent all that money to get here, to furnish the house. Why didn't you tell us if you knew you were going to do this?' Bobby replied, 'Well, I wanted you to have one last good summer.' He said the car had to be immediately returned by a certain date. Nina said, 'What do you mean? The car is mine.' Bobby said, 'Oh no, the car's not yours. The car is leased.'"

It all sunk in. As of September 1, the mortgage payment was due on their New Jersey house—also a house Bobby had told Nina he was buying for her but had then reneged on and had only paid the down payment for. Nina was no longer employed by Bobby. She had no car, no job, and no money.

The family raced the car back to New Jersey and returned it. Two weeks later the assistant manager of the car dealership called Nina and said, "You know, I don't know why Mr. Darin had to surrender the car. He bought a three-year lease and he still has to pay the entire lease whether he uses the car or not. It's a closed-end lease." Bobby had them frantically go 3,000 miles to return a car that did not have to be returned at all. "My mother," Gary says, "had less than a month to find a job, get a car, and have enough money from whatever job she could get to pay the house mortgage that was due on the first of September. Bobby was punishing the whole family."

BOBBY HAD SPENT THE YEAR liquidating most of his holdings. He sold his real estate and sorted out his possessions. He put boxes into storage and gave away the rest of his possessions to friends or charities. "I want to get back to basic reality," he told the press.

"One morning he came over to my house," Carol Lynley remembers, "and he sat me down and he said, 'Carol, I'm going to die.'

"I said, 'Oh Bobby, we're all going to die.'"

"'No,' he said, 'I've just been to the doctor. I've been to several of them. I've willed what's left of my body to science.' And eye bags. He willed his eyes to somebody that he knew, and whatever organs were in good shape. He said he was going away for a while. I just started shaking."

"My wife and I visited Bobby on Rodeo Drive before he went to Big Sur," Dick Lord recalls. "People were coming in and saying, 'Bobby, could I have that?' He would say, 'Yeah, take it.' He was giving everything away, his clothes, chandeliers, coffee tables. I still have this little old-fashioned candy-ball machine where you put in the money and get the candy ball out. He said to me, 'Take that.' I said, 'Bobby, I can't. I can't stand it. People are coming in and taking everything out of your house. I don't want it.'

"He said, 'Okay, I'll tell you what. You take it and give me four hundred. Would that make you feel better?' So I said okay, I'll take it. I still have it in my office."

THERE WAS TURMOIL WITHIN HIM and turmoil outside. Each week brought arrests, trials, anti-war demonstrations, and demonstrations by GIs opposed to the war.

"When RFK was murdered, that's when Bobby went to Big Sur, threw the show-business thing away to become a political musical satirist, and find his way and become a poet," says Tony Orlando. "The shock of RFK's death never really left Bobby Darin. I think it had a lot to do with making him even more tired. I think a piece of the shrapnel of that bullet entered Bobby's spirit."

"He gave up his house in Rodeo Drive because he wanted a simpler life," says Carol Lynley. "He lost all his money. He was very angry. Then his career bottomed out because no one wanted to see him in jeans playing a guitar. They wanted Bobby Darin."

BOBBY WENT INTO SECLUSION in Big Sur, a Pacific shore community some 150 miles south of San Francisco where the Big Sur River meets the sea. There was a 50-mile stretch of beautiful coastline just below Carmel.

"He moved to a 14-foot trailer in an apple orchard in Big Sur," says Steve Blauner. "Now the trailer that he lived in was a tiny ugly thing, but it was on a piece of farmland owned by a man named Jan Brewer in an area known as Fifer's Beach. Brewer's farm was two steps away from this arbor of Cyprus trees that you walked through onto a beach like you've never seen in your life, with white sand, nobody there. And he just lived in that trailer. Chopped wood and went to the library a lot."

It was a time of reflection, of taking stock, of seeking the peace that would always elude him. He wandered the beach, strummed his guitar, and read books at random at the library in Carmel. But he was, as always, restless, and when he was offered a two-week run in Vegas, he took it.

"Bobby got an engagement at the Sahara in Vegas," Quitman Dennis says, "and came back from Big Sur just for the two weeks. He had a full-size cutout poster of him based on the image used on his new *Commitment* album. The poster was placed beside the front of the door coming into the Sahara's Congo Room, and his billing on the marquee was 'Bob Darin,' not Bobby Darin. People were dissatisfied with what Bobby was doing. The material was going over their heads. Soon I could see people leaving, filing out of the room."

Bobby told Al Aronowitz of the *New York Post*: "As I walked out on the floor, they walked out of the audience. That's the key thing I remember, the total feeling of rejection, like I had come down with the plague."

Don Gregory became Bobby's agent at APA (Agency for the Performing Arts) in 1969. "Bobby said, 'You know, I want to perform. But I'm not going to be Bobby anymore. If you're my manager, I want you to go into this with your eyes open. I'm going to be Bob.'

"I said sure. I didn't know exactly what Bob Darin meant, but I figured he's going to bring his charisma to whatever he does. So I booked him at the Sahara Hotel. The booking person there had the same reaction I had: 'Bob, Bobby, what's the difference?' Bobby sat on a stool for 45 minutes and bored everyone to death. Everyone came out in shock."

"When Bobby started going back on stage in denim tuxedos," says Jimmy Darren, "we would talk and I would say, 'What the fuck is that? What the fuck is that? A tuxedo made out of Levi material? Give me a break.' And Bobby would say, 'What the fuck do you know? This is hip; this is the way it's gonna be.'"

After the Sahara, Bobby went back to Big Sur and decided to try his hand as a filmmaker. Bobby came up with a story idea that paralleled his experience in the music industry. The script, titled *The Vendors*, was about a folk singer-songwriter, a heroin addict, trying to break through, who wins a contract with a music publisher in New York. They want him to dilute his lyrics, take any topical or political bite out of them, and make them more commercial.

"I remember that the protagonist (played by Gary Wood) was held captive trying to churn out these hits," recalls Terry Koenig. "He was chained to a chair in a room writing songs. As though he's a vendor. If it wasn't entirely about Bobby, it was about what the music business had evolved into. After all, Bobby came up through 1650 Broadway that had fabulous talent pouring out the windows. And it was spontaneous fun then. But by 1970 the music business had morphed into something that was much more venal."

Gary Wood met Bobby at a party in Dean Martin's home in Palm Springs. Wood became a close friend. "I was a young actor out from New York—young, dumb, full of testosterone. Bobby had dated my wife in the past, so when he came into the room, it made my blood boil. I didn't say a word. He looked at me and said, 'You haven't said anything. What are you thinking about?' And I heard myself say, 'I think you're full of shit.' The place went dead still. And Bobby just looked at me and he got a grin on his face from ear to ear, and he said, 'That's exactly right. But so are you.' In that instant we became forever pals.

"I got a call the next day from him. 'Hey G,' he said. 'Listen, I'm making this movie. I wrote it. I'm going to have it FedEx'ed to you. Look it over. Let me know if you want to do it. I don't need to have you read, I know you can act.' Just like that. The part was Willy, the lead. It was a very low-budget picture. But it was *Gone With the Wind* as far as I was concerned. We filmed in Venice. The movie was a dark picture. The theme was that everybody was selling something, that this was the underbelly of society. I played a pimp, a music manager, a villainous amoral character who totally relished his own evilness. My character controlled the boy who was the singer and the hooker, Mariette Hartley, who worked for me. The hooker and the boy fell in love, and I made their lives miserable.

"Bear in mind I was completely broke. But in the movie I'm playing a guy who's very, very flush. There's no double for my suit. I've got one suit. It's a beauty, a Brioni, it cost a thousand dollars in 1970. And we had a scene to shoot at the beach at sunset. A five-minute take. No cuts. We rehearsed all day, and we only had one shot at it. That's it. Sunset only happens one time. We didn't have the police security you usually have.

"But there was a big crowd around. We're rehearsing the scene. I'm concerned about not making any mistakes in a one-time-only take. All of a sudden, there's a bum standing there who's stoned on downs. 'I don't like Bobby Darin; who does he think he is?' He thinks I'm Bobby Darin. Because I'm sitting in a big beautiful Cadillac convertible in a Brioni suit. I look like a million bucks. Bobby you wouldn't even notice. He's this little short schlemiel with a fishing hat covering half his face and shades. So this bum thinks I'm Bobby and he hates me. He's interrupting every take and talking. We ask him to please be quiet. It means nothing. He's stoned; he's enjoying the attention he's getting.

"Now he starts walking into the shot, trying to hit me. He's trying to walk in from my back where I can't see him. It was scary. Finally we do the take and the guy comes for me. And I see him. I'm not thinking about the movie anymore; I'm back in Brooklyn. I unhook myself from the microphone and I get out of the car. And I hit him with a solid left to the body and a right to the head that picked him up and spread him across the car. He gets off that car and looks at me and smiles, like Lee Marvin. I shit in my pants. I'm 185 pounds, I'm ripped, and I'm in shape. I hit this guy with the two best punches I had and he smiles at me bleeding. All of a sudden I hear on a megaphone someone shouting: 'No! The suit! Save the suit!' It was Bobby. The crew gets around me to protect me, or protect the suit. They take the guy and handle him. And Bobby strolls up to me casually and he says, 'Hey G., what happened?' I looked at Bobby and I said, 'I don't know. Must have lost my punch,' and we laughed. We shot it another time.

"When Bobby finished the movie, he hoped Columbia would put it out. It was so dark they didn't want to go near it. Bobby was so pissed off and offended that instead of researching and finding a release for it, he just decided fuck it. He didn't want a failure. He wouldn't even let me see it. I got into a fight with him about it. So he showed it to me. It really was too black. In my death scene, Bobby was poking at me with a stick to give me a specific point of reference to where I was being stabbed. A guy that was as bad as me had to die a horrible death. So I'm stabbed like 35 times which Bobby just shot in a close-up of my face. Under the camera he was hitting me with the stick."

Bobby returned from Big Sur to Beverly Hills in May 1970 and set about reclaiming his career and finding a distributor for *The Vendors*. The movie went nowhere. There are no prints surviving of the film, but those who saw it unanimously agreed that it was an inchoate mess. He wanted to get back to performing in nightclubs, but nightclubs did not want Bob Darin.

"One night we went out," Gary Wood recalls, "and I sat down with him and said, 'You know what, Bobby? You're totally fucked up. What's the point you're trying to make with Bob Darin? I know you don't want to feel like a monkey, pleasing the Man. But who's getting ripped off by you not going on stage and doing all your stuff? You are. You like to do that. You do it all the time with me. Why are you denying yourself the pleasure that you get from it? Why is it important for you to go out and spit in the eye of the audience? What is the payoff for you?' Literally from that moment, he started to go back to being Bobby Darin. He said, 'You're right, G.' That's just how Bobby was. If you reached him and he got what you said, that was it.

"Two things: Bobby always wanted to be Frank Sinatra. On the other hand, Bobby hated all those wiseguys. He didn't like any of that stuff. He had his opportunity. Bobby didn't want to be owned by anybody. I think that Bobby felt he was a talented enough singer to not need to do any of that stuff. As a performer, he was this whirling dervish and did all these things and was so entertaining. But I think he wanted to be able to just walk out there and sing and everybody would just flock to him. I think he felt a little bit maybe like a dancing bear."

"Then Bobby came back to Hollywood and asked me if I could get him back into Las Vegas," Don Gregory remembers. "I said it would be hard. He said, 'Well, it won't be Bob Darin.' I said, 'Is it gonna be Bobby Darin?' I said, 'Look, you don't have to wear a tux. Have a tailor-made denim suit made.' So he went to this tailor in Beverly Hills and had a couple of them made. And he looked great. 'Maybe you could do 'Mack the Knife' your way, with those four musicians,' I said. So he wound up doing that. I got him into the Landmark Hotel. He did a beautiful mix; he did 'Bridge Over Troubled Waters.' And he did 'Mack.'"

Terry Koenig first saw Bobby perform at the Landmark. "The Landmark was off the strip; it didn't have the prestige. Bobby was in desperate straits. He had no money when he started back. It was a 'get started' move. His rooms at the Landmark were horrible, not your normal Vegas rooms with mirrors on the walls. It was closed in; they just had drapes. It was shabby for him. I think he looked at it as 'I'm coming out of nowhere; I'm coming out of retirement; I'm lucky to get this.' It wasn't what he was used to, but he was a trouper. He was still wearing denim. He was working on his identity. He still had his moustache and wasn't wearing a toupee."

Bobby's compromise was working for audiences. He augmented his four-piece band. "Bobby called me," Quitman Dennis recalls, "and said we were going into the Landmark. He was adding seven horns: three tenors, three trumpets, and a baritone sax. He wanted me to add horn arrangements on ten songs, maybe even 'Long Line Rider' and some of the stuff from the *Commitment* album. The Landmark engagement was actually successful enough. I think Bobby adjusted right off the bat and didn't push the Arkansas protest songs. He just kind of let those slide, because he wanted to stay on stage. And they rebooked us. The second time I got the phone call from him that said, 'The rhythm section shouldn't dress casually now; we should get tuxedos.' Bobby was giving up little pieces at a time."

Bobby's return was welcomed with relief by audiences. If it was not the familiar, pure, and unadulterated Darin that audiences loved, they would take what they could get, even a piece of him. There was still enough recognizable about him now to embrace. To the extent that Bobby allowed himself to reemerge into some semblance of what they regarded as his true self, they were overjoyed.

And then Bobby met a true love. "One day we were horseback riding," says Carol Lynley. "This was after Bobby gave up the acoustic guitar and went back to snapping his fingers and making money. Bobby said, 'I'm in love.' And he said, 'I've met a girl named Andy.'"

Chapter Fourteen

ROMAN CANDLE

BOBBY WOULD EXPERIENCE extraordinary triumphs and defeats, frightening illnesses, and amazing recoveries and comebacks in the next period of his life. He would bound back with a superhuman resilience. His was a flame that burned very brightly, like a roman candle that burns the brightest before it extinguishes itself.

Bobby's love life was compartmentalized among his real relationships, his flings with glamorous celebrities, his fantasies and daydreams, and a private swinging side. Like everything else he did, Bobby's sexual appetite was gargantuan. "Hey, it didn't matter what," a friend says, "he liked it. Watch, not watch, listen. He'd listen to a couple having sex by putting a glass against the wall. 'What are ya doin'?' I said. Bobby replied, 'Don't you ever listen? Oh, it's a turn-on.' In the final years, he would go to a house called Sandstone up in the hills of Malibu. He would sneak in the back way to conceal his identity and enter a room that was totally dark with writhing bodies on the floor.

"Bobby and the band would have what they called these little freaking parties," Bill McCubbin recalls. "They'd have sex with each other's girlfriends. One time in New York, Tommy was with these three girls. Terry Kellman was there. And Bobby, he just sat around and made small talk for a while. I had never done this, and I was thinking, I don't know if I'm into this or not. Bobby is sitting there and he gets up, goes in the other room, and comes walking out bare-assed naked in front of all of us. This one girl sitting there, he starts talking to her, holding her, caressing her. Her clothes are coming off so fast she doesn't know how to react."

Then he fell in love with Andrea Yeager. "He talked to me about it," Carol Lynley recalls. "'You must meet her,' he said. So I did. Andrea looked a lot easier to control than Sandy. Sandy was a movie star and had a very protected life. Andy looked to me more like a normal girl, and I thought that was good for Bobby. She wasn't a performer. She seemed absolutely thrilled to be around him. She couldn't believe her good fortune."

Those who met Andrea have a very positive feeling about her. "The first time I met Andrea, I fell in love with her," says Steve Blauner. "As a human being. She didn't want anything from Bobby. You couldn't have had a more stand-up person around you. There weren't two people that loved Bobby more than Andrea and myself." This was something new for Bobby: someone divorced from the show-business milieu who loved him unconditionally out of pure motives, who was not looking for anything from him, who was willing to confront the grim reality of his illness and help him in any way she could and stick with him with complete devotion. Sandra had fine qualities, but she was a victim of her childhood.

"Bobby never knew that relationships could bring him real joy in life," Jerrold Atlas says. "He couldn't appreciate that others would care about him. I thought the only time he was getting that sense of joy was with Andrea. There was something so innocent about their relationship. I saw him with Andrea in L.A. I remember Andrea being very quiet and holding his hand every so often. I know that Andrea loved him deeply, and I know that up to three months before he died, Bobby was terribly in love with her. Bobby was so at peace and happy with her."

Quitman Dennis was not so sure. "I think it was more important to Bobby to live a short and bright and flame-out life than it was to be a happy person in a longer-term way. But he had a good relationship with Andrea. And his son. There were good things in his life that this compulsion to a meteoric burn-out was in conflict with."

"Andrea met Bobby in 1970," remembers Terry Koenig, Andrea's sister. "He was just coming out of Big Sur. Andrea was working as a receptionist at a law firm Bobby was using when he had to go down to Long Beach to sign some papers. Bobby had a keen sense of time and taste and chutzpah. And he asked my sister if he could see her. I'm sure she went screaming home. This was like Prince Charming came down off the hill. I know she was dazzled. She adored him. She loved him so much she never said no, to anything.

"First Bobby and Andrea were living in a cottage in Malibu, then a little barn overlooking all of Coldwater Canyon, and then at Paul Newman's house on Heather. What really touched me about Bobby was watching him father my sister's sons and be a good dad. He was a beautiful soul that way. He would listen to them. That was back when people would not listen to children. I'd never seen that before. His spending time and creating space for them—along with Dodd—to express themselves. And Bobby loved Dodd, just loved his little boy so much. He was his treasure. Just the way they talked to each other, like they were men."

Bobby was enraged by the continuation of the war. He took out newspaper ads in May 1970 denouncing President Nixon's decision to invade Cambodia. He took part in an anti-war demonstration on May 12, 1970, at Los Angeles City Hall. And on May 23, 1972, he paid for a full-page ad in *The Hollywood Reporter* in support of John and Yoko Lennon in their fight against ongoing deportation efforts by the U.S. government:

The Hollywood Reporter   Tuesday, May 23, 1972

A COMMITTEE OF ONE SUGGESTS:

LET THE LENNONS STAY

Although I do not know John and Yoko Lennon personally, I feel that I know their hearts.

They are people whose concern for humanity has been proven countless times.

America could use more people like the Lennons. If you agree, a note to your representatives in Washington, D.C., will help.

—Peace,

Bobby Darin

Many of Bobby's own show-business colleagues could not relate to and did not support his political outspokenness. "Bobby was the darkest human being in the world during that Big Sur time," says Steve Metz. "How do you walk away from a career, take your hairpiece off, run around in jeans, and not be in terrible pain?" And Bobby had a new reason to be angry after Big Sur: he had lost $350,000 producing *The Vendors*. He was broke.

T. K. Kellman joined the band when he met Bobby in 1970. "Bobby had just come back from Big Sur. He made that denim tuxedo. He was in a real left-wing mood. It happened that he was playing to a convention for General Motors. The 'enemy.' The guy who sat down in front looked like Klaus Bormann. Real close-cut cropped hair, very Germanic, and Bobby just didn't like him. He was yelling at him that the Germans made cars that just lasted three years and all that stuff. People weren't pleased. Something snapped in him when he saw this guy, and Bobby was picking on him all night. He actually strutted like a Nazi in front of him. It was a tantrum. Bobby was a hot-tempered guy."

Kellman, Tommy Amato, Bobby Rozario, Quitman Dennis, Billy Aiken, Bill McCubbin—the musicians who worked with Bobby in the final years—formed a tight unit of affection. They came to know all his insecurities and fears. "Bobby was like a banty rooster," says Tommy Amato. "One night we're at the Desert Inn. Bobby's moody. He gets a standing ovation for the show. After the show he called me and the guys to come to see him, like he was pissed off. We go to his dressing room, and he's saying, 'Man, what happened? What happened? What's going on out there?' Billy Aiken and I look at each other. There's this gentleman's highboy, this chest of drawers in his room. Bobby starts yanking the drawers out, like having a baby's fit. 'That show! What happened?' We say to him, 'Bobby, you got a standing ovation, man. How bad could it be? I thought it was a great show.' Bobby says, 'Oh, a great show, eh?' He needed the reassurance. He didn't really know. And we calmed him down. He said, 'Oh, it was a good show, huh?'"

"Bobby had a lot of those moments," says Kellman. "And yet he would always tell me that the only time he felt most at home, relaxed, most comfortable in his skin, was when he was on stage."

Bobby's art became a casualty of Vietnam. With the advent of the war, young people, the generation right behind him, saw the tuxedo as slickness. It had vanished so fast: overnight, all of a sudden, Frank and Dean, *Ocean's 11*, the Rat Pack, all seemed ridiculous, dated, trivial. Suddenly, what Bobby had wanted to be all his life, a tuxedo-wearing, slick, hip, finger-snapping Sinatra—better than Sinatra—throwing the microphone up in the air and catching it the way Woody Allen's Broadway Danny Rose taught Lou Canova, the fat crooner, in the movie—the guys who had it made, worried only about getting their cocks sucked and their tans and their booze—seemed silly.

But the tuxedo was an essential part of how he performed and sang. He not only removed the tuxedo, he removed the essence of his voice—his whole soul—in the folk period. He became another person and he throttled the best of himself. He did it with the best of motives, but for the wrong reasons. He was not rejecting his mode of singing—and the beautiful songs of the great American catalog of pop music—for artistic reasons. He was doing it to raise social consciousness, and as a result, he strayed from what he was best at doing, what he was born to do. He confused message with the art.

What Bobby didn't get was that he was the real deal. He was the *last*. He was the last of the giants in the Sinatra and Dean Martin mode. And at his best, he was every bit as good. Sometimes he was better. Sometimes he was so frighteningly good he seemed to come from outer space. He was the last American performer to wear a tuxedo on stage and get away with it. The minute he rejected his identity, he lost his relevance.

The fact of the matter is, the pictures of Bobby in his folk period are pictures of a lost soul.

But in 1970–71, Bobby was slowly making his way back to the show-business and Hollywood milieus he had contemptuously rejected. Anyone who knows the Hollywood scene knows that you don't walk away and come back that easily. The magic gate, with its entry to unbounded privilege and status and money, slams shut. It's like trying to return to a lover you've spurned. But there was something more: the scent of moral censure, of judgment coming from Bobby. The show-business establishment did not want to be told it was immoral and corrupt—especially by someone rattling the gate and begging to be readmitted. Bobby had been loved by show business. Bobby *was* show business. The rejection had all come from his end. He'd said it was all a crock. For the rest of his life, Bobby would practically be impaled on that gate, not quite out and not quite in.

Bobby had become ambivalent, disingenuous. Young people love Dean and Frank today, and they are always hip, because they were totally in earnest, what they were, no more, no less. They were totally real and natural; that was what was so great about them. "You could be a black hip-hop artist," says Bruce Charet, "but nobody's cooler than Dean Martin. And the reason for that is there's not a phony bone in his body."

In 1947, Bobby and John Bravo were watching vaudeville's dying embers at the RKO Royal, Loew's National, and the Bronx Opera House, when they stayed all day and evening to watch it again and again. But even in its death throes, it had the vitality and spontaneity of veteran show people singing their hearts out; it had a profound intimacy and brotherhood in the bond between performer and audience. Polly had introduced Bobby from his earliest youth to the charm of vaudeville. It was in his blood. When he removed it, he removed the life veins from his body.

Bobby did it because he was drawn by good instincts; his search gives him depth and scope. He was emblematic of a whole generation.

It was a righteous failure.

What has survived is the best of Bobby: Bobby when he swung the standards. "Bobby was like a sponge," Bobby Rozario recalls. "He was a great actor. He was a great impressionist. Which meant he could do anything he wanted to do. So that was a gift and a problem to him from my perspective. I think it kept him from focusing on one thing. And that had a lot to do with him not becoming bigger. But today the audience has made the choice about what they like best about Bobby: the swinging stuff. That was unbelievable. Bobby could swing better and harder than any other singer in the business, including Frank and Sammy. Bobby had that instinct for the swing music he got from

Charlie Maffia in those old 78s. When he played drums, he played like Gene Krupa. When you listen to 'Beyond the Sea,' Bobby puts things into it—a phrase, a little riff, *bzee beep bzee za*—that's right off of Benny Goodman's records. Whatever Bobby was influenced by, *he did it better*. Electricity. Everfresh. He could do it all."

But now he had to eat. "When Bobby realized the folk thing wasn't working," Bobby Rozario recalls, "he knew he had to get back and make some money. He was always worried about Dodd. That when he was gone, Dodd had to be well taken care of. Bobby called me and said, 'Listen, I'm putting my tuxedo on, I'm putting back my tupe, do you want to come back to work?' I said, 'Yeah.' I said, 'When do you want me to start?' He said, 'You can start tomorrow.' So I said okay."

"I went to work for Bobby as his publicist when he came back from Big Sur," remembers Mimi Greenberg. "He scrupulously avoided the Hollywood scene, the lifestyle he had lived during his first incarnation there. He certainly seemed to be more stable and happier once Andrea moved in with him. He rented a beach house in Malibu. Andrea was a very kind, sweet person, a very passive person without a lot of fire in the belly. Bobby married the same woman twice. He married women who really needed to have him tell them what to do."

"I think that Bobby was a depressive. He would have swings into mania—that was when he would have a million creative ideas. But I also experienced him at some of the lowest lows—it was frightening the lows that he sank to. When he came out of Big Sur, he hadn't fully hatched the plan, but I think that somewhere in the recesses of his mind, Bobby was either going to make it superbig and become the superstar that he always wanted to be, or he was going to check out. He was very successful when he came back, absolutely. But he made terrible demands on himself. He felt that if he wasn't the biggest thing, that he was nothing. The film he made, *The Vendors*, was really reflective of the very confused and depressed state he was in.

"Bobby wasn't Jewish, but he was the most Jewish Italian I ever knew. He reminded me of a really smart Jewish guy: the passion, the appreciation of irony, sarcasm, futility. And the intellectual capabilities. He had that New York street-smarts thing about him that frequently gets confused with being Jewish. I wouldn't say he was very Jewish; he was very *haimeshe*. I felt like we'd grown up in the same neighborhood, went to the same school, lived on the same block. I genuinely liked him. I thought he was crazier than a bedbug and could be so difficult. He was very mercurial, quixotic. I don't know any woman he put his mind to that he didn't get. He thought he was uglier than sin. He told me that frequently."

Bobby went to Toronto in October 1970 to tape a TV special called *The Darin Invasion*. At the taping of the program, Hesh Wasser discovered just how desperately sick Bobby really was. "That time I saw Bobby almost dead," Hesh says. "He was crumpled on the floor in front of the dressing room door, gasping. Bobby said, 'Hesh, I've just been sitting here for half an hour, not doing anything, but my heartbeat feels as if I'm running a marathon. Hesh, I'm scared. I'm really scared.' He was crying. I put my arms around him. Then Bobby said, 'If anybody finds out about this, I'll know who told them.'"

These attacks had happened many times, but they were becoming much more frequent, and he was terrified. They were called fibrillations. For ten hours at a time his heart would beat 140 to 160 times a minute instead of the normal 60 to 80. Bobby would come down with pneumonia every 18 months or so.

The doctors called for immediate open-heart surgery. Two of Bobby's four heart valves were malfunctioning and had to be replaced. The advanced medical procedure was called cardioversion, involving the use of anticoagulants and a synchronized defibrillator, which would stop the heart and then shock it into the proper rhythm.

Bobby was determined to keep his next engagement at the Desert Inn in January 1971 for six weeks and then go in for the open-heart surgery. He wanted a last hurrah. He did not expect to survive.

"Bobby came to me," Steve Blauner says, "and he says, 'I'm going back into the tuxedo.' I say, 'Why?' 'Because I don't want to stand in line for medical treatment.'"

It was not really the old Bobby at the Desert Inn, but a hybrid. Bobby dropped all of his own protest songs except "Simple Song of Freedom" for this engagement. The lineup of songs represented a reluctant concession to what Bobby was known for. But the tug on Bobby was still overwhelmingly toward the new. He sang Laura Nyro's "Save the Country," James Taylor, Dylan, and the Beatles.

"That was a 28-day engagement, two shows a night, and there's no break in there anywhere," Quitman Dennis remembers. "Bobby was not appearing to be well. We didn't see him very much. He seemed like he could barely muster the strength to do the show. He was eating steak and spinach and nothing else. He'd stay up late after the show and watch old Marx Brothers movies. Sleep during the day and come back for the next show. A lot of his old friends were coming to visit. Dick Lord, his old buddy, was the opening comic. People coming and going in the dressing room, because word was getting out that Bobby's not having a comfortable time physically."

"At the Desert Inn," Dick Lord says, "he would stay in bed all day and just get up and do the shows, and then go back to bed. And I would sit with him until maybe five in the morning. He had Andrea with him. We would just talk, watch a movie. One night he said to me, 'I'm not going to make it through this operation.' And I said, 'What are you talking about? Of course you are.' He said no. He called the hospital: 'Nine out of ten operations are successful.' I said, 'So. There you go.' He said, 'You don't understand. I'm the tenth one.'

"And then on closing night, the outer dressing rooms were filled with reporters, all the good wishes, fan club president, whatever. And I walked in and Bobby said, 'Everybody has to leave the dressing room, if you don't mind.' So I was about to leave. He says, 'Dick, could you stay a minute, please?' I walked into the inner dressing room, and he hugged me and he kissed me like he would never see me again. I was crying.

"Jim O'Neill, the road manager, had set up this little station wagon with a bed in the back, mattress, pillows, books, a lamp, and an ice-cream sundae—that was a big treat for him. And you could hear the audience in the nightclub still applauding. And Bobby went out with Jim O'Neill, got in the station wagon, got in his little bed in the back, and was holding this cup of ice cream. And he was waving to me. And the station wagon drove away."

The operation at Cedars of Lebanon took nine hours. Two plastic valves were inserted into Bobby's heart. Bobby stayed in intensive care for five days, and he recuperated in the hospital for six weeks. Andrea stayed by his side.

Steve Blauner would visit daily. "I'd go see him and come home and tell my wife, 'Oh, he's great. You can come.' So I take her down one night and we walked in the room, and you could smell death. It was awful. And my wife went into shock. I remember she took his hand and kissed it. That freaked him out. We went outside, and on the steps of the hospital, I grabbed her and broke down. And I said, 'I'm never going to see him again. Because he's got to have died.' And then something happened, and all of a sudden, he was fine. The doctors didn't know what to do. And I was told later, these doctors were sitting around, and one of them said, 'Well, whatta we got to lose? Let's change the medication.' Take a shot. It was like shooting crap in Vegas. And they changed the medication, and he improved immediately."

Bobby felt better than he had felt in many years. He felt as if he had been reborn. He had come so close to death once again. He had been put on steroids and gained a great deal of weight. He grew a red beard and put away his hairpiece. After six weeks of rest, Bobby was back in the big time, headlining at Harrah's in Reno. He had a sharp tuxedo on, and a hairpiece, and he was doing some of the show-business shtick that the audience loved, including his impressions. "That's All" and "Beyond the Sea" were back, but trying also to hold on to what he'd spent so much time and effort cultivating, he also sang his three most palatable "folk" numbers: "I'll Be Your Baby Tonight," "If I Were a Carpenter," and "Simple Song of Freedom."

In February 24, 1972, Bobby took the gamble of trying to reclaim his reputation at the biggest and most important nightclub, the Copa. There were fences to be mended with Jules Podell. Bobby called and said he had done a bad thing the last time and that he knew that he was really a saloon singer, that's what he was. He was dynamite at the club; this was his turf, and Podell loved him and had only wanted to forgive him his trespasses all along.

Bobby also returned to another scene of his earlier triumphs, the Coconut Grove in Los Angeles. Jack Giladi was in the audience. "He cut the hair, the moustache, left the guitar," Giladi recalls. "But the response wasn't as strong. The turnout was good, but it wasn't the electrified audience that Bobby had before. If you're in the limelight and you win the World Series, they remember you from that. Next year you might come in second; they don't remember that. I remembered Bobby so well from the nightclubs and that pin spot would open up on his hand and he just clicked his fingers, and you knew that that whole audience was electrified."

Bobby had dropped the torch, and when he reclaimed it, the flame was not quite as bright. The problem Bobby faced was that the minute he turned his back on what he was loved for—and what he loved—and then went back to it, it was never quite the same thing. A cord had snapped—in him, in his relationship with his audience.

OUT OF THE BLUE, Bobby was given a great new opportunity in the summer of 1972. NBC hired him as the star of a seven-week summer replacement for *The Dean Martin Show*. Bobby's show was named *The Bobby Darin Amusement Company*. It seemed tailor-made for Bobby. It would be a variety show—vaudeville, his first love—and he was temporarily filling the slot of one of his idols, the great Dean Martin. There would be comedy skits, ample time for Bobby's singing and clowning, duets with guest stars, and room for spontaneity and inventiveness. It was a real coup for Bobby, considering the ups and downs of his career. Above all, it was the chance to learn and master yet another branch of show business: star of his own variety series. Bobby always thrived on something new, learning new skills. And he did: the show was a free-wheeling, spontaneous affair, relaxed, funny, and engaging on every level. It bristled with creative energy—Bobby's and the talent he assembled. Bobby hired his old pal, Dick Lord, as creative consultant. Bobby was careful not to overwork. After each week's show—four days of rehearsal and taping—Bobby and Andrea went to the country and camped out for three days.

Bobby made the show into a genuine triumph. It scored high ratings.

Dick Bakalyan had become good friends with Bobby when he appeared with him in *Pressure Point*, and Bobby asked him to join the cast of the new TV show. "The producers, Saul Ilson and Ernie Chambers, weren't sure about me," Bakalyan recalls. "They said, 'Dick is a good actor, but we need a comic for this spot.' Bobby said, 'Dickie's an actor. He'll play a comic playing the part.' The busted nose gives me the New York sound. They said my hair was too white; Bobby said, 'Put a rinse in it.' So Bobby gave me the opportunity to do many things that I might never have had the chance to do. 'Carmine and Angie' was Bobby's idea, the old Italian neighborhood in the Bronx. In fact, the stoop, the set, was actually a replica of the front of the brownstone in the Bronx where Bobby grew up. Walden Robert Cassotto."

"Carmine and Angie" would become the most popular, most loved, and most remembered segment of the program. Bobby returning to his Italian-American roots and exploring his Italian background with tenderness and affection. The skit conjured up the daydreams, yearnings, and vain hopes of two neighborhood pals just goofing their lives slowly away. In the skits, Bobby was dressed in a Mets cap and jacket. He played Angie, the more cynical of the two young men, married, world-weary. Dick Bakalyan was the more innocent Carmine who lived with his mother and was in love with all of the girls in the neighborhood. They both spoke with lightly tinged New York–Italian accents.

"Bobby was continuing his childhood or his teenagehood in those skits," Dick Bakalyan goes on. "He was hitting on something. We got a lot of mail on it. Not just guys from the city, but people from all over that understood friendship and pals. Chums. That's why when he would go, 'Ey, stay out of the street, Anthony'—he'd throw out lines like guys playing stickball. It reminded him of who he was there, himself, not the celebrity. And he loved my character, Carmine, because it reminded him of a lot of the guys that wanted to leave the old neighborhood. In the sketch there was always a broad with me, always a chick I met and wanted to jump, and he talked me out of it. Made me realize the reality here."

The skits became a mainstay of the program. They were by no means outright farce. They were gentle, humorous, low-key, sharply observed vignettes of lived immigrant experience and they were filled with affection.

NBC was delighted with the show and renewed it for a regular season run starting in January 1973. That was when things started to go awry. Bobby didn't want to go on with it. He told Dick Lord he was tired of "auditioning." But he reluctantly agreed to continue.

Meanwhile he was headlining all over the country. Terry Koenig, Andrea's sister, was working as Bobby's valet, overall assistant, and gofer during the tour. Sometimes she would forget to lay out Bobby's three condoms.

"Terry came into our dressing room," Bill McCubbin remembers, "and said, 'Oh God, I forgot the condoms.' I'd never heard that before about anyone else. Before or since. I remember one time there was some lady out of the audience who just had to meet Bobby. She was like just squirming in her chair. And I walked her up to his dressing room. And Bobby was walking around, he was just pulling off his pants. He didn't care. He turned around and dropped his shorts and he pulled the condom off, right in front of her. And her eyes kind of opened up. She couldn't talk for about two minutes. And he just casually pulled his pants on. Then he said, 'Hi, how are you?' She was just stammering. Wetting her pants."

"But Bobby's heart was starting to go on him again," Terry Koenig says. "What I saw about him was his courage and his intellect take over when he had this rotten heart inside of him. Just watching him tackle it as though it were a problem to be solved. He got right in there, rolled up his sleeves. That last year, we did the TV show, and Vegas again in February 1973."

Bobby wanted Dodd to know where he had come from, and so in February 1973 he took Dodd on a tour of the old New York neighborhoods. Charlie Maffia drove the limousine. Bobby showed Dodd the Bronx streets where he'd played stickball, Clark Junior High, the Bronx High School of Science, Baruch Place, and the Catskills. When they were near Baruch Place on the Lower East Side, Bobby pointed to a young boy shining shoes and said, "If it weren't for me, that could be you." Dodd wasn't impressed. That trip still enrages Bobby's brother, Gary, for he regards it as an example of Bobby spitting on his family and his past—and particularly on the mother who had borne both of them.

"Bobby was showing Dodd all the places he'd lived and the scum that he came from," recalls Gary. "Bobby told Nina in the car later what the day with Dodd had been like. Nina said that her mother, Polly, was the most brilliant person she had ever known. And Bobby said again that if Polly was so brilliant, how come she had lived in those slums all those years and never gotten out of them? And my mother started to cry. I was 16. And despite all the things that Bobby had done to her, she had never cried in front of him. And Bobby said, 'What are you crying for?' Charlie didn't stop the car, but he turned to Bobby and said, 'You have no right to say anything about Polly.' It was the first and only time I saw Charlie talk back to Bobby. Bobby didn't reply, because he'd won. He'd made her cry."

"In December 1972, Bobby came to see me," Steve Blauner recalls. "He wanted me to manage him again. He said he made a million dollars last year, which was more than he made when he was hot. But he didn't sell any records. He said, 'Look, I need you ten minutes a day from your office, beep beep beep.' What I did was come up with a deal. I wasn't going to say no to him; I didn't have the heart. But I was going to get him to say no to me. So I said, 'Okay, I'll manage you, but this is the deal: 1) We gotta have a contract in writing; 2) I want a million dollars guaranteed whether you ever work a day or not in your life, against 20 percent, and 3) I don't travel anymore. I've got a wife and a kid. You can't call me after six o'clock at night and never on weekends.

And if your lawyer lets you make this deal, we gotta fire him and sit down and figure out who we're gonna get to manage you instead of me.' And Bobby looked up and said, 'You got it.'

"And I remember going home to my wife and I say to her, I was like in shock, 'We're now managing Bobby Darin.' And she put her arms around me and said, 'Only you will know when to walk away.'"

"I think Bobby was looking for shelter when he went back to Steve," Terry Koenig says. "I just think he knew time was running out and he could not afford to be fucked up or fucked over."

The Bobby Darin Show premiered on January 19, 1973, on NBC. It lacked the comic energy of the earlier show from the start. This was partly Bobby's fault. He claimed he didn't want a variety show, but a straight music show instead. Something vital was gone from it. "Carmine and Angie" was retained, but the level of writing was not as high and the sketches were undeveloped. The level of guests fell, and so did the ratings. Bobby was not even doing his hits; again, the contrary and perverse side of him was calling the shots. He insisted on a monotonous chess segment in which he made chess moves against a computer.

Much of Bobby's irascibility was due to his declining health. Once more he was experiencing heart fibrillations and felt weak and drained. He was constantly using the oxygen mask.

In April 1973, NBC announced that it was canceling the series. There would be just four remaining shows. "He calls me up," Steve Blauner says, and he says, 'Look, I want out of this show. I want to walk off. It's not creative. It's bullshit. It stinks.'

"And I'm freaked. What had I walked into? The four shows that they had finished at NBC weren't very good or creative. I said to him, 'Look, let me tell you something. All your life you've thrown tantrums and gotten away with them. A lot of them probably stem from the fact that you were sick as a kid. But for once in your life, see something through to the end. And then you'll be a man, my son.' And I got up and walked out of the room. The next day he showed up at NBC. He drove through the lot, but he was ill. And I said, 'This fucking guy.

What is he doing? He's now gonna take it out on all of us for my not saying 'oh yes' to him. Had I known he was going to die, I would have gotten him off the show in an instant. And then, after a while, I said to myself: Wait a minute. I believe that he's a good actor. But not this good. I called shrinks, I called doctors. They were all hedging.

"The show was $250,000 over budget. Well, I certainly wasn't going to let it cost him money. And he was sick. There were no rehearsals. And he came out with his head down and his hand in a claw. And the lights went on and he started singing: he did 70 percent, but only I knew it was 70, that's how good he was. And I doubled the shows up: two a week. By the time we finished the 13 shows, not only was he not behind a quarter of a million, he was ahead about a quarter of a million."

It is difficult to understand how Steve did not perceive how sick Bobby was. It was widely known in the industry and had been for years. It is Hesh Wasser's theory that Steve did not want to know, that he could not bear it. Many people, like the show's producers, Ilson and Chambers, thought Bobby was feigning illness. But Steve was as close as a brother to Bobby.

Blauner says, "It got to the point where you'd walk down the street with Bobby and he'd walk into a wall. They didn't know what it was: the brain, the this, the that."

Chapter Fifteen
THE CURTAIN FALLS

The last year of Bobby's life was a phantasmagoria. It was all spinning out of control.

Bobby went to the dentist and for the first time in his life he did not take the antibiotics in advance that he'd always known were necessary to ensure that bacteria did not invade his bloodstream. "Bobby had contracted a rare blood disease," Steve Blauner recalls. Bobby was enraged with his condition, wondering what the point of the surgery was. He was terrified of the prospect of having to go through yet another operation. He had also been taking prescribed steroids, and early in 1973 he stopped taking them, too. He also ceased taking an anticoagulant called Coumadin, which prevented clotting.

"Before this happened," Terry Koenig says, "Bobby was coming together again. Sometimes you have to go out of your mind to come back to your senses. When he came back from Big Sur, I never met a more together man, from 1969 through 1973. The heart surgery in 1971 had made him stronger."

"I would go and pick Dodd up after school and bring him to Bobby," continues Koenig. "I would bring a check from Bobby for Sandy. Sandy would come to the door in a beautiful 1950s red chiffon tight-at-the-waist dress and a long matching red chiffon scarf. Her hand came around the door, took the check with the chiffon scarf draped over her arm, went back, and Dodd came through the door. He was coming from an altered reality that had nothing to do with real life."

In the early months of 1973, the worst symptoms came and went. Bobby was very sick, but could somehow function. "Bobby's heart would go out of rhythm," Steve Blauner says, "and he would go to the hospital. And they'd shock it, and then he'd go back to work."

Early in the year Bobby gave two of the greatest performances of his life. An episode of *The Midnight Special*, a weekly TV rock concert, was being shot at NBC. Bobby opened his performance with "If I Were a Carpenter" and "Dream Lover." Then he moved into a wild version of "Splish Splash." Bobby ripped it up with wailing harmonica solos and blistering piano breaks. "Now mind you," Jimmy Scalia says, "the audience is compromised of 19- or 20-year-old kids. Bobby starts getting worked up. Now his eyes are almost shut; he just doesn't look good. *But his body is moving, he's playing. The beauty is, while he's playing, if you listen to the audience, they don't just clap for a second. It builds after that in one stretch. Now watch the band; they're getting pumped, okay? And I'm realizing, they're movin'! Now he's not getting up, but he's sitting at the piano bench, and his legs are up! They're going up and down, he's pumpin'. Bobby's picking up the harmonica, he's throwing it down. Midnight Special* used to shoot the show so you'd get a back view of the band. And you could see the mirrors on the back of the stage almost shaking. It was wild. And the irony was that Bobby had started with 'Splish Splash,' ran away from it all those years, and at the very end, he was accepted as a rock star again."

On April 27, Bobby did the last show for his cancelled series. He jettisoned the show's standard format and did a 70-minute concert. It remains a masterpiece. It is preserved on video and it will endure for all time. Bobby summoned up every ounce of strength he had left and the effect was mesmerizing.

"The show was done with no rehearsal," Bobby Rozario says. "He realized that was an amazing concert. He broke down afterwards because Dodd couldn't be there. Sandy wouldn't let him. Bobby kept looking for him in the audience. He cried. He knew he had done a fabulous show. He wanted Dodd included. And little does he know that Dodd is part of it—posthumously. Dodd has seen it umpteen times now.

"When he came to the piano, he put his head down on it and said to me, 'We can't do it, Bobby, we never rehearsed.' And he gave the best show of his life. The moment the lights went up. He was so weak, I thought we'd never get through it. What we did was his live nightclub act. And the band had never done it because they only played the regular TV shows. But this was a whole concert; he did 14 songs. He left the chart and improvised. 'Can't Take My Eyes Off of You' is unbelievable. 'Bridge Over Troubled Waters'—the orchestra had never rehearsed it. I was so tense. It was perfect. At the end of 'Beyond the Sea,' he cues up the trombone player. Because he knew the trombone player didn't know where to come in, Bobby goes 'Be bop bop, beetle bee'—a sailor's hornpipe, so he would know exactly where to come in. He was just so musical."

"The man is dying right there on the stage," recalls Terry Koenig, "and he's giving his absolute, every ounce of energy in his body. And he came off the stage and literally hooked up to oxygen."

"Right after that television show," Bobby Rozario says, "we worked the Hilton in Vegas. Bobby literally crawled up the steps on his hands and knees. He was that weak. And I thought he couldn't do a show. And the curtain would go up and he was like all of a sudden a different person. Superhuman. The moment the lights hit and the music started, there he was."

"I went looking for him afterward and I couldn't find him," says Terry Koenig. "And he was in the deepest bowels of NBC crying, sobbing like a baby. Why? Because he knew this was a unique thing he had done, and Dodd didn't come to see it. That night he was very sick. His body was betraying him. I think he knew it was really one of the last times he was going to perform."

Steve Blauner had set about finding the ultimate deal for Bobby that would free him financially for the balance of his life. "I went to Vegas to make Bobby's insurance policy," he recalls. "I told him I would make a deal between Vegas and Tahoe where Bobby wouldn't have to work again except in those two places for the rest of the year. I was going to get him twelve weeks a year in Vegas and maybe a week and two weekends in Tahoe. So I now go to Vegas. I hadn't been there in years. I hadn't managed since like 1965, and this was 1973. Different people, different faces. I leave at eight in the morning and I'm going to hit every hotel. The first place I went was to the Sands, where they had a guy that worked for Howard Hughes for years. He was now buying the talent for five hotels. I finally made a deal at the MGM that was almost unbelievable. It was 27 weeks over three years, seventy-five thousand a week, plus they covered his backup singers and musicians. A two-million-dollar contract. That was enough money that he wouldn't have to work another day in the year if he didn't want to."

As a result of not taking the antibiotics before the dental work in February 1973, an infection entered Bobby's bloodstream. "The infection that was unleashed into his heart literally withered it," Terry Koenig relates. "From June through December, he was rotting. His body was in a shutdown. He couldn't evacuate all the water; they were using heroic diuretics on him." Bobby was admitted to Cedars of Lebanon Hospital with septicemia—blood poisoning. There were complications. Bobby experienced a series of mild strokes. The doctors found that Bobby had developed several small blood clots on the brain that were caused by Bobby's cutting out the Coumadin. The strokes were a result. Bobby was directed by the doctors to resume all of his medications.

His heart stopped beating on several occasions, but emergency treatment restored his life. He was released from the hospital after six weeks, warned that he would have to be very careful in his physical activities.

He continued to perform. "I don't know how he did it," says Koenig. "He found the strength to go out on stage. Dr. Martin Levy flew to Vegas a few times because Bobby was having trouble breathing. His heart and lungs were letting him down. I was buying portable oxygen tanks. But it didn't stop him from giving absolutely 200 percent."

When he got out of the hospital, Bobby proposed to Andrea. They had been living together for three years. They were married on June 25, 1973, in Walnut Grove, California, and honeymooned in Micronesia. "It was near Guam," Steve Blauner says. "A guy that sick to go to a place like that!" On the way back, Bobby became very ill again with heart fibrillations and entered Cedars of Lebanon for treatment.

Andrea and Bobby were divorced in October, and Bobby was dead by December.

"BOBBY WENT TO TAHOE for a four-day engagement at the Sahara," Steve remembers. "It was one of those incredible nights. Women were throwing keys up on the stage, throwing notes. When the show ended I went back to see Bobby. He said, 'You know, I'm out there, and I've got the audience in the palm of my hand, and you know what I'm thinking, Steve? The whole time? How am I going to tell Steve I can never play here again?'"

"At the Sahara Tahoe," Bill McCubbin says, "he would sit down at the piano and the circulation in his hands was really bad. He'd make a joke out of it. We were the only ones who knew. The audience wouldn't be close enough to pick up. He'd look at his left hand and he'd slap it with his right and he'd go, 'Work, damn it, work!' And he would shake them, to try and get the circulation going. Every other song he would take a false bow and go offstage and get the oxygen tank. He was having a hard time breathing."

"I saw Bobby in Vegas about six months before he died," says Jerrold Atlas. "He was so tired. I said, 'Bobby, you don't look good. You don't need the money. Why are you doing this? You know that after the surgery you're supposed to relax . . . ' Bobby had this very plastic face. It could convey all kinds of emotion and attitudes. You could always read his face—when he wanted you to. And for the first time in his life with me he just lost all affect, became totally blank and leaned close and said, 'Jerry, I need the applause.'"

On July 18, he opened at the Hilton in Las Vegas. His engagements there in July and August were the last times he would perform in public. "Elvis Presley used to come in and watch him," Bobby Rozario recalls. "He'd sneak into a booth and sit there quietly. Because he thought it was unbelievable what Bobby did. He said, 'Jeez, I can't do any of this stuff.'"

Back in Los Angeles, his health got steadily worse. He was losing his memory, including what he had said minutes before.

"He would call me up at ten o'clock on a Monday morning," Steve Blauner remembers. "He'd say, 'Meet me at Westwood at such and such.' He was going to try and find a new business, because he was never going to be able to work again. Okay, I'll be there. At noon he'd call me. Same day. Exact same place, same city, same reason. Like he hadn't told me an hour before. Okay, I'll be there. At one o'clock he'd call me again. It was like Alzheimer's, senility. Once during this period, he took Dodd to buy him a bike. Dodd was still a kid, ten or twelve. Bobby said, 'I'll be right back,' left Dodd in the bike store, and didn't come back."

"Bobby knew that without medication he was likely to get an infection," says Mimi Greenberg. "I think what happened was self-willed. If you have a heart condition, if you stop taking your medication, you know you are going to get a secondary infection. And he did. And he got it at a time in life when he was miserable. He was miserable with the television series; he felt like he was a failure. In my last conversation with him, he called me at home and said, 'The TV series isn't going. I've decided I'm going to go into radio.' 'Radio?' I said. He replied, 'Why not? I've failed at every other medium. I've only got one left to fail in.'

"What we saw on stage was that very hip, glib guy. But in his private life, he was really depressed. I know that he was in analysis with Dr. Jonah Perlmutter but that he would often not keep his appointments."

"When Bobby came to his dying days," says Hesh Wasser, "he really needed help. I think what he didn't want was that help. His estrangement from Andrea, I don't think, was a lack of caring. I think it was a matter of giving up. I think Bobby took his own life. Most people, including Steve, didn't know how sick he was. He kept his illness under wraps always. Only he knew. But there came that point when he couldn't hide it anymore. And when that point came, I really believe that he felt, 'This is it.'"

"Five years ago I caught up with Andrea, and we talked about Bobby," Mimi Greenberg says. "At the end she really felt she was a nurse, that Bobby wasn't a companion anymore; he was a patient. She was carrying him around. And she said that regarding the medication, that was an old story with him. He would take it, he wouldn't take it. The doctor told him he could not do this, because each time there was surgery, not taking the medication compromised the outcome, and there would be a point at which there could be no more surgery. He didn't accidentally forget to take his medication—Andrea was there reminding him. This was a very cleverly crafted plan on his part so that nobody would know it was suicide. But there was this other side of Bobby that felt triumphant every time he cheated death."

"He was in and out of hospitals," says Steve Blauner. "I visited him at Midway, a private hospital. He had these intravenous tubes in him. One day I got there and he said, 'I'm getting out of here.' He pulled the tubes out of his arm, got dressed, and was leaving. And he said, 'They're not doing right.' He traveled with a medical book in his car, he kept track of everything. He said this wasn't right, that wasn't right. He said, 'I can't live this way because I'm not in control.'"

He was flailing around desperately. He was drowning.

"One day I was in Bobby's house," Dick Lord remembers, "and I don't know where Bobby is. I go into the garage, and he's rummaging through the files. I said, 'What are you doing?' He said, 'I'm looking for all those letters you wrote to me.' 'Why?' He said, 'Well, I want to publish them. They're very funny and I have to do it now.' I said, 'Okay, but why now?' And he took his cap off and he was really balding. And he said, 'I'm gonna die soon. I'm not getting enough oxygen to my head. I'm not getting oxygen in my brain.'"

"Bobby called me," says Steve Blauner. "He said he wanted to see a shrink. He said that Andrea was coming with him and he wanted me to be there as well. 'She'll go in and do some time, you'll go in and do some time, then when it's time for me, he'll know all about things,' Bobby said. Okay. I said fine.

"The three of us walked in. And the shrink took Andrea in by herself. So Bobby and I went for a walk around the block. When we got back, the shrink came out and he didn't call me in, he called us both in. And he said to Bobby, 'Listen. I've reserved a place for you at UCLA.' Somehow it was the psychiatric division, but he would go in as a heart patient. And I'm dying. I was sitting there, thinking, oh no, it's the wrong way to handle Bobby. You don't infer that he's crazy.

"Bobby said to Andrea, 'Is that what you think?' And she said, 'Yes.' When he asked me, I choked on it. I knew this was a terrible thing that was happening. But I said, 'Yes.' Because we needed to get him off the street. He jumped up and said, 'Okay.' And he stormed out. At the elevator with him pushing the button, I said, 'Bobby, what is the matter?' He had now conjured up that we were trying to have him committed. I said, 'Bobby, what are you carrying on for? This is your call! You're the one that had us come here! This is your idea. Are you blaming us for this?' And he goes tearing off, leaving Andrea and me on the sidewalk. And the next day somebody called Andrea and told her, or she read it in Army Archerd's column in *Variety*, that Bobby was getting a divorce.

"Bobby showed up at my house that night," continues Blauner. "He came to tell me it was a wrap. I couldn't believe it, like he was crazy in the head, and so I was sort of making fun of it, which only got him madder. The last thing I did was, I leaned into the car window, kissed him, and said, 'You can't legislate love. I'll always love you.'"

Bobby flew to Las Vegas for the divorce. Kay Rozario, Bobby Rozario's wife, picked him up at the airport and drove him to the courthouse.

"My wife said he was concerned that people would recognize him," recalls Bobby Rozario, "and he didn't want the divorce on the news. But she said he was so weak and he looked so bad that nobody would recognize him. She said he looked like an old man. He even smelled like a person dying. She said, 'I literally had to hold him up, and we went up the court steps and got the divorce.' 'Oh my God, Bobby,' she said to me, 'he's dying.'

"I had gone to work for Tony Orlando; that was Bobby's wish. Because when he was so sick at the end and decided to stop working, Bobby decided to put the band on a retainer. In other words, he wouldn't be working but he would make sure we were on a salary. I know he didn't want to die. He was very sad about it."

And then Bobby turned to the most unlikely place for help: his own family. "Bobby called Nina, and Vee was on the other phone," Gary Walden recalls, "and he was in tears and said he couldn't believe his supposed best friend could do this to him. He told her the whole thing about Andrea and Steve and the shrink. So Nina and Vee were comforting him. 'It will be all right, sweetheart,' my mother said. My mother and sister went all over town cashing checks like crazy and got in their Chevy Suburban and drove immediately out to see Bobby in Vegas. Because my mother knew that Bobby needed somebody to lean on.

"Bobby now had no problem telling Nina exactly in no uncertain terms how he felt toward her. They were in Ralph's supermarket.

They're going up and down the aisles to get what Nina needed in order to prepare the food for dinner. Bobby suddenly said, 'How could you have lied to me? How could you keep this a secret from me all of these years?'

"There were people all around. Bobby was famous. He was wearing sunglasses and a hat because he didn't have a toupee, but still people would recognize him. My mother at this time was very overweight, so she was very, very big. This scene went on up and down the aisles.

"And she finally turned to him and said, 'Sweetheart, you hate me.' And Bobby said, 'What I will tell you is there is a little man inside of me that will always hate you for what you've done to me.' They finished shopping and went home and Nina went into the kitchen and cooked dinner. And Bobby was going to go to L.A. to see his lawyer to change his will and finalize the divorce from Andrea. And before he leaves, he tells Nina: 'When I come back, Vee is more than welcome to be here. But I don't want you here.' When Bobby left, my mother called me. She was heartbroken.

"Nina could not make the trip back, a woman alone driving 2,500 miles back to New Jersey. She had driven like a lunatic from Jersey to Vegas. She and Vee had cashed checks all over because they didn't have credit cards and couldn't get a cash advance. So they decided to fly me out and have me drive back with Nina. And that's what we did. Vee would stay with Bobby. So I flew out to take Nina home."

There was still the contract that Bobby had signed with Steve Blauner to deal with. "Now there's a meeting in Gerry Lipsky's office," Blauner recalls. "Lipsky, Bobby, and me. This is the first of what I know about what's going down. He's stopping working. He let everybody go. And he looks at me in front of these people, very cavalierly, and he says, 'Well, timing is everything, Steve.' About me. Well, I wasn't going to hold him up for the million, or whatever was left of it.

"I felt he wanted to cut the ties with all the people that he loved. So they wouldn't mourn his death. Me and Andrea. I always loved him so much that I told him the truth. Andrea loved him so much she never said no."

"He paid Andrea off," Terry Koenig says. "I think she got ten thousand dollars and a car."

BOBBY WAS BEGINNING to wall himself off. "Bobby was leaving Vegas," Tommy Amato remembers. "He was going to L.A. This was 1973. He came over to my house. It was winter. He comes over and knocks on the door. He's frail; he must weigh 80–90 pounds. I never saw him looking so bad. I had some friends over; we were playing darts. Bobby tried to throw a couple of darts and he was real weak. He was cold. I had to put an Afghan shawl over him. So he brings over this box full of liqueurs, scotches, single-malt stuff. Later I knew it was his way of saying goodbye. He said, 'Tommy, we're supposed to open Bally's with MacLean Stevenson. But I ain't gonna make it, man.' I said, 'Ah, bullshit, you've been telling me that for the last five years.' I thought it was jive, because he was always saying that. And he was so vital onstage; the contrast was between the reality of the sickness and the way he seemed onstage. I never knew anybody who worked like that up until the day they died. He was still active, he was cramming it in there, I guess, man. And I don't know how he willed that little weak body to do that, but he did. He did."

He had lost so much weight and aged so much, and he was seeing fewer and fewer of his friends. "When Bobby was really sick at the end," says Hesh Wasser, "he didn't want to talk to people like me." Bobby made out a new will in October, leaving his entire estate to Dodd, with the provision that Dodd would only get the income from the estate, not the principal, until he was 65. Bobby's lawyer, Gerald Lipsky, was named executor.

"Bobby had rented the house on Rexford to be close to Dodd so that Dodd could come over after school," recalls Terry Koenig. "He was probably there for 90 days. There was nothing in it but two beds and an oxygen tent. The shades were drawn; it was dark. He was too weak to go to the bathroom. I would empty buckets of urine. I would drop by and take care of his details. I used to go and pick Dodd up and bring him to Bobby when he felt healthy enough. He never really got up and wandered around. I'd bring him food.

"He was defecating in bed," Steve Blauner recalls. "He was just quivering, not getting out of bed in this room with the blinds closed. I ripped the blinds open and said, 'What the hell have you got to be feeling sorry for? So you'll never go on the stage again. So you'll direct, so you'll write songs, so you'll produce people on records.' I said, 'Come on, it's about time, get up, stop it.' He said, 'Thanks, Steve. On your way out, close the blinds, will ya?'"

"After a while he wouldn't see Dodd," Terry Koenig says. "He didn't want Dodd to see him swelling like that. He had the heart of an 80-year-old inside the body of a 37-year-old.

"I was kind of a go-between between Andrea and Bobby. She was so traumatized. They talked on the phone. He wanted to clear the estate for Dodd. He paid off Andrea virtually nothing. And that was not important to her.

"One time it was too much and I finally had to drive him to Cedars of Lebanon Hospital. On December 10. Oh my God. I saw his heart jump out of his chest. I saw the heart beating arrhythmically—pounding—on his chest cavity. Because he was very slight. He let me look at his chest. He just had a tee shirt on and his bathrobe.

"I did not stay at the hospital. I saw him to his room, got him set, then Vee moved in. She made it known that she was taking over. He was there about a week."

"Near the end," Gary Wood recalls, "Dick Bakalyan and I went to visit him in the hospital together. I put on a doctor's coat and a stethoscope and I came in and I lifted his gown and I put it on the head of his dick. And I said, 'Ah, I think you're going to be fine.' Just clowning and joking. He laughed his ass off. But the truth is it took everything I had in me as an actor to do it. Because I hadn't seen him for a while. Bobby had been pushing everybody away. When I walked in that room, it blew my mind. He'd become an old man. He'd become old right in front of my eyes. It took only a few months for that to happen."

Andrea stayed with him at the hospital for two days, and then he sent her away. "If you can't stay with me without crying, you'll have to leave," he told her.

Bobby's sister Vee stayed by his side. Bobby wouldn't see Andrea, Sandra, or Dodd again. Bobby called Dodd for the last time on Dodd's 12th birthday, on December 16, from the hospital. Dodd wrote, "When I heard his voice, I almost couldn't tell who it was. He was part hysterical, part sobbing, almost unintelligible. I eventually understood that he was calling to wish me a happy birthday. He told me that he loved me and that he was very sorry he couldn't be with me, but his manner distressed me so much, I cut the conversation short . . . I wrote my dad a note telling him I loved him, which Vee took to him in the hospital."

Bobby called Andrea before he went into surgery. He said, "I'm not going to make it. This is it, kid. I really love you." They said their goodbyes and told each other they loved each other.

"Andrea was genuine," says Terry Koenig. "Bobby had been used to an entirely different kind of woman in the entertainment business. She was guileless. She hadn't wanted him to give her money, anything from him but love. So for Bobby that had been intoxicating. She still loves him today. He was the great love of her life." After Bobby's death, Andrea almost immediately married Bobby's friend and business associate Steve Burton, who was the son of Ed Burton, Bobby's agent at Csida-Crean who later became vice president and general manager of T. M. Music.

George Burns once said of Gracie Allen, "Then, in 1928, I got my big break, and I married her. And we were together a long, long time." Andrea was Bobby's big break, but it didn't work out the same way.

"BOBBY AND I had been estranged," Dick Lord says. "One day I was working in Buffalo, New York, and the phone rang. It was my ex-wife, Ellen. She said, 'Bobby's here, at the house. He's quite ill. We called Steve Blauner and they're going to meet him at the airport in L.A. with an ambulette. He's going right to the hospital. He wants to talk to you." So I'm holding the phone. I remember exactly what he said. He said, 'I can't even think of something funny to say.' And I said, 'I really love you.' And he said, 'I love you too.' And that's the last I ever spoke to him.

ON DECEMBER 18, Bobby whispered to Vee, "Save Dodd from the wolves." Later he smiled and spoke his last words: 'Cypress 2-6725." That was Bobby's first phone number in the Bronx. He was re-experiencing the moment of joy he felt as a boy when the family phone was installed. Vee tried to talk about it, but he put his fingers to his lips and said, "*Shhh.*" He repeated the number and fell into a coma.

On December 19, Bobby underwent an eight-hour surgery. He was kept alive by a heart and lung machine. His doctors performed an arteriogram, in which a catheter is threaded through an artery into the heart. The doctors discovered that one of his artificial valves had been malfunctioning. Attempting to repair the damage by opening up Bobby's chest, they discovered that the entire heart muscle had deteriorated from his infection. Most of the left side of Bobby's heart had been cut away during the 1971 surgery. There wasn't much left to work with.

He died early in the morning on December 20, 1973.

Bobby had requested that his body be given to science. His remains were transferred to UCLA Medical Center.

There was no funeral service, no proper mourning. Jackie Cooper and his wife invited Bobby's friends to their house and boozed it up while watching a tape of Bobby's final TV show. Sandy, Dodd, and Vee spent Christmas together, eating Kentucky Fried Chicken.

BOBBY LEFT HIS ENTIRE ESTATE to Dodd. Gerald Lipsky told Vee, "You're not getting a thing."

"GERALD LIPSKY, THE LAWYER," recalls Terry Koenig, "said to me, 'Look, Vee wants to go to Bobby's house in Vegas. You go, make sure she doesn't take anything.' I was so distraught. She brought empty suitcases and she just piled them full of Bobby's clothing, took paintings off the wall. I thought she was going to open up a curio shop. I couldn't confront her, I was so devastated. To me it was a temple. I called Lipsky and said, 'What do I do? She's taking things off the wall.' And I guess he just let her do it."

"PROBABLY THE ONLY TIME I ever saw Bob Rozario crumble," recalls Tony Orlando, "was when the news got out that Bobby died. We were working in the Blue Room in New Orleans. I was going to his room to tell Bob that Bobby died, and as I approached his door, I heard the wailing of a crying man. It was guttural. I went to put my hand up to knock on the door and I thought, no, this is not the time. And all I kept hearing him do was 'Bobby, no! Bobby, no!'"

Bobby was saying his goodbyes to the people he loved. "Bobby saw me and Bobby Rozario on the street," Tony Orlando remembers. "He came out of the car and said, 'I'm on all this medication. I can't take it anymore.' Telling us he wasn't going to take his medication. I didn't know he was going to die. When he said it, I just got the feeling like 'I'm tired, I give up.' Later I understood. And he weighed nothing that day. He was so skinny. And he said to Bobby Rozario, 'I want to tell you something, Bobby. I want you and Terry [Kellman] and Tommy [Amato] and the entire rhythm section, if anything happens to me, I want you to work for nobody else but Tony. Tony has a future that is bright, he understands what show business is about, kind of like a student of mine, and I'm bequeathing this band to you, Tony.' For me this was an honor, as though a young soldier just received a medal from Patton. And Bobby Rozario went on to be my musical director. When I sang 'Tie a Yellow Ribbon,' I said to my producers, 'I'm gonna sing this as though Bobby was going to sing it. I'm coming home, I've done my time,' that's Bobby.

"Then," Orlando continues, "in 1974, Dick Clark announces that I'm the winner for Entertainer of the Year. Bobby had not been dead long. I walked up and said, 'Ladies and Gentlemen, I accept this award in the memory of Bobby Darin.' And you know and I know how Dick loves Bobby Darin. Dick has tears in his eyes and I have tears in mine.

We hug each other, and as I pull away from Dick, I've got the award in my hand and I walked down the aisle. The first person to come up to me was Roger Miller. He said, 'I can't believe that you did that.' I said, 'Why?' 'You had Bobby on your mind with 'Yellow Ribbon.' Roger said, 'Well how about this: "Trailers for sale or rent..." [King of the Road]—I was doing Bobby on that!' As he says that, Diana Ross walks over and goes, 'Bobby! What are you talking about?' She puts her arms around me and said, 'Bobby, he taught me everything I know about being an entertainer.' Now this is like a train going, you couldn't believe how it went from one to the next to the next—everybody. It was awesome. Every single performer there was touched by his talent or taught by his talent."

"I was like his right arm," Terry Koenig remembers. "He called me 'my right arm' toward the end when he was so sick. I had like a hysterical paralysis; I couldn't lift my right arm up. As soon as he died, I could swing it around the room. But I was lost."

"All I could think of," says Hesh Wasser, "was this was a person who changed my life, who changed the lives of the people around him, and that there wasn't anyone who could take his place. He was bigger than life. You start to think of all the wonderful times and all of the difficult times you had in dealing with him. It was the sadness of his not being in my life any longer that was almost too much to bear. And more than that I don't think I can say."

"When he died," Carol Lynley says, "he loved the ocean, and he loved Malibu, so I rented a hotel room there and I just couldn't stop crying. I was laying out on the balcony. You know when you cry so much you get sleepy; at least I do. I was just lying there, and a seagull came down, very close, and I looked at it. Oh my God, it's Bobby's eyes. Bobby had these fantastic eyes. They weren't pretty, he wasn't a pretty guy, but they were lively. They took in everything."

Andrea Darin has a free spirit like Bobby's. Today she works as a paperhanger and house sitter in Malibu. Bobby has never left her, and she cries when speaking of him. "Thirty-one years ago and it's yesterday," she says. "I'm still carrying around a plant he gave me."

Unlike others who suspect that Bobby committed a kind of suicide by not taking antibiotics before his dental appointment, Andrea believes that Bobby neglected to take them because of a series of undiagnosed mini-strokes he suffered which incurred temporary memory loss. "He would call me and say, 'Honey, I don't know where I am.' So I think inadvertently he didn't take his medicine; it was not deliberate. He would just forget things.

"I couldn't smile when I saw him in the hospital," she says. "I couldn't be cheerful. And Bobby said, 'If you can't get it together, don't come back.' I love him as much now as I ever did, and he was a handful. He was a little pistol. He was a spoiler. But he was fair. Never a dull moment. Three years with Bobby was a lifetime with your average guy. The mind was going all the time. Always old. And street smart. And just brilliant.

"A fluke. A person came into my life out of left field. He was dressed in his jeans from head to toe, glasses so he could see, a cowboy hat and moustache. And I didn't know who he was! He didn't look like the Bobby Darin that I remembered. And he opened the door for me, and clowned around. We got together: it was like a pair of your favorite old slippers or sweater. It was so comfortable from the beginning. He picked me up at the Vegas airport the first time. I was coming down the escalator, and we just hugged like we'd been doing that forever."

STEVE BLAUNER AND HESH WASSER are not alone anymore. They are keeping the Darin flame alive on both coasts, and today it has ignited across the country. With the release of the movie *Beyond the Sea*, with the scores of CD's and DVD's on sale nationally, with Bobby's voice on movie soundtracks and baseball stadium loudspeakers, Bobby's influence is everywhere. "What we're seeing in the musical world today," says Len Triola, "is that Norah Jones is doing the same thing that Bobby did. These people are crossing over like Darin. He was so curious and adventurous. And now closet Darin guys are all over the place: the announcer at Yankee Stadium who plays 'New York on

Sunday.' They really dig him and what he's done. Bobby copped a hell of a lot of fucking life in 37 years."

There was a time when Steve would walk into Tower Records on Sunset Boulevard and find no Bobby in the racks and he went home crying and his wife wrapped her arms around him. Or if there were perhaps a handful of CD's in the "Oldies" section or pocketed away on some obscure shelves, Steve would swoop them up and redeposit them in the "Vocalists" section in the most prominent positions. He would ask to speak to the manager and insist that the records were in the wrong place and that there weren't enough of them. He now visits the same Tower store, or any record store in the country, and finds scores of Bobby's CD's on display. The movie, from its inception 18 years ago in earlier incarnations to its production and release in 2004, had Steve's involvement and input at every stage.

"When I was five years old," recalls New Orleans disc jockey and singer Ron Cannatella, "I had singles of Bobby's that my sister and I would play over and over again. He had just died. For years you'd have to go into a collectible-record shop to find a mint copy of Bobby; it was like finding the Holy Grail to find a good, unscratched copy. My own copies had been circulated to family members for years and looked like they had been through World War III. That was the only way you could get to hear Bobby. But now all the record companies are releasing everything. I've got a whole shelf of CDs, and there are 50 albums in the stores."

GREATNESS is not a relative term. Bobby had true greatness, in the sense that Sinatra, Garland, Ray Charles, Sammy Davis, Dean Martin, George Burns, and Jolson had it. Bobby didn't perform for the money or the glory. He did it for the love of it. And when he got tired of something and didn't love it any more, he wanted to move on. He needed to love what he did.

In a PBS documentary about Bobby, Ahmet Ertegun said, "He was extraordinary. He wanted to be the quintessential American singer, actor, bandleader, musician, songwriter, the whole thing."

Dodd Darin added: "I miss him immensely. What I really miss was what I know would have been such a blast of knowing him. I'd do anything to have that. Not just as the son. But just to be a fly on the wall and be part of it, the excitement, the fun, that he brought to life."

One can glean from these two tributes a sense of his scope and depth. The cofounder of Atlantic Records and the son of Darin each reflect an awareness of Bobby's greatness. Ertegun cites every single facet of show business to encompass what Bobby was reaching for. His son, with great longing, wishes somehow to have been a part of Bobby's world in any capacity, knowing how enriching, how procreative, it was.

Each person stretches to express somehow what Bobby meant to him.

He was never what he seemed. In the fifties, when rock reigned, he was not a typical rock-and-roller. In the sixties, he was not a typical swinger. He took the old "You Must Have Been a Beautiful Baby" and made it ecstatically, rocking new. He took swinging ballads like "Fly Me to the Moon" and invested them with slow, haunting, romantic feeling from an earlier age. He was Presley on "Mighty Mighty Man" or "Sermon for Samson" and sometimes he was Ray Charles or Sinatra. You couldn't catch him. You were still digging his treatment of the standards and he was gone, veering to folk and country-rock and protest songs.

He had the inspiration that comes with having a great passion for the things you love. He loved them all, and he was like the product of all of them. As Ron Cannatella puts it, "Bobby was the past, the present, and the future, every variety performer and song-and-dance man. Roll them up and you get Bobby."

The effect could be maddening. The public could not separate out all the Bobbies. Perhaps Bobby couldn't separate out all the Bobbies. When he was hooked on something, you couldn't stop him. It was a kind of mania. And it didn't always work. "He was right even when he was wrong," says Rudy Clark. You couldn't argue with him. The same ferocious messianic determination to go to Watts in 1964 was the stubbornness that drove him into other obsessions. He was motivated in his work by where he was emotionally in his life. And emotionally, Bobby was a volcano.

Here is a measure of how far Bobby had climbed: Going out as an actor and exposing oneself to the public again and again is a gamble and risk that no performer ever becomes oblivious to. Tens of thousands of people do it. A few are successful at it to the extent of making a minimal living. Think of the hierarchy in films: those at the bottom are "wavers"—those who are hired to simply wave at the camera—and above them are the extras. Then you move up to the cameos and the tiny parts and so on up the ladder.

The same principle applies to all the other entertainment genres. Bobby was initially a nightclub performer, singing in lounges and bars. He sprang to the very peak of his profession almost overnight, becoming a headliner, a star, then a superstar. By the 1960s he was show-business royalty; he was in his early 20s. He had the Jolson thing: that maniacal feel—Bobby was a little bit crazy like Jolson—and partly the Judy Garland thing. It was a little like going to a hanging.

Borrowed time created Bobby Darin, the character the public perceived as the boldest, brashest, cockiest performer in show business. He carried with him at all times his own insecurity about his health. He was always cheating death. But he wasn't pathetic. Garland wore it on her sleeve and bled on stage. But what was motivating Bobby at all times was conquering the fear of death, defying it joyously, celebrating life with melody and dance and humor and sexuality and swing and impressions and the harmonica and drums and bitchin' piano. He *was* a monster, as the great singer and drummer Grady Tate put it. There was a sense of electrifying urgency in everything that he did. It was now or never. The audience didn't understand all they were responding to, nor should they have. But it was present in all his work.

His rise was so meteoric that it must have created incredible pressures within him. He saw the reality of the roar of applause from every audience, the ecstasy he evoked. Once he made it with rock, he had to make it with standards, country rock, as a movie star, a songwriter, a producer. He snagged the gold prize in Hollywood: Sandra Dee; at the same time, he was prodigiously active with other women. He had it all.

And from the start, his knowledge of mortality and his superior intelligence set him apart. His awareness of death curtailed his greed and expanded his commitment to values and a compassion for others, a questioning of how he could leave a meaningful legacy behind when he was gone. His roots in poverty made him sympathetic to the struggles of the poor and fueled his love of black music and the blues.

His was a separate journey. Knowing it would be a short one, he jumped to the sounds of music, not to the jingle of coins. He dodged every comfortable niche that came his way, infuriating the business people who wanted to profit maximally from his incredible talent. He had to feel it to do it, and watching his smile expand as he created a song like "Rainin'" is to watch a mother viewing her newborn, a poet finding the perfect word, lovers discovering each other.

In his attempt to grow, to be contemporary and relevant, Bobby went backward in his art. The road to hell was, as always, paved with good intentions. The nobility of the attempt makes Bobby's failure heartbreaking. He never understood the trap inherent in choosing to do protest music. He felt it conveyed a deeper reality and honesty.

Bobby did go beyond the protest-song period, and in the final years of his life, he recreated the old magic. But it was never the same. He'd broken the circle of love that had embraced him with such fervor. His failure was a consequence of the eternal debate about art as a weapon versus art as the thing in itself, intertwined with his endless inclinations to be an impressionist. When Bobby muted his voice, put on his leather cowboy hat, moustache, and sideburns and sang mournfully of dusty roads and buried bodies of convicts in the Arkansas dirt, he did a reasonable impersonation of Dylan, Dave Van Ronk, Arlo and Woody Guthrie, and Pete Seeger. But why? An artist's obligation is to probe his own soul, not impersonate the souls of others. No one—not Sinatra, not Garland, not Jolson, not Prima, not Tormé, not Tony Bennett, not even Ray Charles—could do "Mack," "Lazy River," "More," or a hundred other gems like Bobby did them. They did what they did. And Bobby killed what he could do best.

Bobby's lofty intelligence, his social awareness, his intellectual curiosity and probing honesty tricked him. As audiences deserted him, he never understood what happened or why.

AND THEN HIS BODY turned completely on him. His supercharged energy, his doubly burning candle, defying the odds and encompassing beautifully every facet of music—for Bobby was simply one of the greatest entertainers of all time—flickered out.

And what are we left with? It is Bobby—not Dolly—who "will never go away." The records can engulf you, singe you, burn you, thrill you, haunt you, make you swing and dance and fly and know and feel you are alive. They kick ass, do they ever: "Mack," "More," "Mame," "Artificial Flowers," "Call Me Irresponsible," "Splish Splash," "Beyond the Sea," "Some of These Days," "Clementine," "Bill Bailey," "Down With Love," "That's All," "Two of a Kind," "Ace in the Hole," "I Ain't Gonna Give Nobody None of My Jellyroll," "My Cutey's Due at Two-to-Two Today," "You Must Have Been a Beautiful Baby," "Lazy River," "Baby Face," "Hello Dolly," "Long Line Rider," "Just Friends," "I Guess I'll Have to Change my Plans," "A Nightingale Sang in Berkeley Square," and scores more. And they will haunt you, from "Simple Song of Freedom," "Don't Dream of Anybody But Me," "My Buddy," "Dream Lover," "She Needs Me," "Fly Me to the Moon," "Through a Long and Sleepless Night," and "You'll Never Know," to "Change," "I Can't Give You Anything But Love," "What a Difference a Day Makes," "When Your Lover Has Gone," and "The Gal That Got Away."

They will never become dated, never seem tired, never stop glowing and burning into your soul.

And just to confound you, as Bobby always did, check out some of the bluesy songs from his uncelebrated "message" period: "Jive" and "Distractions." They're wonderful, and they have no message at all.

They are all Bobby's true legacy, torn from his soul, from his need, from his love, and created faster than the speed of life.

The Best of Bobby: A Selected Guide

ALBUMS:
That's All (Atco)
This Is Darin (Atco)
Darin at the Copa (Atco)
Bobby Darin and Johnny Mercer: Two of a Kind (Atco)
Love Swings (Atco)
Oh! Look at Me Now (Capitol)
From Hello Dolly to Goodbye Charlie (Capitol)
In a Broadway Bag (Atlantic)
Bobby Darin Sings Doctor Doolittle (Atlantic)
Inside Out (Atlantic)

COMPILATION ALBUMS:
The Lost Big Sur Masters (Varese Sarabande)
Aces Back to Back (CD and DVD) (Hyena)
The Bobby Darin Story (Atco)
The Best of Bobby Darin, Volumes One and Two (Atco)
Biography: Bobby Darin (Capitol)
If I Were a Carpenter: The Very Best of Bobby Darin (Varese Vintage)
Live at the Desert Inn (Motown)
The Curtain Falls: Live at the Flamingo (Capitol)
Classic Masters: Bobby Darin (Capitol)
Great Gentlemen of Song: Spotlight on Bobby Darin (Capitol)
As Long as I'm Singing: The Bobby Darin Collection (Rhino)

Acknowledgments

My deep thanks to Jerry Wexler, Andrea Darin, Bruce Charet, Ahmet Ertegun, Chris Potash, Bobby Rozario, Gary Walden, Len Triola, Dick Bakalyan, Ronnie Zito, Frankie Avalon, T. K. Kelman, Grady Tate, Roger McGuinn, Julius La Rosa, Tommy Amato, Shirley Jones, Bob Crewe, Robert Greenwald, Gary Wood, Gene Lees, Carol Lynley, Gary Smith, Bill McCubbin, Quitman Dennis, George Nestor, John Bravo, Andy DiDia, Jerrold Atlas, Roger Kellaway, Dick Lord, Leon Axelrod, Bobby Rydell, Gerald Wilson, Joel Dorn, Rudy Clark, Buddy Bregman, Jack Gilardi, Will Friedwald, Paul Anka, Stella Stevens, Errol Dante, Mimi Greenberg, Zach Fried, James Darren, Hubert Cornfield, George Carpinone, Joe Vicari, Carol Lees, Jeff Weatherford, Bobby Ramsen, Carol Fellenstein, Keely Smith, Jimmy Scalia, Terry Koenig, Joyce Becker, Tony Orlando, Bob Marcucci, Neil Sedaka, Linda Charet, Arthur Resnick, Walter Raim, Hal Taines, Robin Lorring, John Capotorto, Jim Stone, Rona Barrett, John Primerano, Vickie Eaves, Theodore Mitrani, Michael Cuscuna, Dick Clark, Fred Gardaphe, Tony De Nonno, Don Gregory, Ira Howard, Jan Thalberg, Joanne Romeo, Toni Alciade, David Isaac, Eric Wilson, Janet Groth, Tommy Culla, Jimmy Lategano, Eugene Allen, Laurel Newmark Falcon, Rita Dillon, Arturo and Bette Guinta, Steve Metz, Pete Cavallo, Ron Cannatella, Karen Janszen, Myra Cohen Klenicki, Steve Lawrence, Joyce Lerner, Ron Langel, Stephen Gregg, Bob Jones, Ina Wood, Judy Tannen, Gloria Ramsen, Edward Blau, and Patricia Zimmer.